WALKING DISTANCE

Extraordinary Hikes for Ordinary People

The Camino de Santiago traverses some of the most beautiful pastoral landscapes in Europe.

WALKING DISTANCE

Extraordinary Hikes for Ordinary People

Robert and Martha Manning

Photographs by Robert Manning

Maps by Ryan Mitchell

Oregon State University Press   Corvallis

Front cover photograph by Robert Manning (Colorado Trail)

The paper in this book meets the guidelines for permanence and durability of the Committee on Production Guidelines for Book Longevity of the Council on Library Resources and the minimum requirements of the American National Standard for Permanence of Paper for Printed Library Materials Z39.48-1984.

Library of Congress Cataloging-in-Publication Data

Manning, Robert E., 1946-
Walking distance : extraordinary hikes for ordinary people / Robert E. Manning, Martha S. Manning.
    p. cm.
 Includes bibliographical references.
 ISBN 978-0-87071-683-6 (alk. paper) -- ISBN 978-0-87071-684-3 (e-book)
 1. Walking. I. Manning, Martha S. II. Title.
 GV502.M26 2012
 796.51--dc23
                        2012015117

Oregon State University Press
121 The Valley Library
Corvallis OR 97331-4501
541-737-3166 • fax 541-737-3170
http://osupress.oregonstate.edu

To those who manage and maintain the trails we walk—thanks for all your good work.

The nineteenth-century prophets of Romanticism sent legions of walkers out of their gardens and into the wider and wilder landscape where they searched for beauty and solitude. (Colorado Trail)

Now shall I walk
Or shall I ride?

   "Ride," Pleasure said:
   "Walk," Joy replied

          —W. H. Davis

Many long-distance trails offer walkers close inspection of archaeological sites not otherwise accessible. (Inca Trail)

Contents

Coastal walks feature the dynamic and dramatic interface between land and sea. (Lycian Way)

Introduction

About ten years ago we decided to walk the aptly named Long Trail in our home state of Vermont. This was the first long-distance trail in America, running 273 miles along the spine of our beloved Green Mountains from Massachusetts to the Canadian border. Many small country roads cross the trail, and this allowed us to walk it in sections, often a day or two at a time, as schedules and weather permitted. The trail took us to places that reminded us of why we're so fortunate to live in Vermont and to portions of the state we'd never visited. We looked forward to every opportunity to get back on the trail, and we used the map in our guidebook to keep track of our progress by coloring in the sections we'd just completed. It was immensely satisfying to color in that last section; we'd finished what we set out to do—a long and sometimes challenging walk the length of our state. We'd enjoyed the adventure of walking one of the world's great long-distance trails and now had a much richer sense of the place we live, one that comes only with the pace and intimacy of walking. But we missed our weekends on the trail and started looking for other walks …

Since then, walking has played an increasingly important part in our lives. Like most people, we walk every day, but now we try to be more deliberate about it, walking to work and back, around our neighborhood, to the market. Walking is so simple for most people, but paradoxically it can also be profound: the evolution and mechanics of walking are unique parts of what make us human, walking is infused in our history and culture, and walking is such a personal and often joyful way to know the world.

Our walking over the last ten years has taken us to many places to hike the world's great long-distance trails. For the purposes of this book, our definition of a long-distance trail is a named trail that can be walked in a few days to a few weeks. While the notion of a long-distance trail might sound intimidating, it shouldn't. Our purpose in preparing this book is to emphasize the accessibility of walking in general and walking the trails we describe in particular. As the subtitle of our book suggests, these are extraordinary hikes for ordinary people. The trails we describe in this book are well marked and managed. Many offer commercial services, if wanted, including accommodations, rides to and from trailheads, even guides and luggage transfer. These trails can be walked, in their entirety or in sections, by *ordinary* people like us—and you.

"The sum of the whole is this: walk and be happy; walk and be healthy. The best way to lengthen out our days is to walk steadily and with a purpose."
—Charles Dickens

If you haven't tried long-distance walking, we hope this book will encourage you to consider it. And if you're already a confirmed walker, we hope the book will stimulate your thinking about where to walk. The first part of the book includes three chapters that address why, how, and where to walk; we hope this will help prepare you for your walking adventures. The second part of the book—its heart—describes our favorite walks on six continents. These are walks through the great cultural landscapes of the world where nature and culture are intertwined in harmonious, pleasing, and sustainable ways. We've made a deliberate effort to offer a diversity of choices in terms of attractions, geography, and length, and the presence, type, and level of commercial services. We've been purposeful in not including any of world's super-long-distance trails such as the 2,200-mile Appalachian Trail, as walking these trails is not feasible for most (ordinary) people. However several of the trails we include are parts of these very long-distance trails; for example, the southern third

Local foods help fuel walkers along many long-distance trails.
(Cape Winelands Walk)

of the Long Trail is part of the Appalachian Trail (one of the best parts in our opinion!).

Long-distance walking is good for you and good for the earth. It promotes personal health and is one of the most basic and sustainable forms of recreation. In our increasingly complex and frantic world, walking is a way to simplify our lives. Walking guru Colin Fletcher wrote that walking is the yin that can complement the more hectic yang of our everyday lives. Walking is also adventurous; one is never quite sure what's around the next bend in the trail and every day brings new and sometimes unexpected experiences. We sense a growing yearning among many people for more "authentic" experiences and walking allows more intimate and genuine contact with local places and people. Walking vacations can also help protect local places through their economic impact, especially when using local services such as B&Bs, small inns, and refuges and eating local foods. But most of all, walking is a joyful celebration of life and the diverse, beautiful, and curious world in which we live.

We hope we'll cross paths with you soon.

Bob and Martha Manning
Burlington, Vermont

PART 1: WALKING DISTANCE

The long-distance trails described in this book are well-marked and managed. (Cotswold Way)

"Walking distance" is a double entendre: it usually means that places are close enough to easily be walked, but it can also suggest walking a long way. We use it both ways in this book. We want to encourage readers to walk from place to place along the world's great long-distance trails, appreciating the best that nature and culture have to offer, and walking a relatively long way in the process. But why would one walk rather than ride? How should one prepare for long-distance walking? And where would one walk? The three chapters comprising Part 1 of this book attempt to answer these questions. They set the stage for Part 2, the heart of the book, which describes thirty of the world's great long-distance trails.

Previous page: Churches and other historic buildings are common along many long-distance trails. (King Ludwig's Way)

Why Walk?

Why walk, indeed? History can be read as a millennia-long struggle to free ourselves from the need to walk. Freedom from walking has always been highly coveted, coming first to the rich and powerful; slaves carried their masters, knights rode horses, the rich owned carriages, and the upper and now middle classes drive cars. Today, only the less fortunate are forced to walk. Most people prefer to sit and ride rather than walk, or so it's been.

But things are changing, as some people are now *choosing* to walk instead of ride, and this is most pronounced in leisure time as a form of recreation, and maybe something even more substantive. The choice to walk is in response to an apparent yearning to be more active and healthy, to do things in a more sustainable way, and to be more directly in touch with the world around us. The deliberate pace of walking allows us to more fully sense the world, to see its richness of detail, to touch, hear, smell, and even taste it. Like the more general "greening" of leisure, recreation, and travel, often called "ecotourism," the choice to walk is based on principles such as appreciation of natural and cultural diversity; direct and authentic contact with people and the places they live; a need to slow our everyday, hectic lives; protection of the distinctive places that make our world so interesting; and investment in these places through direct economic benefits.

Walking the great natural and cultural landscapes of the world is an ideal way to pursue all these objectives. Walking's deliberate, human-scale pace encourages a deep understanding and appreciation of nature and culture, and this ultimately leads to preservation of special places. Walking contributes to personal health and fitness and has relatively little environmental or social impact. The small scale of walking makes use of facilities and services provided by local people, and resulting economic benefits flow directly to these communities and places. And walking is one of the most democratic and accessible recreation activities, demanding no extraordinary athletic ability, requiring relatively little cost, and it's appropriate for nearly all ages.

But to more fully appreciate walking, let's take a brief stroll through history ...

Pilgrimages represent one of the oldest forms of long-distance walking. (Camino de Santiago)

All parts of the world have great cultural landscapes where people and nature have been intertwined in distinctive, harmonious, enduring, and sustainable ways, and many of these regions can be walked on safe, well-marked, and managed trails. (Cinque Terre)

Walking Through History

The history of walking is a paradox; walking is integral to human development, but the practice of walking has declined precipitously. In important ways, walking is one of the things that makes us human. While scientists debate the origins of walking, it's generally agreed that walking on two feet or "bipedalism" emerged several million years ago as an evolutionary adaptation. There is more consensus on its implications. In her book *Wanderlust: A History of Walking*, Rebecca Solnit writes that "[t]he only given is that upright walking is the first hallmark of what became humanity" and "[w]hatever its causes, it caused much more." It freed what are now our arms, allowing humans to evolve into the ultimate tool maker, and our brains responded accordingly. Science writer John Noble Wilford writes, "Anthropologists and evolutionary biologists are now agreed that upright posture and two-legged walking—bipedality—was the crucial and probably the first major adaptation associated with the divergence of human lineage from a common ancestor with the African apes." And renowned paleoanthropologist Mary Leakey wrote:

> One cannot overemphasize the role of bipedalism in hominoid development. It stands as perhaps the salient point that differentiates the forbears of man from other primates. This unique ability freed the hands for myriad possibilities—carrying, tool-making, intricate manipulation. From this single development, in fact, stems all modern technology. Somewhat oversimplified, the formula holds that this new freedom of forelimbs posed a challenge. The brain expanded to meet it. And mankind was formed.

To reject walking is to turn our backs on our evolutionary history and character. But just as importantly, walking is a miracle—a biological and mechanical marvel and an aesthetic triumph. Of course, most of us take walking for granted; it's simple, even "pedestrian." But in reality, it's a symphony between our highly developed nervous, skeletal, and muscular systems; the balance and strength to hold ourselves upright on our two relatively small feet while moving one foot in front of the other for miles on end, over all sorts of terrain, without falling, and doing all this with little conscious thought. The aesthetics of walking were widely appreciated for the first time with publication in the 1870s of Eadweard Muybridge's photographic "motion studies," which used a battery of linked cameras to record the act of walking. Geoff Nicholson writes in his book *The Lost Art of Walking* that "for me the walking pictures reveal the magical nature of something we take so much for granted." We should appreciate and celebrate this gift by taking a daily walk.

While walking is thought to have contributed to development of the brain, there is no question that it has stimulated our thinking across recorded history. Aristotle is an early example, walking as he thought and taught in the Lyceum of ancient Athens. Other philosophers followed suit in what is known as the Peripatetic School (peripatetic meaning "one who walks"). More recent examples include the philosophers, poets, and writers of the Romantic Movement in the eighteenth and nineteenth centuries. French philosopher Jean-Jacques Rousseau set the stage for Romanticism by questioning western society's march toward increasing industrialization and urbanism. Joseph Amato, in his book *On Foot: A History of Walking*, calls Rousseau "the father of romantic pedestrianism." Rousseau's principal books, *The Confessions* and *Reveries of a Solitary Walker*, encouraged readers to return to nature and simplicity and were informed by his own long walks. He wrote that "[t]here is something about walking that stimulates and enlivens my thoughts" and "I can only meditate when I'm walking … When I stop I cease to think; my mind works only with my legs."

Other great walker-writers of the Romantic period include William Wordsworth, Henry David Thoreau, and John Muir. Wordsworth walked extensively in England, particularly in the Lake District. His colleague Samuel Coleridge estimates that Wordsworth walked 180,000 miles over his adult life, often accompanied by his sister, Dorothy. Wordsworth had the remarkable ability to develop insights and compose his poetry while he walked. Author Christopher Morley wrote, "I always think of him as one of the first to employ his legs as an instrument of philosophy." It's reputed that when a traveler asked to see Wordsworth's study at Dove Cottage, his home in the Lake District, his housekeeper replied, "Here is his library, but his study is out of doors."

> **"If you are seeking creative ideas, go out walking. Angels whisper to a man when he goes for a walk."**
> **—Raymond Inmon**

Thoreau took up the Romantic mantle in America, walking extensively throughout New England and more intensively around his home in Concord, Massachusetts, and his retreat at Walden Pond. Eloquent (but often cranky), he advanced his transcendental philosophy, urging Americans to preserve remaining pockets of nature and to walk in the landscape to find manifestations of god and higher truths. His essay *Walking* is his classic statement, in which he wrote, "I think I cannot preserve my health and spirits, unless I spend four hours a day at least,—and it is commonly more than that,—sauntering through the woods and over the hills and fields, absolutely free from all worldly engagements." And in his sometimes arrogant but endearing way he wrote that "I have met but one or two persons in the course of my life who understood the art of Walking, that is, of taking walks,—who had a genius, so to speak, for *sauntering*."

John Muir carried the Romantic tradition westward, walking a thousand miles from Indiana to the Gulf of Mexico, then walking extensively in the Sierra Nevada Mountains of California throughout much of his adult life. His walks offered him deep insights into human relationships with the natural world, and he used walking as a metaphor near the end of his life when he wrote that "I only went out for a walk, and finally concluded to stay out until sundown: for going out, I found, was really going in."

> *"... an unwalked city is a dead city; arguably it is no city at all."*
>
> **—Jane Jacobs**

The rich set of ideas associated with walking, along with the very act of walking itself, have advanced an array of political causes. For example, the Romantic philosophy of Rousseau suggested an inherent value in the individual and this in turn offered a powerful argument against the tyranny of a wealthy minority. These ideas helped inspire the Women's March on Versailles in 1789 to protest the scarcity and price of bread, and this was an important precursor of the subsequent French Revolution. Other prominent examples include Mohandas Gandhi's 200-mile Salt March in 1930 (protesting British taxes), Dr. Martin Luther King Jr.'s 51-mile march in 1965 from Selma to Montgomery, Alabama, to protest unjust voting laws (this route is now memorialized as the Selma to Montgomery Voting Rights Trail), and Cesar Chavez's 340-mile March for Justice in 1966 in California to protest treatment of farmworkers. It's no coincidence that the autobiographies of King and Nelson Mandela are titled *Stride to Freedom* and *Long Walk to Freedom*, respectively. The marches noted above are a few of many over a long history of protests, demonstrations, and parades with strong political agendas: peace, civil rights, cultural pride, and much more. There have even been walks to protect walking as when several hundred people staged a mass trespass in 1932 on Kinder Scout in the Peak District of England, ultimately leading to legislation to assure the historic "right to roam." Joseph Amato suggests that walking in this way adds important elements of "earnestness," "solemnity," and "humility" that help to advance political causes, and that walking is thus "a form of public discourse," while Rebecca Solnit says that "walking becomes testifying."

One of the political causes closest to many walkers is conservation. The prophets of Romanticism sent legions of walkers out of their gardens and into the wider and wilder landscape, where they searched for beauty and solitude. In this way, walking evolved into an attraction, not just a means to an end. Of course, this meant that walkers needed wild places to walk in. Walkers banded together in what have become powerful social forces, such as the Scottish Rights of Way Society (founded in 1845), the Commons Preservation Society (founded in England in 1865), the Appalachian Mountain Club (founded in America in 1876), the Sierra Club (founded in America in 1892), Wandervogel (founded in Germany in 1896), and the Ramblers' Association (founded in England in 1935, now known simply as Ramblers). These organizations have been instrumental in environmental conservation and preservation, and organize trips for millions of walkers each year.

Walking and conservation have a parallel track in cities as well as in wilderness. (In fact, it's not uncommon to read about urban areas as wilderness of a different kind.) Walking in cities also appeals to those with a sense of adventure. In Paris, it was the flaneur or bohemian who famously explored the city's nooks and crannies and, in the words of Walter Benjamin, went "botanizing on the asphalt" in the nineteenth century. But Charles Dickens may have been the ultimate urban walker, logging as many as 20 miles a day in his native London, giving him welcome respite from his writing desk and providing his writing with observations of the often grim details of city life. The golden age of city parks in America—such as New York's Central Park, Philadelphia's Fairmont Park, and San Francisco's Golden Gate Park—occurred during the same period as the Conservation Movement, and with similar causes and consequences: residents of densely populated cities demanded open space and safe, clean places to walk, and this led to development and conservation of many of the world's great urban parks.

Walking also has a strong spiritual dimension that is most evident in the pilgrimage. Pilgrims have been walking for centuries to holy sites around the world to seek spiritual guidance, to be healed, as a form of penance, or to fulfill religious obligations. The oldest and largest pilgrimage is the Hajj; all Muslims who are physically able and can afford to do so must travel to Mecca, Saudi Arabia, to participate in the Hajj at least once in their lifetime. Two-to-three million pilgrims annually participate in the Hajj. It's thought the Hajj dates to the time of Abraham, around 2000 BC. Most pilgrims join others in large groups on their way to Mecca, and once there walk counter-clockwise seven times around the Kaaba, the holy building that Muslims face during prayer. Christian pilgrimages to Rome, Jerusalem, Santiago, and other holy sites began in medieval times. Today, many of these pilgrimages are walked for cultural as well as religious reasons. It's thought that mazes and labyrinths may have a spiritual origin and they are first mentioned in Greek mythology. Labyrinths are condensed forms of the Christian pilgrimage; they are often found in churches or churchyards. The labyrinth at Chartres Cathedral in France may be the oldest of this type, dating from the third century. Geoff Nicholson notes that there are currently a number of labyrinths in American prisons designed to instill peace and calm in those who choose to walk them.

The Fall and Rise of Walking

Despite the significance of walking in history, it's suffered a steep decline over the last hundred years in response to the revolution in transportation. While all forms of mechanized transportation have allowed increasing numbers of people to ride rather than walk—a choice most people have exercised when presented the option—it's the car that relegated walking to the back seat. Most people drive back and forth to work, to the store, running errands; most children take the bus or are driven to school, socializing them to mechanized transportation. In the process, we've transformed much of the world to accommodate the driver—and at a cost to the walker. City streets are straightened and widened for more and faster traffic, making walking difficult, unpleasant, and often dangerous. And vast suburbs have been developed on a car rather than human scale: distances from home to work and shopping are beyond the reasonable range of walkers and there are often no sidewalks. American historian Lewis Mumford wrote that the car is responsible for "the end of the pedestrian" and that "[i]n America we have pushed the elimination of the pedestrian to its ultimate conclusion—the drive-in market, the drive-in movie theater, and the drive-in bank." Even vacations are often spent driving for pleasure. Offices and public buildings also discourage walking as most are equipped with elevators,

Long-distance trails often offer opportunities to observe iconic wildlife such as storks nesting in church steeples along the Camino de Santiago.

Mountain refuges offer walkers camaraderie and five-star views. (Alta Via 1)

escalators, and other "people movers." Even the modern home with en suite bathrooms and other conveniences is designed to reduce walking; for example, multiple bathrooms reduce trips throughout the house.

The decline of walking has caused considerable angst among people who choose to walk (or who would like to have that choice). Rebecca Solnit suggests taking an ecological approach by considering walking an "indicator species for various kinds of freedoms and pleasures: free time, free and alluring space, and unhindered bodies." In this context, walking might be considered "endangered." She argues that modern transportation and technology lead us to transcend space and time, alienating us from the material world, and leaving us "disembodied." "It is the unaugmented body that is rare now," she writes, "and that body has begun to atrophy as both a muscular and a sensory organ." Joseph Amato suggests that the car has altered our relationship with the world, making the walker "feel like a trespasser on the earth," and that

in the process it has "transformed … human senses of space, time, and freedom." Social critic Marshall McLuhan warned us against allowing technology to rule our lives, observing that cars have transformed cities into places where traditional walking patterns now constitute illegal "jaywalking." In science fiction writer Ray Bradbury's short story "The Pedestrian," the protagonist is rousted by the cops because he's found to be walking. Sociologist Jean Baudrillard observed, "As soon as you start walking in Los Angeles you are a threat to public order, like a dog wandering in the road."

But this doesn't have to be the future of walking, and trends suggest that walking is entering a new phase in which increasing numbers of people are choosing to walk for many of the reasons outlined above. At the beginning of the twenty-first century, most countries have established extensive systems of public parks, forests, and trails, and these demand exploration and the close inspection that is only possible on foot. Government agencies and non-profit citizen groups continue their good work toward expansion of these places and the opportunities they present to walkers. All parts of the world have great cultural landscapes where people and the environment are intertwined in distinctive, harmonious, enduring, and sustainable ways, and many of these regions can be walked on safe, well-marked, and managed trails, served by public transportation and local facilities and services. Many cities are working hard and successfully to accommodate the needs of walkers through pedestrian malls, better sidewalks and lighting, and greenways to connect home, work, and recreation. Citizens groups such as First Feet in Seattle, PEDS in Atlanta, Philly Walks, Walk Austin, and Britain's Ramblers and Reclaim the Streets are helping to lead the way, as well as the New Urbanists, a philosophical school of planning that wants to place pedestrians at the center of an urban renaissance. Private enterprise is playing an important role as well by providing walkers better shoes and clothing, lightweight equipment, guidebooks, and a host of other commercial support services.

This increasing suite of walking opportunities is responding to changes in society. Obesity and related health issues are an epidemic in America and other places, and walking is an antidote, an exercise that is accessible to nearly everyone and universally recommended by the medical community. Parents are worried about their children losing contact with nature—what Richard Louv calls "nature deficit disorder"—and walking in parks and related areas can reconnect people with the environment. Adults of all ages caught in frantic lifestyles are looking for ways to slow the pace of life and walking offers life at a more human scale. Walking guru Colin Fletcher wrote that walking is the yin to life's more hectic yang, and we need to find a balance between the two.

Walking the Talk

Walking is simple; Geoff Nicholson writes that walking is analog in a digital world. But it can also be profound. We began this chapter by interpreting its title as a question: why walk? We can now restate the

> **"Walking is the natural recreation for a man who desires not absolutely to suppress his intellect but to turn it out to play for a season."**
> **—Leslie Stephen**

title in declarative form: we walk because it's a celebration of our evolutionary heritage, it stimulates our thinking, it's a form of political expression, it contributes to conservation and sustainability, it deepens our understanding and appreciation of the world, it can be a means to explore spirituality, and it makes us healthier and happier in the process. But in today's world, walking is a choice we must consciously make; it's more conventional and easier (in some ways) to sit and ride. In an especially appropriate turn of contemporary phrase, we must "walk the talk." By choosing to walk, we make a lifestyle choice, fulfill a commitment to ourselves and to the environment, and make a political statement about what we think is important.

This book is designed to encourage a particular kind of walking: long-distance walking—walking the great cultural landscapes of the world. Walk across England, around Mount Blanc, along the coastlines of North America and Australia; follow the Inca Trail to Machu Picchu; walk with pilgrims to Santiago de Compostela; walk among the world's great mountains—the Sierra Nevadas, the Rockies, the Appalachians, the Andes, and the Alps; walk through the Grand Canyon. And much more. Walk part or all of these trails, walk a few days at a time or for a few weeks, walk from inn to inn or backpack. These extraordinary trails are accessible to ordinary people. This book tells you how and describes many of the world's great long-distance walks.

A few years ago, we read some material from contemporary American comedian Stephen Wright who offers a string of social commentary. In his thoughts about walking, he says, "Everywhere is walking distance if you have the time." This is funny, but it's also potentially profound. We'd change this aphorism only slightly: everywhere is walking distance if you *take* the time. We hope you'll find our book convincing and helpful.

Trails can be metaphors—literal and figurative pathways into nature and human nature, into history and natural history. (C&O Canal)

How to Walk

We're often asked how to do long-distance walks: how to prepare, make arrangements, select clothing and gear, find commercial services, and related questions. Most of it's pretty straightforward, and preparing for a long-distance walk is a vital and enjoyable part of the walking experience. This chapter offers some guidelines and tips about how to prepare for and enjoy long-distance walking. If you're already an experienced walker, scan through the chapter and read sections that interest you. If you're not yet experienced, well, start right here …

Preparing Physically

You're intrigued with the idea of "walking distance," but how do you start? It's really pretty obvious: in order to walk a long-distance trail, you need to practice walking—more often and farther. Most people can walk just fine; getting in the habit of walking more builds strength and endurance, and a little time spent learning a few strategies and techniques will make the whole experience more pleasurable and successful. By walking more in your everyday life, you'll gain the confidence that comes with knowing first-hand that by continuing to place one foot in front of the other you *will* reach your destination. Better yet, you'll enjoy the journey and that's what it's really all about. In fact, for walkers, the journey *is* the destination.

Of course we have to start with the usual disclaimer: when beginning a new program of physical activity, or stepping up an existing one, it's recommended that you check with your physician. But, of course, most doctors *recommend* walking. Then it's time to incorporate walking into more of your life, aiming to gradually increase the time spent walking. Once you set your mind on walking, you'll find lots of opportunities. The next chapter on Where to Walk is full of suggestions.

Current medical recommendations suggest that healthy adults should walk at least ten thousand steps per day, translating to about 4 to 5 miles, depending on stride length. Pedometers can be useful in this regard; we love ours and use them almost every day. Ten thousand steps may sound like a lot, but try your pedometer for a few "normal" days and see how many steps you average. Then increase your total a bit on a week-by-week basis. Be patient—it's much better to have small improvements over a period of time than it is to overdo it at the beginning and end up discouraged or injured. When the situation allows, carry a pack to get used to it and to enhance the aerobic quality of walking, and include some walking on varied terrain. Ultimately, you should be able to walk about 3 miles per hour under ideal conditions, which will probably translate to about 2 miles per hour on the trail over the course of a day of walking.

If you're heavier than you'd like, think about how much easier it would be to walk with less stress on your body—and start losing weight. Walking is a good way to shed pounds, almost universally recommended, inexpensive and enjoyable. Walking is an especially good exercise because it helps you lose weight, and when you lose weight the walking becomes easier, a reinforcing cycle. A rough calculation is that a 150-pound person burns 100 to 125 calories per mile when striding purposefully.

If you're already an experienced walker, just keep on walking! We've found that the more we walk in our daily lives, the more we enjoy our long-distance walks, and using our pedometers faithfully on a daily basis helps us feel confident that we'll be successful on our long-distance walks. Walking along any of the great long-distance trails described in this book feels shorter than covering a similar distance at home because there's so much of interest along the trail. And when you've done your walking "homework," you can relax into your long-distance walks with the assurance that you can do them. Preparation and confidence breed success. If you feel you need more guidance in your walking program, we recommend consulting some standard references, including Therese Ikonian's *Fitness Walking* and Maggie Spilner's *Prevention's Complete Book of Walking*.

Planning a Long-Distance Walk

Ultimately, you'll want to leave the comforts of your neighborhood and head out—perhaps to one of the long-distance trails we recommend

> *"Afoot and lighthearted*
> *I take to the open road."*
> **—Walt Whitman**

in this book. We suggest starting slowly by choosing one of the less challenging walks or maybe walking a section or two of one of the longer trails. We started our long-distance walking by day-hiking sections of the Long Trail in our home state of Vermont.

When we're exploring the possibility of walking a trail, we usually start with an Internet search and see what information we can gather. Most long-distance trails have Web sites and these include helpful information such as support services and amenities in nearby towns. If there's an organization that supports and manages the trail (a government agency or non-profit group), they can be wonderful sources of assistance. A little more searching might come up with a company that leads walks or you may find diaries (blogs) of people who've walked the trail. An Internet search combining "guidebook" with the name of the trail leads to even more information. Pretty soon you'll find much of what you need to know about the trail that interests you. We've compiled a list of useful references, including Web sites and guidebooks, at the conclusion of each of the trail descriptions in Part 2 of this book.

Planning the route and logistics of long-distance walking can be an important part of the experience. We've enjoyed many hours at home poring over maps and guidebooks, planning and anticipating our upcoming walking adventures. However, commercial services can be used to simplify the process. Though we don't recommend particular businesses, examples of some that operate on an international scale include Backroads, Boundless Journeys, Classic Journeys, Country Walkers, HF Holidays, Mountain Travel Sobek, REI, Ryder-Walker, Sherpa Expeditions, Wayfarers, Wilderness Travel, and World Walks. But there are many others at the regional, national, and international levels

Boardwalks are sometimes constructed to help protect native vegetation and to keep walkers dry. (Overland Track)

and they range from basic to luxury. Membership organizations such as the Sierra Club and Ramblers also offer popular walking trips. Commercial companies cover a wide range of services and can support you whether you walk independently or with a group. There are bare-bones businesses that simply take you to the start of the trail and/or pick you up at the end. Some companies book accommodations for you and transport your bag from lodging to lodging. Some offer the services of a local guide in addition to lodging and baggage transport; you can book a guide just for you or make new friends by walking with a group. And finally, there are commercial companies that do everything from meeting you at the airport to pouring a glass of local wine after a day on the trail.

Commercial services will often personalize the trip for you. If you want to skip some trail sections, ask if that's possible—and if the company will arrange transport for you over that distance. You can squeeze a long trail into a short time period by doing what might be called "best of" trips; on lengthy walks like the Coast to Coast Trail (which is traditionally walked in two weeks), a company might offer six days "hitting the highlights." These shortened trips can be a good way to experience the essence of a trail.

A convenience for walking long-distance trails is to mail yourself resupply packages containing food, fresh clothes, and other items. Post offices will hold mail addressed to your name plus "General Delivery," and accommodations will usually hold packages for guests.

Be aware that permits are required to walk several of the long-distance trails included in this book, and we've noted this in the respective trail descriptions. In some cases, permits may need to be reserved well in advance and this needs to be taken into account when planning some long-distance walks.

Clothing

We use lightweight multi-use clothing on our walks. We want to be comfortable but carry as little weight in our packs as possible. And we want our clothes to be field tested before a trip; if something's going to chafe, for example, it's better to find out ahead of time. There's an old saying among walkers that "cotton kills," and cotton is a poor choice for anything you wear while walking; once wet, it tends to stay wet, conducting heat away from your body and potentially leading to hypothermia (a dangerous drop in body temperature). This long drying time is a real disadvantage if you want to wash anything at night, too. Wear clothing made of synthetics as these materials tend to wick moisture away from your body and dry much faster. Outdoor stores and catalogs are full of this type of clothing. Arc'teryx, Columbia, Eddie Bauer, ExOfficio, Granite Gear, Marmot, Mountain Hardwear, Patagonia, and The North Face are among the popular brands.

Shop for clothes that have built-in adaptability, clothes that can be used for more than one purpose. For example, hiking pants that zip off just above the knees to become shorts give you 2-for-1 versatility. Use a lightweight rain jacket as a windbreaker or as the outer layer of clothing to keep the warmth in when needed. Plan your clothes to allow you to dress in a series of layers so you can adjust your clothing quickly in response to changes in weather and activities—take your vest off when walking uphill, for example, and put it back on at the end of the climb. We try to limit ourselves on long-distance walks to two basic sets of clothes—one for walking and one reserved for after we've cleaned up at the end of the day. We hand-wash our walking clothes as often as possible, usually every night since they're fast drying. Long-distance walkers tend to emphasize function over fashion.

We often walk in long sleeves and long pants to protect ourselves from the sun, even if the weather is warm (special sun-block pants and shirts are very lightweight and their wicking properties are cooling). We recommend that everyone wear a hat with a wide brim and liberally apply sunblock to protect against sun damage, a special problem for anyone who enjoys the out-of-doors.

The most important item of clothing is boots/shoes. If your feet are happy, chances are the rest of you will be happy, too. Although some outdoor outfitters still push heavy-duty expedition type boots constructed of leather, please don't buy them unless you're going on an expedition.

> **"You can't see anything from a car; you have got to get out of the god-damned contraption and walk."**
>
> **—Edward Abbey**

The trend is to lighter footwear, and we endorse this, often walking in trail running shoes; they're like running shoes with beefed-up soles. Shop at the end of the day when feet are probably a little swollen and shop only where there are salespeople to help you with the fitting. You should fit your boots/shoes with medium thickness socks, but should also carry thinner socks in your pack for use at times when your feet may be swollen. We always have two or three choices of socks in our packs so we can do a lot of adjusting as conditions dictate, even sometimes wearing unmatched socks to meet the individual needs of our feet. Wear your new boots/shoes on your training walks as much as possible. If anything needs to be adjusted, it's best to deal with it at home.

There's another old adage among walkers: "There's no such thing as bad weather, just bad clothing." Think about where you're going as the key to what you'll need. Mountaintops have entirely different weather than valleys, for example. If you're hiking somewhere like Scotland, you'll want "real" rainwear made of breathable, waterproof fabric. If you're going somewhere that precipitation is unlikely—Tuscany in the summer—perhaps a lightweight inexpensive poncho is adequate. Any time you're going out for a walk, consider "What if … ?" and bring clothing to match. Being too cold, too hot, wet or otherwise unsuitably prepared could be very uncomfortable—and even dangerous. It's not much of a burden to build in a margin of safety in your pack, especially if your clothing is selected to be lightweight and multi-purpose.

Gear

Of course, you'll need some equipment for long-distance walking, and the kind you'll need depends on the type of walking you're doing. Obviously, if you're staying in B&Bs or other commercial accommodations, you'll carry a different assortment of things than if you're backpacking. And if you're having your luggage transported, you'll carry even less. In every case, your gear has to be functional, but it doesn't have to be heavy! We don't consider ourselves "gear heads" and don't suggest you have to keep up with the very latest trends. But the evolution (maybe even revolution) to lighter weight equipment demands attention.

Since you'll carry your gear in a pack, let's start there. Day hikes and walks where you're sending luggage from one lodging to the next require only a daypack. If you find it uncomfortable to wear a pack on your back, consider one of the lumbar packs on the market; this may be just the solution you need. If you're backpacking, you'll need a larger pack that can accommodate your needs for several days. Whatever your pack needs, consider the lightweight options. When we first started backpacking, our conventional external-frame packs weighed 7½ pounds apiece—empty! Several years ago we converted to an ultra-light pack that weighs 1½ pounds, saving 6 pounds on our backs and feet for each of the thousands of steps we take each day on the trail.

If you're backpacking, you'll need a tent and sleeping bag. We had what we thought was a lightweight tent that weighed 4 pounds, but replaced it with one that weighs 2 pounds. Our new sleeping bags weigh 2 pounds each. We've continued to replace old gear with ultra-light versions and other walkers often stop us on the trail and ask about our small, obviously lightweight packs and the gear they contain. These folks are invariably overloaded and struggling while we're operating with a more comfortable workload (and maybe having more fun). When backpacking, we now carry less than half the weight we used to and have no loss of utility or safety. The new gear is less rugged than the old, but the cost of

"A vigorous five-mile walk will do more good for an unhappy but otherwise healthy adult than all the medicine and psychology in the world."
—Paul Dudley White

Most long-distance trails can be walked in sections that may include one to a few days at a time. (Camino de Santiago)

exercising a little care with it is well worth the reward. An ideal pack weight doesn't exceed 10 percent of body weight, but you won't be able to approach this ambitious guideline without lightweight gear. Small companies on the Internet are often good sources of ultra-light gear; examples include GoLight, Gossamer Gear, and Tarptent.

If you're staying in a B&B, inn, or hotel, you have the luxury of leaving the bedding to them. If you're staying in a refuge or hut, usually all you'll need is a sleeping sheet (sometimes called a hostel sheet). This is like an uninsulated sleeping bag with a pocket for the pillow. You sleep in the sack and use the pillow and duvet provided by the refuge. We prefer the sacks made of silk because they are lighter and pack smaller; consider getting an oversized one if you're a larger person or like more "wiggle room."

If you're camping, you obviously need a sleeping bag and insulated pad. Down sleeping bags are lighter, but are not recommended for wet weather conditions as they lose their insulating qualities when damp. Some sleeping bags are cut in a slim "mummy" shape; these weigh less because they require less material, but may not be suitable for someone who prefers more space. Some folks like the comfort of an air-insulated self-inflating mattress, but these are heavier than pads made of closed-cell foam. Does the comfort of the air mattress outweigh the disadvantage of its weight?

Keep asking yourself: Do I need this item for comfort or safety? If so, what's the lightest weight version of this item that will be useful? For example, we always carry small flashlights, and our old ones (bought at an outdoor-gear store) weighed 3.75 oz. apiece; each seemed quite small compared to the other flashlights at our house. But now we carry pinch flashlights (from the same store) that weigh 1/4 of an ounce. Saving less than 4 ounces per person may not seem like much, but the weight difference is appreciable in your hand, and the savings add up in the pack.

Please note: we're not advocating the extreme minimalist philosophy that some ultra-light backpackers have adopted. Their point sometimes seems to be to carry the least and walk the farthest fastest, and one wonders how much these ultra-light walkers appreciate the trails they travel. While we don't share their philosophy, we do appreciate their gear; we advocate adapting and appropriating it to more conservative— and enjoyable—uses.

It's easy to get consumed with the latest equipment and products, but we don't recommend this. Even Colin Fletcher, author of "the Bible" on walking gear, wrote, "Equipment and techniques are mere means to an end." Sometimes the choice of which item to purchase isn't obvious—and this is where a good outdoor-gear store can help. And folks who've done a lot of walking (members of walking groups, etc.) are full of opinions

and happy to share, and they may be the best source of all. The more experience you have, the more you understand what will work.

It can be useful to consult some reference books on equipment. *The Complete Walker IV* by Colin Fletcher and Chip Rawlins will tell you all you need to know (and then some!) about outdoor gear, particularly in a wilderness-oriented context. It's an excellent reference, though certainly not the kind of book most people read cover to cover. Other useful reference books on outdoor gear and related topics include John McKinney's *The Joy of Hiking*, Mark Harvey's *The National Outdoor Leadership School's Wilderness Guide*, and Andrew Skurka's *The Ultimate Hiker's Gear Guide*. For lightweight gear, we find Ryan Jordan's book, *Lightweight Backpacking and Camping*, useful, as is the Web site www.backpackinglight.com. The last two of these sources are focused on ultralight backpacking and can be

The deliberate pace of walking allows walkers to more fully sense the world, to see its richness of detail, to touch, hear, smell, and even taste it. (South Downs Way)

a little extreme for our tastes, but both have good ideas to cull, and they stimulate thinking about ways to reduce the weight you carry. Magazines can be good sources of information, too. For example, *Backpacker Magazine* and *Outside* regularly review outdoor clothing and equipment.

Don't feel you have to buy everything at a specialty store catering to walkers and other outdoors people. Sometimes you'll find the things you need at the grocery or hardware store. For example, we long ago replaced the special rain covers for our packs with plastic bags (trash compactor bags are best) from the grocery store that we use to line the *inside* of our packs—lightweight, cheap, and quite effective. We find the liners work better than the exterior covers anyway, and we only use them on days there's a threat of rain. Zipper bags, especially the ones designed for the freezer, are always handy for carrying food, medicines, and other small items; we like to stick a few extra in our packs. Small carabiners from the local hardware store were intended for key rings, but work beautifully to corral loose items in the pack.

Of course you'll want a first aid kit and making your own allows you to customize to your needs and to keep it light. One of our favorite products on all walks is flexible plastic first-aid tape (e.g., Nexcare) and we routinely pre-treat any place on our feet that might become a "hot spot" or blister. Another strategy is to use an anti-chafing product (primarily used by runners and bought where they shop) or lanolin (used by nursing mothers) to coat any sensitive areas that might chafe. Treat potential problems before they become real problems. In your first aid kit be sure to include a few of the kinds of medicines you use at home. If you regularly need an antacid, for example, you'll probably want a few doses during the course of your walking adventure. Always have various ways to treat your feet—they're your most important resource!

Prepare yourself with the place-specific information and supplies you'll need. Consider where you're going and what challenges might present themselves. If you're on a short practice walk where there are lots of other walkers, you probably don't need elaborate first aid supplies. But it's a different situation if you're walking the John Muir Trail. When we first decided to try some multi-day backcountry treks, we took a first aid course from our local hiking club and it's been invaluable for peace of mind; we haven't had serious problems on the trail, but feel prepared. Paul Auerbach's books, *Wilderness Medicine* and *Field Guide to Wilderness Medicine*, and Tod Schimelpfenig's *NOLS Wilderness Medicine* are the standard medical references for the out-of-doors.

Walking (or trekking) poles have become popular in recent years. Lightweight and collapsible, they offer a bit of steadiness when needed and, by allowing the walker to transfer some of the load to the upper body, reduce leg fatigue and strain on creaky knees. We often take poles with us, but generally use them only for rough areas and steep downhill stretches. Reading a guidebook for the trail should give you a good sense of whether trekking poles are appropriate.

Water is one of the heaviest things you'll carry and you need adequate water to function well; we suggest taking full advantage when water is available to hydrate yourself. We always drink a little extra every morning, allowing us to carry a little less. Instead of loading up our packs with water for the whole day, we determine where we can get water along the trail (purchased or from a natural source) and plan to resupply accordingly. If we're getting water out of a stream or other natural source, we always purify it before drinking. We used to use a pump filter, but now treat with either iodine (which leaves a bit of a bad taste and is not recommended for extended use) or a chlorine dioxide two-part mixture especially designed for walkers, both of which are very lightweight. We also bypass conventional water bottles in favor of the bladders used in personal water-delivery systems; we just don't bother with the hose and mouthpiece. Again, we're going for the lightweight option.

Some walks require more specialized items in the pack. An area known for its birds might demand binoculars, and many walks are more fun if you can identify the flora and fauna; local identification guides can be very helpful and make the walk more interesting. In the height of insect season your time outdoors will be more pleasant with insect repellent and/or head nets at the ready.

> **"Walking would teach people the quality that youngsters find so hard to learn—patience."**
> **—Edward P. Weston**

Look for stores that specialize in hiking and outdoor gear and that have a large selection and knowledgeable staff. We've found Eastern Mountain Sports (EMS), L. L. Bean, Mountain Equipment Co-op, and REI to be useful. All of these stores offer Internet catalogs.

Food

One of the delightful aspects of walking through landscapes that are new to us can be appreciating the "tastes" of the trail; every region of the world has its distinctive terroir. Savoring local food and drink can add a layer of sensory experience to walking, and we're always glad when we can supplement any food we've brought with us with local foods that are fresher and more flavorful. Regardless of whether the food you eat is purchased on the trail or brought from home, food is an important source of energy for walkers. In addition to planned meals, we encourage you to take calorie-dense snacks in your pack—and more of them than you think you'll need. One of us is a constant grazer when walking, so plastic bags of dried fruit and nuts are kept close at hand, and they're crucial in maintaining an even energy level. Eat before you feel the need and your walk will proceed more smoothly.

We used to eat commercially prepared freeze-dried meals on our backpacking trips, but never found any we really enjoyed, so now we shop in the grocery store for food for our walks. There are lots of dried options and the choices may be more palatable than the tasty-sounding camp meal. (Unfortunately, when you add boiling water to a foil bag that's labeled "Spicy Southwestern Chicken Taco," what you end up with is *not* a taco!) We'd rather cook pasta with Parmesan cheese and red pepper flakes, a more pedestrian choice perhaps, but one that's

> *"My father considered a walk among the mountains as the equivalent of churchgoing."*
> —**Aldous Huxley**

comforting and nourishing. We've sometimes admired the dehydrated meals prepared at home by fellow walkers. If bringing your meals from home is of interest to you, there are many books on the market; some of the best include *Lipsmackin' Backpacking* by Christine and Tim Conners and *Simple Foods for the Pack* by Claudia Axcell. If your pack is as light as we suggest, you can afford a small weight allowance for some fresh food. Always take more food than you expect to eat because you'll be hungry, and you'll want a little extra just in case something unexpected makes the trip a bit longer.

Of course, if you're walking inn to inn, or staying in refuges that offer meal service, most of your food is already provided, and the food we've most enjoyed is that purchased en route. Some of our fondest trail memories are the local foods we've eaten—cherries purchased along the Camino de Santiago, goat cheese on the Tour du Mont Blanc, olives and wine in Cinque Terre, monk-brewed beer along King Ludwig's Way, fish and chips on the South Downs Way. We enjoy shopping in grocery stores in different parts of the world, another way to learn about other cultures. If towns are sparse along the route, peanut butter brought from home can add nourishment to an otherwise skimpy meal. We repackage all foods in plastic bags or other lightweight containers.

Wayfinding

Of course, you'll want to take along maps, guidebooks, and a compass. Guidebooks can be heavy, but are sometimes divided into two sections, describing the trail in both directions. Once we've decided in which direction we're going to walk, we cut out the unneeded section to lessen pack weight and bulk. Outdoor clubs and stores can help you gain proficiency with map and compass. There are also several reference books that can be useful, including David Seidman's *The Essential Wilderness Navigator* and Bob and Mike Burns' *Wilderness Navigation*. Global Positioning System (GPS) technology can be very useful, but be aware that satellite coverage is not available everywhere. The long-distance trails we recommend in the second part of this book are generally well marked and easy to follow. However, walkers are obliged to be observant on the trail, watching for blazes, cairns, and other trail markings. John Brierley, author of the guidebook we used for the Camino de Santiago, reminds us, "When the mind wanders, the feet will follow."

Walking a Trail in Sections

Most of the trails described in the second part of this book can be walked in sections that range from day hikes to several days. How can you make that work? First, using maps and guidebooks, look for obvious break points along the trail, usually roads that cross the trail. For example, roads roughly every 10 miles apart cross the first several days of the Colorado Trail near Denver and this enabled us to do a series of day hikes. Another option is to find a driver to shuttle you and there are commercial services available on many trails, some strictly for hikers, some offering related services. On our walk of the Colorado Trail, we wanted a ride into the town of Buena Vista, which is a short distance off the trail. We couldn't find a listing for a commercial service, so we called the town Chamber of Commerce to ask for suggestions. At the end of the conversation the president of the Chamber said, "If none of these options work, call me back and I'll give you a ride myself," which we found both charming and most accommodating. One of her suggestions was a professional hunting guide, and we arranged for him to pick us up at a road crossing at an agreed-upon time. We had to move an elk hide out of the way to get in the truck, but that was part of the fun and it was an interesting ride as he told us all about his native Buena Vista. We've also gotten short rides from many B&B owners who were willing to drive a little in order to guarantee a night or two of business. We've almost universally found local residents to be helpful; long-distance walking seems to resonate with many folks. People in the walking community sometimes call this "trail magic." Of course, when we ask for help, we're ready to pay a reasonable fee for services rendered.

When looking for someone to provide a ride or other services, first check if there is an organization that supports the trail, such as The Superior Hiking Trail Association, which manages the Superior Hiking Trail. We've listed these organizations at the end of each trail description in the next part of this book. These organizations can be a wealth of information about the trail and off-trail services as well. (Consider joining these organizations as a way to repay these efforts and help support the walking community.) Ask at your lodging and at places where outdoor equipment is sold and activities offered. A few times we've gotten a ride with fishing guides, for example. We've found that even small communities often have someone who performs this and related services. Perhaps a summer employee would like to supplement his or her wages.

Another way to walk long-distance trails in sections is to hike with others. If two couples are walking, they can start at opposite ends of a trail section and trade car keys in the middle. Or one person can be the designated driver while the others walk; the driver gets to explore the region off-trail, the others on-trail, and everyone shares experiences at dinner. Switch roles the next day. Public transportation is often a good option for positioning yourself to walk—to get to and from the trailhead or skip trail sections if wanted or needed. Options include buses, trains, ferries, taxis, and ski lifts—we've used them all. Think creatively as you look at your route and study your guidebook.

Walking Ethics

Walking is one of the most sustainable forms of outdoor recreation, having very little impact on the environment. However, that doesn't mean that walkers can be careless about the potential environmental impacts they

"Bear boxes"—steel lockers to store food—are often provided at campsites in bear country. (West Coast Trail)

Walkers often rely on many forms of local transportation. Here a local Sami guide provides a ride across a broad lake. (Kungsleden)

may cause. For example, walkers should generally stay on maintained trails to avoid trampling surrounding soil and vegetation, should never feed wildlife, and should dispose of trash in an acceptable way (use trash receptacles or carry it out with you). The ethics of walking generally follow commonsense guidelines. However, the old saying "take only pictures, leave only footprints" has been superseded by more advanced efforts to think through these ethical considerations. These guidelines can be useful to walkers in carrying out their obligations to the environment and future generations of walkers.

For example, the non-profit group Leave No Trace has partnered with trail management agencies such as the U.S. National Park Service to develop a set of seven principles that should guide walkers and other users of public lands:

1. Dispose of waste properly
2. Leave what you find
3. Minimize campfire impacts
4. Plan ahead and prepare
5. Travel and camp on durable surfaces

6. Respect wildlife

7. Be considerate of other visitors

These principles are discussed and illustrated in more detail on the organization's Web site (www.lnt.org). A related program of ethics for walkers has been developed in Britain and is known as the Countryside Code. A series of five principles is suggested to help walkers respect, protect, and enjoy the countryside:

1. Be safe—plan ahead and follow signs

2. Leave gates and property as you find them

3. Protect plants and animals and take your litter home

4. Keep dogs under close control

5. Consider other people

These principles are discussed and illustrated on the Web site for the organization Natural England (www.naturalengland.org.uk).

There are also several good books that offer useful discussions of ethical practices that can help walkers be good stewards of the land. We recommend Guy and Laura Waterman's *Backwoods Ethics*, Will Harmon's *Leave No Trace*, and Rich Brame and David Cole's *Soft Paths*.

"Going" in the Woods

We find it surprising how often the subject of the "bathroom" comes up as we talk to people about walking. There may be opportunities to use conventional indoor facilities when trails pass through towns and other developed areas. "Going" outdoors is something we tend not to think of much anymore because it's gotten to be no big deal. Obviously, there are differences by gender, and most men seem to instinctively know to "find a tree"; all you have to do is get off the trail, turn your back, and you're fine.

Women seem to have a harder time of it. Try and get over your initial reluctance and your fear that you're going to get caught or seen—after thousands of trail miles Martha has been embarrassed only once, when she chose a bad site. Besides, most folks simply look away if they happen to see someone off the trail tending to their needs. Here's a procedure for women that's trail-tested. Carry fresh tissues in a plastic bag in one of your pockets and an empty plastic bag in the other—zipper bags are best. Remove enough tissues for the task at hand as you're selecting your spot. Remove your pack and find a screened area. Wait for any foot traffic to pass and then, facing the trail, urinate as quickly and efficiently as possible. Keep your head down—it makes you less noticeable. Drop used tissues on the ground beside you, get your clothes back in place, and then pick up the tissues and put them in the other plastic bag. Next time you'll just add to this bag. If you always have clean tissues on the left and used ones on the right, there's no fumbling or confusion. If you don't want to walk around with a bag of used tissues, tuck them in your pack when you return to the trail. Feminine "urinary funnels" are available and some women swear by them (after practicing a bit at home); with a funnel you don't have to remove any clothing.

We use code phrases when we're in a group and one of us wants to take a bathroom break. "I'm going to step off the trail" works (and everyone knows what it means), but our favorite is "I'm going to take a wee break," a phrase we picked up walking in Scotland.

A few tips: always have extra tissues in zip lock bags in your pack. Tiny bottles of hand sanitizer are lightweight and a good way to freshen up, and, if used by everyone in the group, a good way to prevent the spread of germs.

If you are leaving some solid waste, please follow the Leave No Trace guidelines and dig a cat hole 6 to 8 inches deep and at least 200 feet from the trail, water, and campsites. Again, if you get everything set up ahead of time, there's little time spent in a vulnerable position.

Walking Companions?

Will you walk with someone? Maybe you have a walking partner in mind—a spouse, friend, or family member who is interested in sharing the experience. If not, consider joining hiking and trail clubs in your area or find one online for the area you'll be visiting. Outdoor-gear stores sometimes sponsor group outings; at the very least they may suggest people and organizations in your community that are active in walking. An advantage of going with an organized outing is talking to other walkers—you'll learn so much from their experiences and (like us!) they'll love offering advice and tips.

Or maybe you want to enjoy the solitude of walking by yourself. We've met a number of solitary walkers on the trail and this seems to work well for them. Wordsworth, Thoreau, Muir, and other great walkers often went by themselves, thinking great thoughts along the way. But be aware that walking by yourself raises important safety issues; be sure to tell a friend or family member where you're going and when you expect to return (a good idea for all walkers).

Happy Trails!

Let's not make all this harder than it is—walking is pretty basic. Try to walk more often and farther in your everyday life to prepare for long-distance walking. Choose your clothing and gear to maximize utility and minimize weight. Smart food choices will enhance the whole adventure. You now know how to deal with the logistics of a long-distance trail and you know how to behave once you're there. By "practicing" at home, you'll be confident in your abilities and ready to go.

Two final pieces of advice. First, walk *your* walk—tailor walking to your individual needs and interests. Some people get great satisfaction out of testing themselves, walking challenging trails in long days. But others prefer to linger and stay closer to developed areas and this is just as valid. Some people backpack while others enjoy local inns and B&Bs. Some enjoy planning the logistics of their walks and others leave the details to commercial companies. How do you want to walk? We find

"The best remedy for a short temper is a long walk."
—Jacqueline Schiff

that our tastes change from time to time and from trip to trip, and we've wound up doing many kinds of walks. You'll find that reflected in the trails we describe in the second part of this book.

Finally, we've discussed lots of logistics in this chapter—clothing, gear, food, etc. But the most important thing you can bring on a walk is a sense of curiosity about the interesting world in which we live. See places and meet people in the intimate way that only walking allows. We think you'll find this enjoyable and highly rewarding.

Where to Walk

Deciding where to walk is an important part of the walking experience—will you stroll among the ancient villages of Cinque Terre, join the spirit of gold rush prospectors as they scramble up and over Chilkoot Pass, follow in the footsteps of Alexander the Great along the Turquoise Coast of Turkey, walk John Muir's beloved High Sierra, or perhaps just walk around your neighborhood? In fact, planning a walk can be one of the most enjoyable parts of walking— researching the many alternatives that are available, reading guidebooks, consulting maps, making travel arrangements, and anticipating the walk. This book addresses long-distance walking primarily, but also offers encouragement to walk more in everyday life as a way to prepare for long-distance walks and to adopt a healthy lifestyle, add interest to life, and lessen our impact on the environment.

From Global to Local

"Think globally and act locally" is an old environmental adage that suggests we inform ourselves about environmental issues and then conduct ourselves accordingly in our everyday lives. Perhaps there's an analogous way of thinking about walking: you appreciate the joy and value of long-distance walking, so consider how you might walk more in your daily activities. Is it feasible to walk to and from your place of work? Or to the market? How about a stroll around your neighborhood (or someone else's neighborhood) in the morning, in the evening, or on the weekend? When it's feasible, take the stairs instead of the elevator. Explore your local parks. Some folks are "mall walkers" and this can be a good option, especially when the weather's bad. Others use a treadmill or other exercise equipment to simulate walking. Walk outside when you can, even when the weather's less than ideal, as this will prepare you for the eventualities of long-distance walking.

By walking locally, we follow in the footsteps of great walkers like Henry David Thoreau. Thinking about his native Concord, Massachusetts, Thoreau wrote, "My vicinity affords many good walks; and though for so many years I have walked almost every day, and sometimes for several days together, I have not yet exhausted them." He continued:

An absolutely new prospect is a great happiness, and I can still get this any afternoon. Two or three hours' walking will carry me to as strange a country as I ever expect to see. A single farmhouse which I had not seen before is sometimes as good as the dominions of the King of Dahomey. There is in fact a sort of harmony discoverable between the capabilities of the landscape within a circle of ten mile's radius, or the limits of an afternoon walk, and the three score years and ten of human life. It will never become quite familiar to you.

Cities offer a different kind of wilderness and are best explored on foot; think of their sidewalks as a vast system of trails representing unlimited walking adventures. Follow in the footsteps of the nineteenth-century flaneurs who "botanized the asphalt" and contributed to the reputation of Paris as one of the great walking cities of the world. Phyllis Pearsall walked the 3,000 miles of the 23,000 streets of London in the 1930s. These are ambitious models. Pay close attention to historic canals and railways, as many have been converted into appealing trails that cover larger areas of geography. Increasing numbers of "greenways" now form linked systems of trails that connect home, work, parks, and attractions.

The long-distance trails described in this book are extraordinary, but can be walked by ordinary people. (Overland Track)

Long-distance trails are routed to include many iconic natural features. (John Muir Trail)

From Local to Global

Beyond the local is the greater world—states, provinces, regions, the globe. These are big places that should be walked on weekends and holidays and days stolen from work. All states, provinces, etc. have systems of parks, trails, and other reserves that offer years' worth of walking opportunities, and these may even include walks in the wilderness. Get in touch with your state or provincial parks department and ask for a list of parks and related areas. There's at least one book that describes trails and walks for nearly every state, province, and region. Many states and provinces have walking and trail clubs and related organizations; consider joining one and participating in organized walks, maybe even eventually giving back by leading one.

At the national and international scale, there are still more choices. Nearly all countries have extensive systems of national parks, forests, and other reserves that offer many lifetimes of walking adventure. Many countries have national-level trail systems and participate in international trail networks. For example, the U.S. has a National Trails System that includes all fifty states and totals nearly 60,000 miles. England and Wales also have a system of National Trails that includes fifteen trails totaling nearly 2,500 miles. Several European countries have a system of multinational long-distance trails called *Grande Randonnees* (often abbreviated GR) and these are very extensive; France alone includes over 37,000 miles. Australia has thirty-nine long distance trails totaling over 8,000 miles. And there are many great walking cities all over the world. A little time in your local bookshop or on the Internet researching walking opportunities will return great rewards. As noted in Chapter 2, there are many companies that offer guided and independent walks all over the world, and their catalogs and Web sites are also good sources of ideas.

No matter where you choose to walk—from around home to other continents—think of the world as a great cultural landscape waiting to be explored, places where nature and culture are intertwined in diverse and interesting ways. The harmony of nature and culture is a subtle but often overlooked refrain in the environmental literature. Our greatest nature writers have made strong statements admonishing us to save the environment from human encroachment. Thoreau, for example, wished to "say a word for nature" and concluded that "in Wildness is the preservation of the World." But a closer reading suggests that balance and moderation were his ultimate goals. The "half cultivated" bean field at his Walden Pond retreat is a useful metaphor of the need for elements of both nature and culture. "I would not," he wrote, "have every part of a man cultivated, any more than I would have every acre of earth." He went on to write, "The natural remedy [to the relationship between civilization and wilderness] is to be found in the proportion which the night bears to the day, the winter to the summer, thought to experience." Contemporary environmental philosophers continue to warn about the false and potentially dangerous dichotomy between humans and nature.

Like Thoreau's bean fields, trails can be metaphors as well. They are literal and figurative pathways into nature and human nature, into history and natural history. The landscape is natural (at least, for the most part), but the trails themselves are human entities, often with important historical meaning, and always with good intentions. They are gifts from one generation to the next, and they reflect the societies that create and nurture them (we call it trail building and maintenance in our mundane and understated everyday language). We're well served to take the time to stop and more fully appreciate our trails and the cultural landscapes through which they pass. Just as we often botanize when we walk, stopping to identify and appreciate the beauty and complexity of the natural world, we should engage the cultural diversity of our outdoor spaces and places, recognizing and honoring the people who live, work, and play there, and the cultures that are reflected in the trails they've given us.

Long-Distance Walking

That brings us to the long-distance trails we recommend in this book. We've taken this assignment seriously and devoted ourselves to a decade of "field work." In the next part of this book we describe thirty of what we consider the world's great long-distance trails; these are our favorites. As we noted in our Introduction to the book, we define a long-distance trail as one that is named and can be walked in a few days to a few weeks. We've purposively not included any of the super-long distance trails like the 2,200-mile Appalachian Trail because these are generally not an option for most ordinary people (including us!).

"Everywhere is walking distance if you have the time."

—Steven Wright

However, several of the trails we recommend are part of these very long trails, often the best parts.

We've organized these trails in alphabetical order in the table at the end of this chapter. For each trail, we list its location, length, type of accommodations, availability of baggage transfer, ability to walk the trail in sections, and our assessment of the challenges associated with walking the trail. With regard to length, we suggest you read the description of the trails in which you may be interested in Part 2 of the book, because some of these trails are rarely walked in their entirety. For example, we've listed the length of the Kungsleden in the table as 270 miles (its full length), but few people walk this distance. The northern half of this trail is by far the most interesting and this reduces the effective length of the trail to about 120 miles, and we make that clear in the trail description.

We've described accommodations as falling into three categories: commercial (e.g., inns, B&Bs), huts and refuges, and backpacking/camping. Commercial accommodations provide private rooms and often include breakfast. Huts and refuges (there are other names for these facilities in some countries) are usually basic facilities that may include either private or communal sleeping, bathing, and cooking areas. Many serve breakfast and/or dinner. Some trails must be backpacked.

Mountain refuges are sited an easy day's walk apart along many long-distance trails. (Walker's Haute Route)

You'll notice from the table that many trails offer more than one kind of accommodation.

Baggage transfer refers to the option to send your luggage from accommodation to accommodation by commercial service, and this allows walkers to carry only a day pack. Most trails can be walked in sections that may include one to a few days at a time over at least part of their distance. Our rating of the challenges associated with walking each trail is subjective by its very nature, and most long-distance trails are highly variable almost by definition. We've used a range of challenge for many trails to reflect this. Challenge is usually a reflection of difficulty of walking (e.g., elevation, climbing and descending) but can also be affected by availability (or lack thereof) of facilities and services and other issues. Again, the trail descriptions in the next section of the book offer more information about this.

We've been deliberate about including a great spectrum of long-distance trails in terms of length, attractions, geography, commercial services, and challenge. We advise starting with shorter trails or sections of longer ones and those that have less challenge associated with them. Walk within your abilities and enjoy success and the confidence it brings. Be clever by thinking about ways to add a walk to some of your other business or pleasure travel; the trails we describe are spread across six continents and fourteen countries. If time doesn't allow you to walk the whole length of a trail, walk part of it. We've had a long debate with ourselves about whether it's okay to walk just part of a long-distance trail

> *"Happy is the man who has acquired the love of walking for its own sake!"*
>
> **—W.J. Holland**

if you can't (or don't want to) walk it all. There's no denying the intrinsic satisfaction of walking the full length of a long-distance trail. But walking parts of these trails gives license to experience a diversity of the world's great cultural landscapes.

Please note that the trail descriptions in Part 2 are designed to tell you what you need to know in deciding which trails you'd like to walk. The trail descriptions include maps showing trail locations and offering a sense of the trails' landscape features and geography. We've walked all these trails (and others as well), nearly all of them in their entirety, and we've enjoyed them all. We hope we'll entice you to walk many of them. Once you've decided which trail to walk, you'll need a more detailed guidebook, a map, and related materials for that trail, and we suggest at the end of each description which guidebooks, Web sites, etc., will be most helpful.

We hope you find the accompanying table useful, that you'll find the trail descriptions in the next part of the book to be intriguing enough for you to try long-distance walking, and that you'll enjoy your walks as much as we do. Happy trails to you!

Just as we often botanize when we walk, stopping to identify and appreciate the beauty and complexity of the natural world, we should also engage the cultural diversity of our outdoor spaces and places, recognizing and honoring the people who live, work, and play there. (Colorado Trail)

Extraordinary Hikes

Trail	Location	Length (Miles)	Commercial (e.g., Inns, B&Bs)	Huts/ Refuges	Backpacking/ Camping	Baggage Transfer	Option to Walk in Sections	Degree of Challenge
			Accommodations					
Alta Via 1	Italy	93	Some	Yes	No	No	Most	Moderate–High
C&O Canal	Maryland & Washington, DC, USA	185	Some	No	Yes	No	All	Low
Camino de Santiago	Spain	480	Most	Yes	Some	Yes	All	Low–Moderate
Cape Winelands Walk	South Africa	60	Yes	No	No	Yes	All	Low–Moderate
Chilkoot Trail	Alaska, USA & British Columbia, Canada	33	No	No	Yes	No	No	High
Cinque Terre	Italy	11+	Yes	Some	No	Not Needed	All	Low–Moderate
Coast to Coast Trail	England	190	Yes	Some	Some	Yes	All	Moderate
Colorado Trail	Colorado, USA	470	Some	No	Yes	No	Some	Moderate–High
Cotswold Way	England	100	Yes	No	No	Yes	All	Low–Moderate
Great Ocean Walk	Australia	60	Yes	Some	Yes	Yes	All	Low–Moderate
Inca Trail	Peru	30	No	No	Yes	Porters	No	Moderate–High
John Muir Trail	California, USA	210	Few	No	Yes	No	Some	Moderate–High
Kaibab Trail	Arizona, USA	21	Some	Some	Yes	No	No	Moderate–High
Kalalau Trail	Hawaii, USA	22 (Round-trip)	No	No	Yes	No	No	High

Nature can be dynamic and dramatic on the world's great long-distance trails.
(Lycian Way)

Trail	Location	Length (Miles)	Accommodations			Baggage Transfer	Option to Walk in Sections	Degree of Challenge
			Commercial (e.g., Inns, B&Bs)	Huts/ Refuges	Backpacking/ Camping			
King Ludwig's Way	Germany	80	Yes	No	Some	Yes	All	Low–Moderate
Kungsleden	Sweden	270	Some	Yes	Yes	No	Some	Moderate
Long Trail	Vermont, USA	273	Some	3-sided shelters	Yes	No	Most	Moderate–High
Lost Coast Trail	California, USA	53	Some	No	Yes	No	Some	Moderate
Lycian Way	Turkey	330	Some	Some	Yes	No	Some	Moderate–High
Milford Track	New Zealand	33	Yes	Yes	No	No	No	Low– Moderate
Ocala Trail	Florida, USA	71	Some	No	Yes	No	All	Low
Overland Track	Australia	60	Yes	Yes	No	No	No	Moderate
Paria River Canyon	Utah & Arizona, USA	38	No	No	Yes	No	No	Moderate
South Downs Way	England	100	Yes	No	No	Yes	All	Low–Moderate
Superior Hiking Trail	Minnesota, USA	300	Some	No	Yes	Some	All	Moderate
Tahoe Rim Trail	California & Nevada, USA	165	Most	No	Yes	No	All	Moderate–High
Tour du Mont Blanc	France, Italy, & Switzerland	100+	Most	Yes	Some	Most (Except Refuges)	Most	Moderate
Walker's Haute Route	France & Switzerland	114	Most	Yes	Some	No	Most	Moderate–High
West Coast Trail	British Columbia, Canada	50	No	No	Yes	No	No	High
West Highland Way	Scotland	96	Yes	Some	Some	Yes	All	Moderate

PART 2: EXTRAORDINARY HIKES FOR ORDINARY PEOPLE

Rock cairns of all sizes and shapes are often used to mark trails above tree line. (Chilkoot Trail)

Part 2 is the heart of this book—descriptions of thirty of the world's great long-distance trails. We've been privileged to walk these trails (nearly all of them in their entirety) over the past decade and these walks have been an important part of our lives—learning about other places and people, improving our fitness, and having an adventure (nearly all of them enjoyable!) every day we're on the trail. We've chosen these trails as our favorites and to represent the great diversity of long-distance walking. These trails are found on six continents, represent fourteen countries, and range from cultural landscapes like Cinque Terre and El Camino de Santiago to wilderness walks like the John Muir Trail and the Kungsleden, and a vast spectrum in between. Some can be walked in a few days, others a few weeks. Most can be walked in sections, sometimes even a day at a time. Some allow walkers to stay in B&Bs, small inns or mountain refuges, and others are backpacking trips. These trails are extraordinary, but they can be walked by ordinary people. We hope you'll sense and share our enthusiasm for long-distance walking and these trails in particular.

Previous page: Road crossings along many long-distance trails offer access and welcome accommodations and other services to walkers. (Alta Via 1)

Part 2: Extraordinary Hikes for Ordinary People

Alta Via 1

Location Italy

Length 93 miles

Accommodations
Commercial: Some
Huts/refuges: Yes
Camping: No

Baggage transfer No

Option to walk in sections Most

Degree of challenge Moderate–High

ITALY

Lago de Braies marks the northern terminus of the Alta Via 1.

Our second day on the Alta Via 1 was challenging and we were grousing a little. We'd walked that day up and over Forcella del Lago at nearly 8,000 feet, down a steep descent, and were now walking up again, this time to Rifugio Lagazuoi, perhaps the most dramatically sited refuge in all of the Dolomites and our destination for the night. We were cold and tired and looking forward to a hot shower, a warm meal, and a comfortable bed. But as we climbed to the refuge we passed the obvious remains of the prolonged and brutal mountain warfare between the Austrians and Italians in World War I—trenches, tunnels, lookouts, barbed wire, discarded mess tins, and bomb damage. These soldiers endured unimaginable hardship and had no down jackets, lightweight backpacks, and breathable rainwear. Thinking of the life of soldiers during this awful war put things in perspective and we didn't feel sorry for ourselves any longer—we continued on to our refuge without another complaint.

The Dolomites are a wonderland of jagged mountain peaks and deep green valleys in the eastern Alps, mostly in northern Italy. They are composed of limestone formed at the bottom of an ancient sea; these sea beds were later pushed up by tectonic forces, and finally eroded into their present form by glaciation and weathering. This limestone is what gives them their distinctive and appealing whitish or light grey color. The mountains are laced with trails, many of which had their beginnings as ancient mule tracks and old military roads. The Alta Via 1 was the first of what are now a number of long-distance routes through the mountains, and many walkers think it's the most beautiful. Running for 93 miles between Lago di Braies (an attractive Italian lake near the Austrian

Fixed chains called **via ferrata** *assist walkers up some steep slopes encountered on the Alta Via 1.*

border) to the small historic city of Belluno in the Veneto, the AV1 weaves its way through many of the most famous peaks in the Dolomites. Known for their important role in the development of rock and ice climbing (you'll see intrepid climbers in several locations near the trail), the Dolomites are more popular today for skiing in winter and walking in summer.

Rugged spires and pinnacles mark the 10,000-foot peaks while the trail undulates between scenic high mountain passes and rich alpine meadows filled with wildflowers, with deep forests and blue-green lakes in between. Look carefully for marine fossils in the rocks that signal the mountains' origins. Wildlife includes chamois and ibex (both species of wild mountain goats), deer, marmots (with their piercingly sharp whistles), and golden eagles.

A distinguishing feature of the Alta Via 1, like many trails in the Dolomites, is their *via ferrata* ("iron way") sections: pitches that are steep and/or exposed and for which a series of metal rungs, ladders, cables, or chains have been fixed. A few quite short sections scattered along the Alta Via 1 will give you a taste of what it's like to use *via ferrata*. A major segment in the stage just north of Belluno can be avoided (as we did) by using a variant of the main trail, or you can rent technical mountaineering equipment to help negotiate this section.

We've conveniently romanticized away most of the harder parts of the walk and have fond memories of many places and events: our walk along the base of the massive "wall of walls," a 5-mile long series of impressive

Refuges along the Alta Via 1 offer some of the most dramatic views of the Dolomites.

> *"Walking is the great adventure, the first meditation, a practice of heartiness and soul primary to humankind. Walking is the exact balance between spirit and humility."*
> —**Gary Snyder**

vertical rock walls that are used for advanced rock climbing; our night at Refugio Lagazuoi, the highest point along the trail, with mountains in all directions, where we felt we were literally on top of the world; the unusually clear mountain air; our futile attempts to appreciate grappa, the local spirit; the evening alpenglow that turned the mountains pink; Cinque Torri, five rock towers that continue to support a culture of mountaineering; the chorus of bells worn by countless cows and goats; the 3,000-foot tunnel (called Galleria Lagazuoi) constructed in World War I by the Italian army mountaineers to secretly move troops; the international group of walkers we met along the way.

This would be an especially fascinating adventure for military buffs, as the evidence of former battles is written in the rocks (and this sense of history adds another dimension for all walkers). After all, how many walks feature foxholes and tunnels? One refuge was as much museum as lodging with its collection of shell and mortar casings spilling out onto the large porch. Culturally, the northern portion of the trail still seemed very Germanic (because of its historic association with Austria), and German was spoken more often than Italian; this brought home to us the fluidity of European political borders over the past few hundred years.

Access to the southern end of the trail is relatively easy by train to Belluno. Reaching Lago di Braies is more difficult as it is at the end of long mountain road; we used a taxi service from Belluno, but it was expensive. The trail is marked by red and white painted stripes, and way finding is generally not difficult, though we had to pay close attention to our guidebook in several places. The trail is generally well maintained, though we were happy to have our hiking poles on some downhill stretches and where there was snow and ice on the trail.

The trail is served by a series of refuges (*rifugios*) at higher elevations and small hotels (*albergos*) at periodic road crossings, and this means the trail can be walked more quickly or slowly than the standard ten-day itinerary, and that it can easily be walked in sections. In addition, there are a few ski lifts that can moderate the route, and some companies offer "best of" packages, allowing the walker to pre-select portions of the trail. Camping is forbidden, but the prevalence of so many refuges means one can still walk the Alta Via 1 without spending a lot on lodging. The walking season is generally from mid-June to late September (we walked in the second half of September, right before most of the trail's refuges closed for the year), and reservations at accommodations are recommended in July and August. As on most mountain trails (and maybe even more so here), you must be prepared for all kinds of weather, even in summer. English is not spoken along the trail as universally as in urban areas of Europe and it may be wise to take German and Italian phrase books if only to avoid dinner surprises.

The Dolomites are among the classic mountain ranges of the world and should be on the resume of all serious walkers. The Alta Via 1 is an excellent introduction—long enough to fully immerse walkers in these distinctive peaks and passes and routed to take full advantage of the rich history of this region of the world. Since the walk can easily be done in sections and there are a variety of accommodations (including those dramatically sited refuges), it's an easy trail to customize. And this is a trail that will make you appreciate the hardships of war—and the recent advances in walking gear.

The Dolomites are known for their rugged limestone peaks.

The Alta Via 1 goes up and over several steep passes.

Further Reading

www1.dolomiti-altevie.it/inglese/altaVia/Home.asp

Price, Gillian. *Trekking in the Dolomites: Alta Via Routes 1 and 2, with Alta Via Routes 3-6 in Outline.* Milnthorpe, Cumbria, UK: Cicerone Press, 2011.

Stedman, Harry. *Trekking in the Dolomites: Alta Via 1 & 2.* Hindhead, Surrey, UK: Trailblazer Publications, 2006.

Part 2: Extraordinary Hikes for Ordinary People

C&O Canal

Location Maryland & Washington, DC, USA

Length 185 miles

Accommodations
Commercial: Some
Huts/refuges: No
Camping: Yes

Baggage transfer No

Option to walk in sections All

Degree of challenge Low

UNITED STATES

The towpath separates the C&O Canal and the Potomac River.

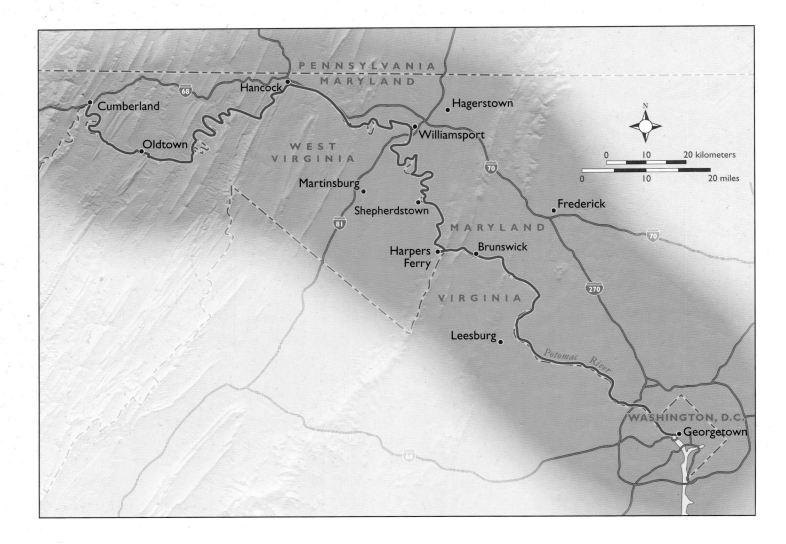

What has seventy-four locks, but no doors? Given the trail we're considering, this riddle isn't very challenging. But we enjoyed watching the elementary school group at one of the National Park Service visitor centers try to puzzle it out. These visitor centers are located at the two ends of the trail (Georgetown and Cumberland) and at Brunswick, Williamsport, and Hancock, as well as at the nearby attractions of Harpers Ferry and Antietam Battlefield. They are rich sources of information about the C&O Canal and the surrounding area, including its human and natural history. They have interesting displays, are staffed by knowledgeable rangers and volunteers, and offer books and other materials. And they're even free! While the C&O Canal is fortunate to have such a rich stock of visitor centers, many of the long-distance trails included in this book have similar facilities, and walkers should take maximum advantage, as these will make your walking more interesting (and sometimes entertaining).

The C&O Canal runs through the historic Georgetown section of Washington, DC.

The Potomac River is one of the largest in the eastern United States and was important to Native Americans as well as colonists and those who traveled westward along its banks. Following the Potomac from the Chesapeake Bay to its headwaters is like following the early years of the colonial expansion of the nation. The lands surrounding this important river have seen it all—peace and warfare, cooperation and confrontation, boom and bust. For years, the river marked the western frontier of the emerging country and separated North from South during the Civil War.

Along the river's northern bank runs the C&O (Chesapeake and Ohio) Canal and its delightfully walkable towpath extending 185 miles from the trendy neighborhood of Georgetown in Washington, DC, to Cumberland in rural western Maryland. The C&O Canal has been called the "most delightful and varied greenway in America," and we can't argue with that. With a total change in elevation of only about 600 feet, it's essentially flat, and the surface is packed clay and gravel and well groomed, all making for easy walking. The towpath and its immediate environs comprise the Chesapeake and Ohio National Historical Park, a unit of the National Park System, which has been called "America's most distinctive national park."

But the C&O Canal didn't have its origins as a park. Early Americans hoped the Potomac River would provide a way westward to the Pacific Ocean. George Washington first wrote of the river's potential when helping with a survey party traveling upriver to the Ohio Valley when he

The Great Falls section of the Potomac River illustrates the need for the C&O Canal.

was only sixteen. As early as 1774 he introduced legislation in Virginia to build skirting canals around the Great Falls area to make navigation of that part of the river possible, and in 1785 he became the first president of the Potowmack Canal Company. Because of these early efforts, he's thought of as "Father of the C&O Canal." Later politicians and industrialists continued to dream of a way to connect the Chesapeake Bay with the Ohio River to make navigation and trade possible between the eastern U.S. and the Midwest. The Potomac River was promising, but the powerful and treacherous rapids made navigation along its length impossible. A canal incorporating a series of locks to raise and lower boats could work, and a towpath constructed beside the canal would allow mules to pull boats along.

The canal was started on the Georgetown end in 1828 just as the Industrial Revolution was coming to a head in America; President John Quincy Adams broke ground. But the project turned out to be harder and more expensive than imagined. The terrain was tough in places; challenges included the need for a nearly mile-long tunnel and negotiation of many small and large steams flowing into the Potomac. Way behind schedule (and way over budget), the canal didn't reach Cumberland until 1850; by that time the Baltimore and Ohio (B&O) Railroad was completed along roughly the same route, making the canal nearly obsolete before it even began to reach its imagined potential.

By the mid-1920s, the canal had been abandoned and fell into disrepair. The federal government purchased the canal in 1938 with the intent of making it a recreation area. After World War II priorities had changed, and Congress considered developing it into a parkway for automobiles. This plan was met with indignation by conservationists and Supreme Court Justice William O. Douglas led an eight-day protest march along the canal in 1954, calling the towpath "a long stretch of quiet and peace." The canal now draws an estimated three million visitors a year, though most of them come from the Washington metropolitan area.

The early history of the area includes use of the Potomac River by several tribes of Native Americans, including the Potomac, Iroquois, Piscataway, and Shawnee, though there is little physical evidence of this today. The word

"Potomac" may be a derivation of the Algonquian name for a tribe in the area and may mean "place of trade." The river was a bountiful source of food throughout the seasons as well as a transportation corridor.

The canal runs directly through much of the military history of America, including the French and Indian War and the Civil War. The impressive Fort Frederick, just off the towpath at mile 112 (the full length of the canal has mileage markers), is an impressive stone structure (most forts at the time were wooden) that was built to defend the western frontier during the French and Indian War. Oldtown, at mile 161, was a key location for both the French and Indian War and Civil War, serving as a wilderness trading post for hundreds of years.

But the town of Harpers Ferry at mile 61 is the historical jewel of the walk. Set just above the impressive confluence of the Potomac and Shenandoah rivers, this town was the site of abolitionist John Brown's famous raid on the federal armory in an attempt to arm a slave uprising, and was the place of the largest surrender of U.S. forces in the Civil War. The Confederate Army used the surrounding heights to shell the town and the Union troops in it, and an empathetic Confederate General Stonewall Jackson said he'd rather "take the town fifty times than defend it once"; in fact, Harpers Ferry changed hands eight times during the war. Other spots along the Potomac saw many troop crossings, skirmishes and battles. Union and Confederate troops clashed again later at Antietam, the bloodiest battle in U.S. history. The battlefield is just two and half miles off the Canal near mile 70. Both Harpers Ferry and Antietam are units of the National Park system.

The walk illustrates the fascinating story of the construction and engineering of the canal, and walking the towpath allows close inspection of this wonder of its time. The seventy-four locks raised and lowered boats along the course of the canal; the swinging miter gates at each end of the locks were derivations of designs by Leonardo da Vinci. The locks were usually lined with locally quarried rock, and much of the stonework is elegant (though some of it has been damaged by flooding). At every lock there was a house for the lockkeeper and his family and some of these

structures remain. The National Park Service has restored a lockhouse and its associated buildings, including a mule barn, at Four Locks (mile 108.8). Several of the lockhouses are now available for overnight stays by walkers and we recommend this option.

"Happy trails to you."
—Dale Evans

There were other impressive feats of engineering and construction. Large culverts were constructed under the canal to allow for the many tributaries of the Potomac to reach the river. A series of eleven large aqueducts was built to contain the canal as it passed over the larger tributaries. The largest of these is the Monocacy Aqueduct, which is supported by seven lovely stone arches. The Paw Paw Tunnel between miles 155 and 156 was the canal's largest construction project, taking fourteen years (instead of the two that had been estimated) and nearly bankrupting the company that developed the canal. This was also the site of numerous labor disputes when Irish, English, and German workers staged walkouts because they were poorly treated (and sometimes not even paid). The tunnel is nearly a mile long and was built as a shortcut to avoid several miles of a winding section of the Potomac. Because construction was so difficult, the tunnel was not built wide enough to allow boats to pass one another. There's a story (possibly even true) that two boats stayed in the Paw Paw Tunnel for days because neither captain would grant the right-of-way, and this backed up canal traffic for miles. Finally, canal officials flushed them out by building a smoky fire at one end.

Boats were specially built to navigate the canal; these wooden boats were 90 feet long and 14 feet wide, the maximum that could be accommodated by the locks. A small mule barn was located on the bow and a small cabin on the stern for the captain and his family. Two teams of two mules could keep 120 tons of boat and cargo moving at 4 miles per hour. Much of the cargo was coal mined in the Alleghany Mountains to be delivered to the Washington, DC, metropolitan area; produce moved upstream. If you'd like to ride in a replica boat, the National Park Service operates canal boats at the Georgetown and Great Falls visitor centers, and there is a third boat on display just south of Cumberland.

Although most people consider the C&O Canal an historical trail, don't overlook its natural history. Landforms change dramatically and include tidewater at Georgetown, where the Potomac empties into the Chesapeake Bay, the fertile rolling Piedmont farmlands (called "the sugar lands" by European settlers), the Great Valley of Maryland, and the Appalachian Mountains of western Maryland. The 20,000 acres comprising the park are considered highly biodiverse. There is good birding along the canal with bald eagles; red-tailed hawks; turkeys; owls; several kinds of woodpeckers, including flickers, hairy, downy, and pileated; warblers and other migrating songbirds in the spring and fall; and lots of water birds, including ospreys, great blue herons, ducks, and geese. It's common to see whitetail deer, but less common to see foxes and beavers, though there's lots of evidence of the latter. Much of the area is heavily forested, primarily in hardwoods, and we especially enjoyed the Osage orange trees with their distinctive fall fruits (look for them on the ground).

"Of all exercises walking is the best."
—Thomas Jefferson

Other highlights for us were the Great Falls area at mile 15, where we took a short detour on the Billy Goat Trail to see the impressive rapids on the Potomac (this side trail is rough), a short section of the trail near Harpers Ferry that is part of the Appalachian Trail, and the Potomac rapids at mile 41.6, where U.S. Olympic kayakers often train. Several restaurants make the highlights list as well, including Betty's across the bridge in Shepherdstown, West Virginia, (where we enjoyed the bean soup with country ham, a closely guarded recipe), Weaver's in Hancock, Maryland (where the chocolate pie and other delicacies are worth the weight in the pack), and the School House Kitchen in Oldtown, Maryland (funky but friendly). You can probably tell we were often hungry!

Logistics for walking the C&O Canal are relatively easy. The walking season is long, with the summer months of June through August generally hot. Long springs and falls offer great opportunities for less crowded conditions; spring includes showy dogwood and redbud and the foliage in the fall is nice. Even winter offers good opportunities for walking sections of the canal when there is no snow on the ground. The entire towpath is very well marked and the mile markers make it easy to keep track of where you are. A series of camping areas are spaced roughly every 5 to 7 miles and include pumps for drinking water (shut down in winter). The towpath meets roads periodically and this provides access to B&Bs and other commercial services and lodgings, though you may need to arrange for occasional rides because these services may be a little ways off the towpath. The walk can be done in either direction, though if you start at the eastern end you walk along with its twenty-two-year history of construction. Walkers, lots of bikers, and occasional equestrians enjoy the towpath, and the canal itself is used in a few places by canoeists and kayakers (though most of the canal is dry). Commercial shuttle service is available and there is train service between Washington, DC, and Cumberland.

The C&O Canal is a wonderful resource for walkers from the busy Washington, DC, metropolitan area and leads ambitious walkers into the hinterlands of rural Maryland. The C&O follows the course of the impressive Potomac River and all its natural history and traces the eventful and important human history of this area over the last several hundred years. With a number of road crossings, it's an ideal trail to walk in sections. The C&O Canal Association offers occasional group hikes and these are a good option. And be sure to take advantage of the visitor centers along the way as they'll make your walk more informative (and keep you entertained!).

Walkers can ride on a replica canal boat at the Great Falls Visitor Center.

The C&O Canal's level, well-groomed towpath makes for easy walking.

Further Reading

www.canal.com

www.candocanal.org

www.nps.gov/choh

Hahn, Thomas. *Towpath Guide to the C&O Canal.* Cumberland, MD: American Canal and Transportation Center, 1994.

High, Mike. *The C&O Companion.* Baltimore, MD: The Johns Hopkins University Press, 2001.

Location Spain

Length 480 miles

Accommodations
Commercial: Most
Huts/refuges: Yes
Camping: Some

Baggage transfer Yes

Option to walk in sections All

Degree of challenge Low–Moderate

SPAIN

*The handsome medieval bridge,
Puente de Peregrinos, brings pilgrims
to the village of Molinaseca.*

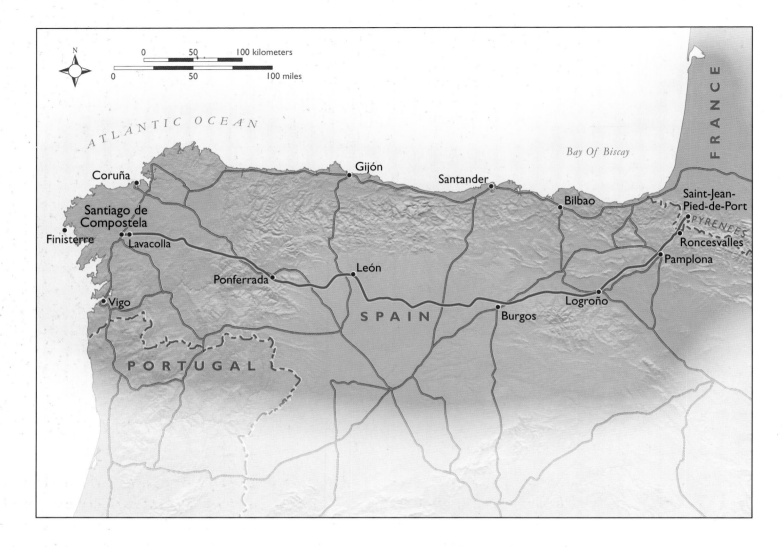

Buen camino. *We'd exchanged this greeting with other pilgrims (or peregrinos) hundreds of times over the course of our walk on El Camino de Santiago. It's an all-purpose phrase that can mean "hello," "goodbye," or many other things, but most of all it means "I hope you find what you're searching for." Of course, many people walk the Camino for spiritual reasons, but others walk during one of life's transitions and are searching for meaning and direction. Buen camino seemed to have a special resonance this morning, the last day of our walk, the day we reached Santiago de Compostela. We'd stayed the night before in Lavacolla, where pilgrims traditionally washed and prepared for their entry into the Cathedral of St. James the next day. It was a short walk into Santiago, where we joined with hundreds of others for the traditional noon mass devoted to arriving pilgrims. During the ceremony priests greeted the congregation in several languages, acknowledging the international nature of this walk. Near the end of the mass, a group of eight red-robed* tiraboleiros *walked*

Pilgrims become more numerous as the camino approaches Santiago de Compostela.

to the front of the cathedral and everyone stirred; we knew we were in for a treat. They were there to swing the famous Botafumeiro, the giant incense burner attached by a very long rope running through a pulley at the top of the cathedral. Over five feet high and weighing 175 pounds, the ornate Botafumeiro is made of an alloy of brass and bronze plated by a very thin layer of silver, giving it a golden sheen. It's filled with nearly 90 pounds of burning charcoal and incense and produces clouds of fragrant smoke. The tradition of the Botafumeiro began in the eleventh century and some people think it was designed to mask the smell of pilgrims, many of whom had walked hundreds or even thousands of miles. The tiraboleiros grasped the free end of the rope, pushed the censer to start it swinging, and then pulled with all their might at the end of each swing. Soon the vessel was swinging all the way across the front of the cathedral and nearly reaching its ceiling. (We read later that the Botafumeiro reaches a height of nearly 65 feet and travels at over 40 miles per hour.) All the while, the cathedral's massive pipe organ was at full volume and the voice of an angelic singing nun was amplified over the cathedral's sound system. Wow! This was a powerful, even magical moment for all the pilgrims who had journeyed to Santiago, a glorious end to a wonderful walk.

El Camino de Santiago is a pilgrim route running west for nearly 500 miles across the north of Spain from the Pyrenees Mountains to the city of Santiago de Compostela. Pilgrims have been walking this route for over a

The Camino often follows country lanes, some of them deeply eroded by centuries of pilgrims.

thousand years. But where does the trail really begin? Originally, pilgrims started from their homes in Europe and joined one of the several routes leading to Santiago, most of them eventually feeding into what is now called simply El Camino. Common starting points today include St.-Jean-Pied-de-Port on the French side of the Pyrenees Mountains or Roncesvalles on the Spanish side, or at any point along the route in northern Spain depending on how far you wish to walk. The Catholic Church requires walking at least the final 100 kilometers (64 miles) to Santiago for walkers to receive a Compostela, certification of having completed the pilgrimage.

El Camino de Santiago means "the road of Saint Iago" or more commonly "the Way of St. James." St. James was one of the twelve apostles and is the patron saint of Spain. While the story of St. James is murky after all these years, it's believed that his remains were found in a boat that washed up on the shores of northern Spain (at Finisterre, the "end of the world"), and were eventually taken to Santiago, where they have been housed since 841. A large and impressive cathedral was built to honor his memory and Christians have made their way to Santiago to pay their respects ever since. A half million or more pilgrims made the journey each year in medieval times, but the numbers dropped off substantially until quite recently; now, more than a hundred thousand people walk a significant portion of the trail each year, substantially more during holy years, years when St. James Day (July 25) falls on a Sunday. Numbers are definitely on the rise.

Santiago is considered the third most important site in Christendom (after Rome and Jerusalem) and El Camino is far and away the most popular Christian pilgrimage. From the Pyrenees, the trail traverses the rolling hills of the Basque country with its distinctive architecture and language, then crosses a long elevated plain called the *meseta*, enters the more mountainous area of El Bierzo, and finally weaves through lush Galicia to Santiago.

The walk is long but not difficult. Wandering across the north of Spain from town to town, the route is remarkably rich in history and culture. Guidebooks to the trail list over 1,800 buildings of great historic, architectural, spiritual, and artistic interest, and the old town of Santiago is a UNESCO World Heritage Site. Some buildings along the trail date from

Part 2: Extraordinary Hikes for Ordinary People

the ninth century. Most of the communities, some large like Pamplona, Logrono, Burgos, Leon, and Santiago, but most small, grew up around the trail and were designed to serve the needs of pilgrims. All towns have at least one church and one or more *hospitales* originally intended to house and care for pilgrims. Many of these are still in use as lodgings and are now generally called *alberques*; they provide inexpensive lodgings for *perigrinos*.

The *Codex Calixtinus* is a further manifestation of the Camino's history. This twelfth-century illuminated manuscript celebrates the life of St. James and includes "A Guide for the Traveler," offering route-finding information for the Camino and identifying places to stay as well as places to avoid. Considered the world's first guidebook, the *Codex* helped popularize the pilgrimages to Santiago de Compostella.

The Pyrenees are one of the world's great mountain ranges and the trail offers at least a glimpse of this region. Pamplona is especially interesting because of the heritage associated with the "running of the bulls." We found Leon to be one of the more beautiful cities we've visited with its cathedral (known as The House of Light), a palace designed by Antonio Gaudi (Spain's most famous architect), medieval walls, and tourist-friendly old town. The province of Galicia is the favorite section of most walkers. It seems very lush and green after the more arid *meseta*, has its own language (related to Portuguese), small-scale agriculture, numerous *horreos* or small elevated granaries, and distinctive Celtic heritage, including use of the bagpipe in traditional music. Highlights of the trail for us were the impressive monastery in tiny Samos (one of the oldest and largest in Europe); the castle of the Knights Templar in Ponferrada (the knights fought the Moors and protected pilgrims); the crosses everywhere fashioned out of stones and tree branches by pilgrims; the storks nesting in the church steeples; and the regional foods (e.g., local cheeses and honey, Caldo Galego and Tarta Santiago) and inexpensive and delightful wine.

Though long, the Camino is not difficult; it is especially well marked (look for the scallop shell motif and accompanying yellow arrows everywhere), footing is easy, and climbs and grades are not excessive (with the exception of the initial climb over the Pyrenees). The route is varied, and includes quiet country lanes, across farm fields and vineyards, through cool forests, and along streams and ancient Roman roads. A few short sections of the route are along busier roads where walkers are usually separated from the traffic, but you must still be very cognizant of safety.

Of course all walkers are excited to reach Santiago and it doesn't disappoint. It's a relatively large city (about one hundred thousand residents), but has a small, walled old town that caters heavily to visitors and especially pilgrims. The Cathedral of St. James, begun in 1075, is especially impressive and meaningful. The old town also includes a five-hundred-year old university, impressive statues and fountains, stately public buildings, more than enough sidewalk cafes, and many shops and carts serving local *helado* (ice cream).

Most walkers acknowledge the pilgrimage by honoring several important traditions, one of which is the custom of identifying yourself as a pilgrim. Historically, pilgrims used a staff and most walkers continue this tradition, though many (including us) have updated it with contemporary hiking poles. And most walkers hang a scallop shell from their pack signifying that they are on a pilgrimage; scallop shells were found on the beach where St. James' body was discovered and they have become the symbol of the pilgrimage. Most importantly, each walker carries a passport or "credential" (*Credencial del Peregrino*) and collects stamps along the walk at local churches, *alberques*, cafes, and other locations. The passport is then presented to the church office in Santiago as proof of the journey and a *Compostela* is awarded.

In medieval times, walking the Camino was an extraordinary, often dangerous undertaking. Many of the larger rivers had to be crossed at the mercy of unprincipled ferrymen, Spain was at war with the Moors of North Africa, bandits made a living by robbing pilgrims, and the region was

"I only went out for a walk and finally concluded to stay out until sundown: for going out, I found, was really going in."

—John Muir

Many walkers on the Camino de Santiago consider the hilly countryside of Galicia to be the most beautiful part of the trail.

Part 2: Extraordinary Hikes for Ordinary People

occupied by wolves. Today's pilgrims have it much easier, but there are still several logistical concerns. The busy season on the Camino is July and August and it can be very busy indeed; it's better to walk in the spring, early summer, or fall, if possible.

Most pilgrims stay in *alberques*, which are hostel-like accommodations with communal sleeping and bathing facilities. They are operated by churches, towns, and as private businesses and are inexpensive, but there are few frills and they tend to fill quickly during the busy season. Because of this, many pilgrims walk very early in the day to claim a bunk or room at the next town. Most towns also have B&Bs and small inns. Though there can be many pilgrims on the trail during the busy season, it's interesting to meet like-minded people from all over the world, and since the Camino is essentially a one-way trail, it doesn't feel quite so crowded.

Be advised that the Spanish have a long tradition of eating dinner late; many restaurants don't open until 9:00 p.m. and sometimes later. This might be a problem for walkers who are tired and hungry at the end of the day, but many cafes offer a "pilgrim's meal" that usually starts at 7:00 and includes a limited (but adequate) menu, including wine, at a reasonable cost. You should not expect locals to speak English (and many don't), so it's advisable to bone up on Spanish—including key words like *panaderia* (bakery), *bocadillos* (sandwiches), *cerveza* (beer), and *vino tinto* (red wine)—and bring along a phrase book.

El Camino is one of the oldest and most significant walks in the world. We were reminded of this in one of our guidebooks that said the trail "still passes through the same villages, climbs the same hills, crosses the same rivers, and visits the same chapels, churches, cathedrals and other monuments as did the route taken by our predecessors in centuries gone by." Another guidebook points out that the some of the deeply incised sections

The impressive cathedral at Santiago de Compostela is the ultimate destination of pilgrims on the Camino.

of trail in Galica and elsewhere have been eroded "by millions of pilgrims over many centuries of walking." It was a privilege and joy to follow in the footsteps of so many pilgrims who have walked the trail for over a thousand years. We hope you'll consider joining in this tradition. *Buen camino.*

> ## *"All truly great thoughts are conceived by walking."*
> ### —Friedrich Nietzsche

···· Further Reading ·····················

www.americanpilgrims.com

www.csj.org.uk

www.santiago-compostela.net

Alcorn, Susan. *Camino Chronicle: Walking to Santiago.* Oakland, CA: Shepherd Canyon Books, 2006.

Brierley, John. *A Pilgrim's Guide to the Camino de Santiago: The Way of St. James.* Forres, Scotland: Findhorn Press, 2010.

Brierley, John. *Camino de Santiago Maps.* Forres, Scotland: Findhorn Press, 2011.

Cole, Ben, and Bethan Davies. *Camino de Santiago Map.* Vancouver, British Columbia: Pili Pala Press, 2010.

Davies, Bethan, Ben Cole, Daphne Hnatiuk. *Walking the Camino de Santiago.* Vancouver, British Columbia: Pili Pala Press, 2009.

Gitlitz, David, and Linda Davidson. *Pilgrimage Road to Santiago: The Complete Cultural Handbook.* New York: St. Martin's Griffin, 2000.

Raju, Alison. *The Way of St. James Volume II: Pyrennees–Santiago–Finnisterre.* Milnthorpe, Cumbria, UK: Cicerone Press, 2006

Rudolf, Conrad. *Pilgrimage to the End of the World: The Road to Santiago de Compostela.* Chicago: University of Chicago Press, 2004.

Cape Winelands Walk

Location South Africa

Length 60 miles

Accommodations
Commercial: Yes
Huts/refuges: No
Camping: No

Baggage transfer Yes

Option to walk in sections All

Degree of challenge Low–Moderate

SOUTH AFRICA

The Cape Winelands Walk wanders through vineyards
and over the Hottentots Holland Mountains.

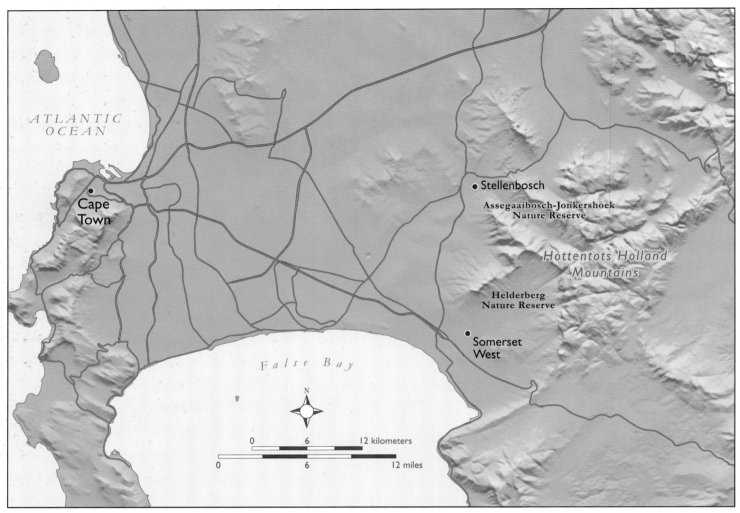

The route of this walk may vary, and walkers must arrange to conduct this walk with World Walks or Walking Holidays SA.

The second day of our walk started in Lourensford, one of the oldest and largest wine estates in South Africa, and, the guidebooks say, one of the most beautiful in the world. The estate has provided the setting for a number of national and international films. Apple, pear, and plum orchards complemented the extensive vineyards. We walked across the estate through the vineyards as we climbed toward a pass in the surrounding Hottentots Holland Mountains that would lead us to another wine estate and our next night's accommodation. Soon the carefully cultivated vineyards gave way to the wilder fynbos, the biologically rich shrublands that make this area famous in the plant world. The weather was warm—in the 80s—but the full summer sun made it feel hot. We lingered in the shade of eucalyptus trees along several mountain streams that crossed the trail, refilling our water bottles at the last stream before the final climb to the pass. We

The Cape Winelands Walk links a series of South Africa's historic wine estates, including Vergelegen.

lunched at the pass as we peered into the next valley to the north and our ultimate destination— the historic town of Stellenbosh and Jonkershoek Nature Reserve beyond. We celebrated our ascent of the pass by pouring one of our water bottles over our heads and felt instantly cooler. After lunch, we followed farm roads down to the smaller, family-owned Dornier Wine Estate, where the historic manor house has been converted to a lodge and restaurant. We were the only guests that evening and we had fun pretending we were the owners, toasting our day at dinner with a cold, crisp bottle of Sauvignon Blanc made from grapes grown on the estate.

There are many reasons to walk the Cape Winelands—the wine, the culture, the distinctive plants and animals, and the rich history of the local area and of Africa more generally. Let's start with the wine. While wine has come to dominate agriculture in a number of regions around the globe, they've been doing it and doing it well for more than three hundred years in the

Portions of the Cape Winelands Walk traverse aromatic eucalyptus forests.

Western Cape of South Africa, a wide swath of some of the world's most productive farmland located about 50 miles outside Cape Town. Here you can follow firsthand the story of wine making from vineyard to glass. There are more than two hundred wine estates in this area, many offering tours, tasting, dining, and lodging. The wine—and the region's other agricultural products, including fruit, vegetables, and cheese—offer a terroir that contributes to the area's distinctive and appealing sense of place.

The town of Stellenbosch, founded in 1679, is the second oldest town in South Africa, second only to Cape Town, the "Mother City." This is the geographic and historic heart of the Cape Winelands Walk. Stellenbosch is nicknamed the "City of Oaks," and many of the town's streets are lined with three-hundred-year-old oak trees, some of which have been declared national monuments. The prestigious University of Stellenbosch is embedded in the town, and includes rows of attractive buildings with red tile roofs, an impressive botanical garden, and its famous Coetzenburg Sports Grounds, including a rugby stadium and historic rugby club house. Other attractions in town include the historic and picturesque Lanzerac Hotel, Rupert Museum, Kweekskool Theological Seminary, Oliver Art Center, a small African market, and the Institute of Culinary Arts (which we recommend for lunch or dinner). We spent a Saturday night in Stellenbosch and it was lively, with downtown streets closed to traffic and live music and dining under the oaks.

> ## "All walking is discovery. On foot we take the time to see things whole."
> ## —Hal Borland

The Cape Winelands Walk has a wilder side as well, including the surrounding Hottentots Holland Mountain Range, the distinctive and important *fynbos* vegetation, and an impressive associated collection of animals. In the world of plant biology, the earth is divided into six plant kingdoms, the smallest and biologically richest of which (on a per acre basis) is the *fynbos*, geographically restricted to the Western Cape of South Africa.

Cape Winelands walkers often see and hear baboons.

This shrubland is composed of an estimated ten thousand species, many of which are endemic (i.e., found nowhere else in the world). Primary plant families include Proteas (large, broad-leafed plants), Ericas (small plants with needle-like leaves evolved to conserve water), and Restios (grass-like plants that have historically been used for thatching roofs). The King Protea is the national flower of South Africa. Many *fynbos* plants are "serotinous"— that is they're adapted to survive periodic fires. These adaptations include seeds that persist for long periods of time and open in response to the heat of periodic wildfires.

The mountains and *fynbos* provide habitat for a variety of interesting and exotic animals, many of which will be seen by walkers, including baboons, bontebok, sugar birds, and sunbirds. Leopards are rarely seen, though their tracks and droppings are clear evidence of their presence. Several species of poisonous snakes, including the puff adder and Cape cobra, inhabit the area, though we didn't see them (despite watching carefully!). Several large nature reserves—Helderberg, Jonkershoek, and Assegaaibosch—have been established to protect local flora and fauna, and these reserves are a vital part of the Cape Winelands Walk.

The Cape Winelands has a rich history that is a microcosm of much of Africa. Colonized by the Dutch and other Europeans over three hundred years ago, much of the country prospered economically, but at the disadvantage of the native black population, which was actively discriminated against. This long apartheid era in South Africa ended officially in 1994 thanks to the sacrifice and leadership of Nelson Mandela and many others, but the country is still plagued by racial problems including continuing tension between the black majority and the white minority and large-scale

Showy proteas are an important component of the distinctive **fynbos** *vegetation along the Cape Winelands Walk.*

immigration from surrounding countries. Sprawling squatters' camps are found along the main road from Cape Town and even in more rural areas such as the outskirts of Stellenbosch. However, the complicated history of the area has left an unusual and appealing culture that blends elements of European and African architecture, arts, food, and language.

The Cape Winelands Walk is about 60 miles, though there are a number of options that can shorten or lengthen it. The walk begins in the Helderberg Nature Reserve in the town of Somerset West, and this is an excellent place to learn about the area's natural history, enabling walkers to more fully appreciate this unusual landscape. The choice of accommodations on the walk ranges from very upscale wine estates to more modest guesthouses and family stays; camping is not an option. Baggage transport can easily be arranged. This part of South Africa has a Mediterranean climate—warm, dry summers and cool wet winters—thus the best months for walking are November through March. Parts of the walk traverse private lands where rights of way have been negotiated, and because of this, this walk must be arranged through South Africa Walks or World Walks. We saw very few other walkers, but always felt secure.

The Cape Winelands Walk is an excellent introduction to southern Africa, its distinctive landscape, history, and culture. The walk includes impressive public nature reserves with exotic plants and animals, private lands in the form of wine estates and other agricultural areas, and lively and attractive towns. Our walk left us glad we had chosen this trail—and we have a strong desire to return to this part of the world.

Further Reading

www.walkingholidays.co.za/node/4

www.worldwalks.com/the-cape-winelands-walk.aspx

Part 2: Extraordinary Hikes for Ordinary People

Chilkoot Trail

Location Alaska, USA, and British Columbia, Canada

Length 33 miles

Accommodations
Commercial: No
Huts/refuges: No
Camping: Yes

Baggage transfer No

Option to walk in sections No

Degree of challenge High

ALASKA, USA &
CANADA

The Chilkoot Trail follows great northern rivers through British Columbia.

Our first day's walk on the Chilkoot Trail traced the length of the Taiya River, from its ocean inlet to Sheep Camp, just below the start of the serious climb over Chilkoot Pass. We'd walked 12 miles through the rich rainforest on the western slope of the coastal mountains, gaining about a thousand feet in elevation. Our plan was to stay at Sheep Camp that night and walk over Chilkoot Pass the next day. We were tired but excited as we pitched our tent and cooked our dinner at the communal kitchen area. After dinner, the National Park Service ranger (we'll call him "Rick") gathered all of the campers (about twenty of us) for the evening talk. He did a good job of explaining the natural and cultural history of the Chilkoot Trail and preparing us for the next day's hike. He cautioned us of the potential dangers, and at the end of his talk admonished us not to die on the hike "because it causes too much paperwork." He continued, "but if you do die, make it epic." We all laughed—he did a good job of breaking the tension we were feeling about the historic and challenging climb in which we were about to engage.

If you've been to Alaska, you've probably noticed the distinctive centennial license plates on many of the cars, a stylistic representation of a long string of hikers climbing up and over a high mountain pass—sort of like ants climbing a gigantic anthill. This is the Chilkoot Trail, an important part of the history of Alaska, British Columbia, and, ultimately, the Yukon Territory. The Klondike Gold Rush of 1898 found thousands of Americans and others traveling frantically to reach the gold fields to the north. The standard route took them by boat to the head of the Taiya River and the boomtown

Flags mark the Chilkoot Trail over the snowfields at higher elevations.

of Dyea, but this was as far as the boats could travel. From there, prospectors had to make their way over Chilkoot Pass to the promise of riches beyond. And this is where the real drama began.

The Chilkoot Trail is 33 miles connecting Dyea, Alaska (just outside the historic town of Skagway), and Bennett Lake, British Columbia. The pass marks the halfway point and is the boundary between the United States and Canada. Prospectors were subject to the "ton of goods" rule imposed by Canada and enforced at Chilkoot Pass by the Northwest Mounted Police; they were required to carry one ton of equipment and supplies into Canada to help ensure they would survive the journey north and a year in the wilderness. However, as it turned out, carrying these supplies over the pass may have been just as difficult as surviving the journey beyond. The "Golden Stairs," as this long pitch is euphemistically called, rise 2,800 feet in the 3.6 miles from Sheep Camp to the pass, with the final push a nearly 45-degree-angle scramble over a huge talus slope. Some "stampeders," as they were called, needed as many as thirty trips to get their outfits across the pass. From the pass, the stampeders walked on frozen lakes and rivers in winter; in summer they used boats and wagons. Over one hundred thousand people started off for the Klondike gold fields, but fewer than thirty thousand made it (most of the others simply gave up).

The rush over Chilkoot Pass transformed the area overnight, with Dyea growing to one of the biggest towns in Alaska with a population of nearly ten thousand with a hundred and fifty businesses catering to prospectors. Sheep Camp boasted sixteen hotels, fourteen restaurants, three saloons, two dance halls, a bathhouse, lumberyard, and post office. At the other end of the trail, the town of Bennett Lake swelled to twenty thousand as prospectors built boats and waited for the ice to go out. On May 29th, 1898, the ice broke and within a week over seven thousand boats departed for Dawson. The next year, the White Pass and Yukon Railroad was completed, opening a new and easier route north and the boomtowns died as quickly as they had grown, fading into their surroundings. Today the Chilkoot Trail is jointly administered by the U.S. National Park Service and its Canadian equivalent, Parks Canada, and commemorates the Klondike Gold Rush that caught the imagination of the world and stimulated a mass migration of humanity.

Few trails in the world offer more dramatic changes in landscape over such a short distance. On the American side, the trail begins at sea level, climbs through the rich Alaskan coastal rainforest, and then emerges above tree line into alpine tundra to reach Chilkoot Pass at 3,525 feet. It then descends through the subalpine boreal forest of British Columbia, past wild rivers and a chain of large lakes, reaching the shores of Bennett Lake. All this in just 33 miles! It's a strikingly beautiful and varied landscape that provides habitat for a rich diversity of animals including black and grizzly bears, mountain goats, river otters, wolves, moose, marmots, pikas, porcupines, wolverines, bald eagles, ptarmigan, ruffed grouse, arctic ground squirrels, seals, and pink and chum salmon.

Of course, the trail has an important cultural component as well—it's "littered" with artifacts of the Klondike Gold Rush. As you walk the trail, it's common to find picks and shovels, boot soles, and tin cans discarded

High mountain lakes dot the British Columbia portion of the Chilkoot Trail.

by discouraged prospectors. We even saw a wood-burning cook stove abandoned along the trail. These items are important evidence of the Gold Rush and should not be disturbed. But long before the Gold Rush of 1898, Chilkoot Pass was used as a trading route by the indigenous Tlingit people, who traded with inland First Nation tribes for moose and caribou hides, copper, and other goods unavailable along the coast. Chilkoot Pass is one of only three glacier-free corridors through the coastal mountains of Alaska.

There were several other highlights of our hike. A short side trail leads to Canyon City, one of the boomtowns along the trail where many historic artifacts can be seen. Of course, our hike over Chilkoot Pass was challenging, but very exciting and rewarding. It was cold (32 degrees at the pass in the middle of August!) and foggy, and we carefully followed poles marking the route over large snowfields. We were the first walkers over the pass that day, arriving at the Parks Canada shelter on top in late morning. No one was in the shelter, but a thoughtful warden had left insulated jugs of hot tea.

When hikers reach Bennett Lake, nearly all ride back to Skagway, the tourist-friendly gateway town just a few miles from Dyea, on the historic White Pass and Yukon Railroad. Most also purchase a welcome hot lunch at the train station at Bennett Lake—stew, baked beans, sourdough bread, and pie. The train ride is especially scenic, passing over high, dramatic wooden trestles and through tunnels. (Hikers are relegated to a special car, presumably so as not to offend the tourists riding the train.) When we got back to Skagway we celebrated with a pizza and enjoyed the "Days of '98 Show," a local musical comedy production (with audience participation) about the history of the area.

There are a number of logistical issues associated with hiking the Chilkoot Trail. Skagway itself is a little off the beaten track. We enjoyed a spectacular ride in a six-seat airplane from Juneau to Skagway and back again. Another option would be to arrive by ferry; the Alaska Marine Highway ferries operated by the state serve the coastal communities of

Alaska, transporting people and freight. Unlike some of these coastal communities, Skagway also boasts road access, and it has become a popular cruise ship destination.

While the Chilkoot Trail is not long—most walkers take three to five days—this is a backpacking trip through a wilderness area. The weather on the Alaskan coast is notoriously bad; lots of rain and wind and snow can occur in any month, and much of the trail is above tree line, exposing hikers to the weather. The trail can be rough, with mud, roots, standing water, and slick and unstable rocks. In some places, it is a route rather than a maintained trail. Large snowfields persist throughout the summer on both sides of Chilkoot Pass, and avalanche hazards persist through mid-July. Hikers may need as long as twelve hours to walk the 8 miles from Sheep Camp, over Chilkoot Pass, and to the next available campground at aptly named Happy Camp. Only walkers who are both physically fit and experienced backpackers should attempt this trail.

A permit (and fee) is required from Parks Canada and permits are limited to fifty people per day. Hikers are required to watch the film on bear safety and related matters before being issued a permit. Almost all hikers walk from south to north to keep the prevailing weather and wind at their backs. Camping is restricted to nine designated campgrounds where food-storage facilities (metal lockers or poles) are provided to keep food away from bears and bears away from the campgrounds. No fires are allowed and all cooking must be done on backpacking stoves in communal areas away from tent sites. Documentation of identity and citizenship must be carried to cross the international border.

The Chilkoot Trail may be unique and is a bit of a paradox. It represents the hardship of the tens of thousands of stampeders, but offers a recreational opportunity of the finest quality to today's walkers in the form of one of the world's most distinctive long-distance trails. It's both a natural and

"Methinks that the moment my legs begin to move, my thoughts begin to flow."
—Henry David Thoreau

The Chilkoot Trail features artifacts abandoned by weary stampeders heading to the Klondike gold fields.

cultural resource, the detritus of the Klondike Gold Rush history deeply embedded in an outstanding natural landscape. And it is an interesting blend of unity and diversity, the trail representing the integrity of the Klondike Gold Rush era, but managed by two agencies that administer it in somewhat different ways. For example, Parks Canada limits the number of hikers, while the U.S. National Park Service does not.

We encourage walkers to prepare carefully and enjoy the Chilkoot Trail, one of the most unusual and interesting walks in the world. We don't know of any trail of this length that includes so much natural diversity along with such a rich and substantive history. Pretend you're a stampeder and try to imagine such a journey with your year's supply of goods. And remember—be considerate of the park rangers and wardens and don't create extra paperwork for them.

Further Reading

www.nps.gov/klgo/planyourvisit/chilkoottrail.htm

A Hiker's Guide to the Chilkoot Trail. Anchorage, AK: Alaska Natural History Association.

Cinque Terre

Location Italy

Length 11+ miles

Accommodations
Commercial: Yes
Huts/refuges: Some
Camping: No

Baggage transfer Not needed

Option to walk in sections All

Degree of challenge Low–Moderate

ITALY

*Five historic Tuscan fishing and agricultural villages,
including Riomaggiore, comprise Cinque Terre.*

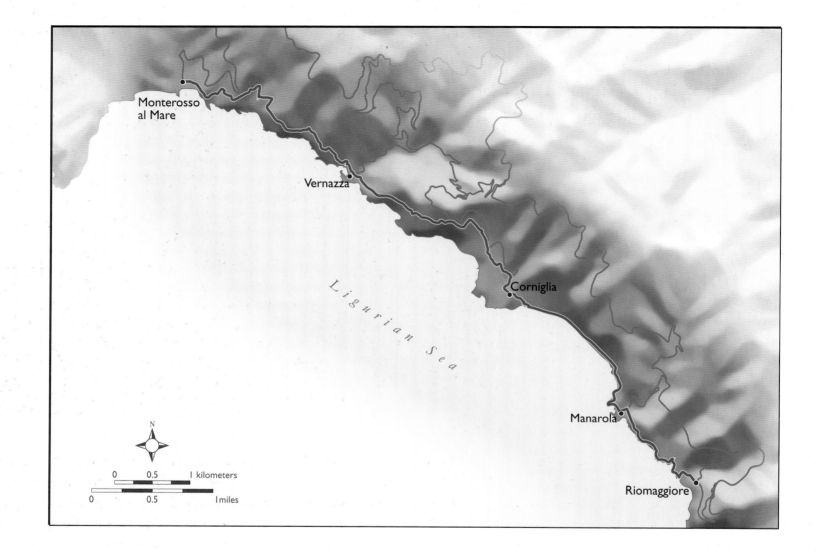

It had been a pleasant high-speed train ride from Rome to La Spezia, where we changed to the local train serving the dramatic coastal villages that comprise Cinque Terre. When we arrived at the town of Manarola, our destination, it was the end of the day and starting to get dark. We walked into the historic town square where a warren of narrow, winding streets and footpaths went in what seemed like every direction, and we wondered how we were going to find the way to our accommodation. As we stood there trying to figure out what to do we heard someone call out our names in a beautiful Italian accent. We turned and saw Marcella standing at the railing of the street above and behind us, motioning for us to meet and follow her. She greeted us warmly and we walked with her to the apartment we'd reserved. There she proceeded to show us around the tiny but spotless apartment with its endless view of the Mediterranean Sea. It's a stereotype that Italians talk with their hands, but Marcella was fluent in this way. She spoke no English

Walkers above Corniglia enjoy spectacular views of both land and sea.

and we spoke no Italian, but when Marcella left us we knew exactly what she'd said: how to operate the quirky refrigerator, where to shop for groceries, and to fasten our wash tightly to the clothes line so it didn't blow out to sea (as she gestured dramatically). Our apartment served as our base of operations for the next week as we walked both the spectacular trail that connects the communities of Cinque Terre and the network of trails that wander up, down, and across the impossibly steep slopes covered in olive groves and vineyards that rise above the seaside towns.

Cinque Terre means quite literally "the five lands"; these are the five towns strung out along this historically isolated region of Italy, hard on the shores of the Ligurian Sea, a large bay of the Mediterranean. These medieval fishing and farming villages rest at the base of cliffs that plunge into the waves. Over the centuries, much of the land above the towns has been terraced to support local agriculture, primarily olive trees, fruit trees, and grapes for wine. The area is so strikingly beautiful and historic that it has been declared a national park and a UNESCO World Heritage Site.

The main trail is short—about 11 miles—and it is not difficult, but it warrants several days of exploration, lingering at each village to appreciate its uniqueness, to fully absorb the rich, elegant atmosphere, and to sample the local foods, including fish, wine, and produce. A local train provides frequent service between the towns, so it's easy to walk from one to the next and return at the end of the day by train. Small ferries also shuttle back and forth and offer a different perspective on the landscape. The streets and walkways of each village wind in complex and pleasing

Tiny hamlets dot the hillsides of Cinque Terre.

patterns, and the buildings are painted in shades of pastel that seem to glow in the reflection of the azure blue Mediterranean. The overall effect is stunning and almost magical.

Riomaggiore is the southern-most village and some say the prettiest. It was established in the eighth century around a small natural harbor, and today fishermen "park" their brightly painted and highly varnished dories on the streets surrounding this harbor. The walk starts here and leads north for a short distance to Manarola. This first section of the trail is called the Via dell'Amore, or Lover's Lane. It's an easy, flat section where sweethearts can often be seen sitting on benches enjoying the unobstructed views of the sea and the striking shoreline (as well as enjoying each other's company). Manarola is the oldest of the five towns, small and especially scenic. We made Manarola our "base camp," walking each day and returning each night, and this worked well. Walking north, the next village is Corniglia, distinctly different from the others. The town is set above the sea and has no direct access to the water; the settlement may date from Roman times. The walk to Corniglia is not long, but it requires climbing the Lardarina Steps—nearly four hundred of them—to reach the town. Local artists cluster on the steps, selling their paintings of the area. The walk continues north to Vernazza, the town some people think of as the best of Cinque Terre. It's a fishing village with a small, dramatic harbor and the medieval Belforte watchtower juts into the sea. Open to the public, this historic tower offers sweeping views of the whole length of the trail. The last section of trail leads to beautiful Monterossa al Mare. This is the largest town with the only swimming beach, and it is always bustling with visitors. The section of the trail from Corniglia to Monterossa is a little steeper and rougher in places than the trail to the south.

Cinque Terre is an interesting blend of old and new. Because the landforms isolated these communities and kept modernity out, they have retained their old world charm; many residents have multi-generational ties.

These people still fish and farm the area and it's fascinating to watch them go about their daily activities. And, of course, the local foods they produce are a delight, including many kinds of fish, fresh vegetables, and several types of wine, olives, fruit, and focaccia. This is the birthplace of pesto sauce, made with basil, cheese, garlic, pine nuts, and olive oil.

"Good walking leaves no track behind it."
—Lao Tsu

These wonderful local foods are served in the restaurants and can be purchased in agricultural cooperatives in each town. Arrival of train service in the late nineteenth century provided easy access to this area and it has become an increasingly popular tourist destination. However, strict regulation of development has maintained the special character of the area. For example, cars are not allowed in the five towns comprising Cinque Terre. Many of the historic buildings are now used for tourist accommodations and restaurants, some of them very upscale.

The coastal path connecting the five towns is linked to a network of trails on the slopes above. There is a continuous ridgetop trail and many other "donkey tracks" that connect to the coastal path. Since many of the higher locations are served by a system of shuttle buses, we sometimes took a bus uphill and walked down, enjoying seeing more of the landscape and the local culture. One day we rode the shuttle bus from Manarola up to the inland village of Volastra and walked down through olive groves, vineyards, and a small pine forest to Corniglia, then took the train back to Mararola, a delightful day trip. Another shuttle bus ride took us from Monterossa up to the interesting Nostra Signora de Soviore (Sanctuary of Our Lady of Soviore) and we walked back to town, a half-day outing. Most visitors are unaware of these shuttles, and we recommend you include them in your Cinque Terre plans.

Cinque Terre can be walked in any season, but early spring and fall are recommended. Summers can be hot and will certainly be crowded,

A network of paths lace the Cinque Terre region.

Much of the Cinque Terre Trail is perched directly above the Ligurian Sea.

perhaps overly crowded as the world discovers this region's appeal. There is a fee for walking in Cinque Terre, but it is nominal and allows unlimited use of the local trains as well as the shuttle buses. Passes can be purchased locally and can cover one or more days; be sure to purchase one as revenues help support management of the area. Besides, there are several stations along the coastal path where you'll need to show your pass, and they are used as train tickets as well. Since the towns are so close to one another, we recommend picking a village and making it your home base, eliminating the need to change your accommodations.

Cinque Terre is a marvel. In many ways it's a model of sustainability— it produces local and distinctive foods, it's inter-connected by train, cars are banned from towns, development is controlled to preserve its history and cultural heritage. Walking is the ideal way to contribute to this sustainability and enjoy one of the finest and most distinctive cultural landscapes in the world.

Further Reading

www.parks.it/parco.nazionale.cinque.terre/Eindex.php

Bardwell, Sandra, Stefano Cavedoni, Emily Coles, Helen Fairbairn, Gareth McCormack, and Nick Tapp. *Walking in Italy*. London: Lonely Planet Publications, 2003.

Girani, Alberto. *Guide to the Cinque Terre*. Genoa, Italy: Sagep Editori, 2007.

Coast to Coast Trail

Location England

Length 190 miles

Accommodations
Commercial: Yes
Huts/refuges: Some
Camping: Some

Baggage transfer Yes

Option to walk in sections All

Degree of challenge Moderate

UNITED KINGDOM

The Coast to Coast Trail is a transect of northern England.

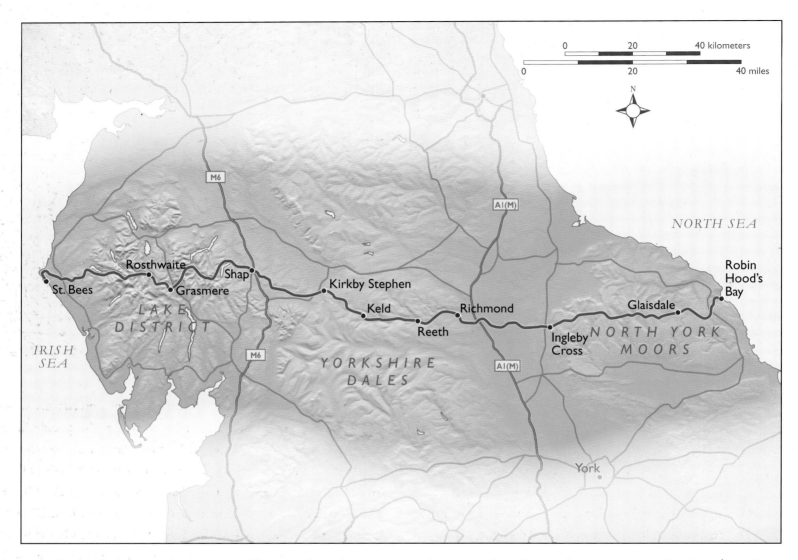

We were tingling with excitement as we arrived by train that afternoon in St. Bees, England, ready to walk the Coast to Coast Trail across the country, a walk we'd been planning for a year. We rose early the next day, enjoyed the traditional English breakfast (eggs, bacon, fried tomatoes, baked beans, mushrooms, and, of course, strong tea—good food to power a long day of walking) and found the beginning of the trail hard on the shore of the Irish Sea. Tradition has it that walkers are supposed to dip the toes of their boots in the Irish Sea, a ritual to be repeated at the North Sea in two weeks time. (Another version of the tradition has walkers carrying a stone from one shore to the other, but we didn't want to carry any extra weight!) It was a great feeling of accomplishment when we arrived at Robin Hood's Bay on the North Sea, and we made our way directly down to the shore for the ceremonial dipping of the toes—a fine celebration of our two-week walking adventure across England.

Walkers enjoy quiet country lanes along portions of the Coast to Coast Trail.

There's something very satisfying about walking all the way across a country, perhaps even more so when you walk from coast to coast. The Coast to Coast Trail, a 190-mile walk across northern England (admittedly, the "skinny" part of the country) is a transect of the national landscape, linking three large and distinctive national parks. National parks in England are not isolated tracts of public land as they often are in North America; instead expect a working landscape with lots of character and historic depth.

The patron saint of this route is W. W. Wainwright, who "pioneered" it in the early 1970s. The trail is locally known as "Wainwright's Way," a tribute to this folk hero of the British walking tradition. (Everyone walks in England; we saw grannies with baby strollers on one section of the trail and even encountered a very elderly man maneuvering his walker.) Elevations along the trail vary from sea level to around 2,500 feet. Although most days involve a modest climb, the footing is good and the degree of challenge is no more than moderate.

What will it be like? On the first day, as you ascend the dramatic headlands, you're introduced to sheep and then more sheep, and stiles of all design, all forms of openings through (or over) the rock and wooden fences that define the British countryside. You'll pass through both public and private lands. The public right-of-way has a long tradition in Great Britain—as does the public's code of conduct when using another's land. (Essentially, the code says to leave things as you found them, and this includes closing farm gates you've opened.) Over the course of your journey, you'll walk on paths and quiet roads, through barnyards and towns, along recreation paths, and on an ancient Roman road, the northern-most one around. You'll walk through pastures with placid livestock and around the perimeter of fields and right down the middle of town—the variety is energizing and fun. We enjoyed watching the landscape gradually change as we walked eastward.

At the end of the first day you'll have entered the Lake District National Park, the most celebrated landscape in all of England. The Lake District

Low-lying hills surround gentle valleys along the Coast to Coast Trail.

includes some of the most "rugged" (by English standards) mountains in the country, and this means a relatively challenging first few days of walking. But the mountains (locally called "fells") are softened by the hill-farming culture, white-washed cottages, and flocks of sheep that flow within the remarkable and striking networks of stone walls constructed over hundreds of years of human habitation. And true to its name, the Lake District is dotted with charming "waters," as lakes are known. Grassmere, heart of the Lake District and home to William Wordsworth, the famous Romantic poet, is an ideal spot for a "zero day," allowing one to rest up from an ambitious start to the walk. It's a beautiful and tourist-friendly town and offers a pilgrimage to Dove Cottage, Wordsworth's home.

On to the Yorkshire Dales National Park. Dales is "English" for valleys, and these strikingly beautiful landforms were carved by glaciers some ten thousand years ago. The local culture is straight out of James Herriot's *All Creatures Great and Small* books and associated television series. The characters are everywhere, and we're sure we saw Tristan visiting one of the local pubs. Here the trail climbs up and over the Pennine hills, which bisect the country on a north-south axis. Highlights of this section are Nine Standards, a series of giant rock cairns thought by some to have been built by Viking raiders, and the historic hamlet of Keld, the halfway point of the hike.

"It is solved by walking."

—Latin proverb

The trail emerges from the Yorkshire Dales at Richmond, the largest town on the walk, and one of the most historic in all of England. There are many Richmonds around the world, but this is the original and maybe the best. Richmond boasts an impressive Norman castle, several museums, cobbled streets, and historic inns; about two-thirds of the way along the trail, it makes an ideal layover.

A long day's walk beyond Richmond the trail enters the North York Moors National Park for the last several days of walking. Sometimes

Leaving St. Bees at the start of the Coast to Coast Trail, walkers encounter dramatic cliffs over the Irish Sea.

described as a bleak landscape, this is an outdated notion for these dramatic moorlands cloaked in heather, though civilization is spotty through this area. The tops of the moors offer exciting first views of the North Sea and the sheer cliffs beside the charming village of Robin Hood's Bay. Down the steep cobbles you go to the water's edge and the ceremonial dipping of the toe.

The Coast to Coast Trail is serviced throughout its length by a ready and varied stock of B&Bs and country inns, and ubiquitous pubs serve hearty meals, good beer, and lots of local color. The primary walking season is July and August, when you must book your reservations well ahead. However, walking can be done in the shoulder seasons as well, with September an especially good choice. Many of the towns along the trail are well connected by a network of local trains and buses. For a modest fee, you can avail yourself of baggage transfer service and walk with only a daypack.

It's easy to get to the start and back from the finish of the Coast to Coast using public transport, primarily trains. Several walking companies will assist you in planning your trip, and your walk could be a single day, a section, or a series of "best of" sections if walking the whole trail is not possible. Two weeks is the minimum recommended if you choose to cover the whole distance—and it would be fun to add in a few rest days.

This is England, not the wilderness, at least not by North American standards, and the nearest road is rarely more than an hour or two away.

The Coast to Coast Trail is a graceful blend of nature and culture.

However, you must be prepared. A good guidebook and maps are a necessity as the trail is not well marked in places. And the weather can (and will) change quickly, limiting visibility and threatening hypothermia, so dress and pack accordingly, including jacket, "waterproofs" (as the British say), and hat.

This is a splendid walk, long enough to allow the walker to relax into the adventure and varied enough to stimulate a high level of energy, excitement, and enthusiasm. With definitive starting and ending points, it's deeply satisfying. It's one of our favorites, and we recommend it in the highest terms.

Further Reading

Bardwell, Sandra. *Coast to Coast: The Wainwright Route.* Dunblane, UK: Rucksack Readers, 2010.

Coast to Coast Walk, Parts 1 and 2. Stirling, Scotland: Footprint, 2003.

Hannon, Paul. *Coast to Coast Walk: The Classic Walk across Northern England.* Keighley, West Yorkshire, UK: Hillside Publications, 1997.

Marsh, Terry. *A Northern Coast to Coast Walk.* Milnthorpe, Cumbria, UK: Cicerone Press, 2006.

Stedman, Henry. *Coast to Coast Path.* Hindhead, Surrey, UK: Trailblazer Publications, 2010.

Wainwright, Alfred. *A Coast to Coast Walk*, London: Frances Lincoln Ltd., 2003.

Wainwright, Martin. *The Coast to Coast Walk.* London: Aurum Press, 2007.

Colorado Trail

Location Colorado, USA

Length 470 miles

Accommodations
Commercial: Some
Huts/refuges: No
Camping: Yes

Baggage transfer No

Option to walk in sections Some

Degree of challenge Moderate–High

UNITED STATES

*The Colorado Trail beckons walkers into the
heart of the Rocky Mountains.*

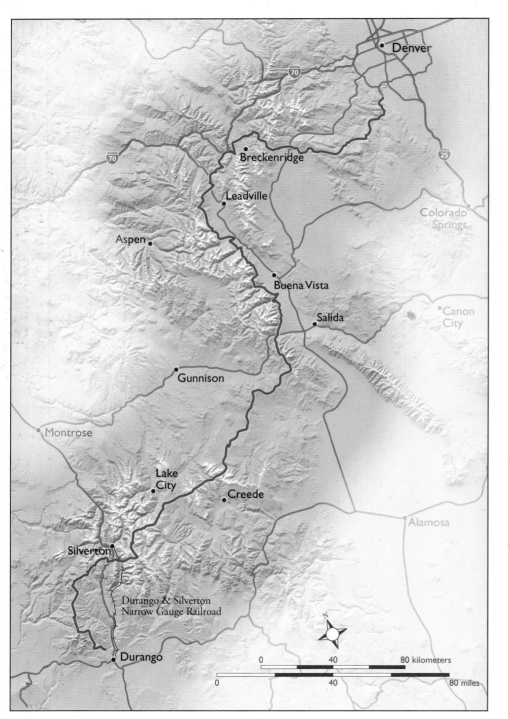

We had camped that night in rugged and dramatic Elk Creek Canyon, a narrow gorge with an abundance of cascades, waterfalls, and inviting campsites. As usual, we were up at dawn, scrambling out of our tent into the chilly mountain air, getting back on the trail as quickly as possible to warm up. But there was a little more urgency than usual in our steps as we headed for Elk Park, a large meadow in the middle of the Weminuche Wilderness. At Elk Park, we were told, the Durango-Silverton Narrow Gauge Railroad stops for hikers—if you know the right signal—and we wanted a ride into Silverton, where we had a reservation at a bed and breakfast, including the hot tub we'd been dreaming about. Don't wave your arms over your head or the conductor will think you are simply sending a greeting. Cross your arms back and forth across your knees (sort of like doing the Charleston) and the train will stop. So when we saw the train approaching, we did our dance in the wilderness and, sure enough, the train stopped for us—and the tourists on the train seemed to get a kick out of the whole thing. It's a beautiful forty-five-minute ride from Elk Park along the Animas River (the "river of lost souls") into colorful and historic Silverton where we enjoyed a welcome respite—clean sheets, a steak dinner, and a long soak in the hot tub— from our month-long walk of the glorious Colorado Trail.

Planning our walk of the Colorado Trail was a bit intimidating for two reasons. First, the trail itself is challenging; it wanders 470 miles through the Rocky Mountains from Denver to Durango, angling south and west. Like the mountains themselves, the trail rises and falls, but most of its miles are spent above 10,000 feet, often well above. Second, much of the

Walkers on the Colorado Trail enjoy views of several 14,000-foot peaks of the Collegiate Range of the Colorado Rockies.

trail is wild, traversing eight major ranges of the Rocky Mountains and five major river systems, crossing seven national forests and six wilderness areas. But like most long-distance trails, a number of roads cross the Colorado Trail as well as side trails that feed into it. And these offer relatively easy access to a string of colorful Colorado towns, including Breckenridge, Leadville, Buena Vista, Salida, Creede, Lake City, and Silverton. We planned our month-long adventure to walk as many miles of the trail as possible, but to take advantage of its small towns as well, learning about the area's history and culture, and meeting its people. We considered our walk to be a "slackpacking" adventure—we backpacked when necessary, but enjoyed the comforts of "civilization" whenever possible. Slackpacking is a wonderful way to break up a longer trail and add variety, and some of our favorite memories involve our times in town.

Much of the trail is directly on the Continental Divide, a long section of which coincides with the roughly 3,100-mile Continental Divide Trail. And much of it is above tree line, crossing meadows filled with world-class displays of wildflowers, including the striking blue columbine, the state flower. The trail passes through pure stands of aspen, isolated clusters of ancient bristlecone pines, stunted krumholtz vegetation (trees that have adapted to harsh growing conditions by staying close to the ground), and alpine tundra. It also passes through historic Camp Hale (now abandoned), home of the famous 10th Mountain Division of the U.S. Army that trained here and fought so heroically in Italy in World War II.

There were many other highlights of walking the Colorado Trail. Walking the high Collegiate Range, whose peaks—Mounts Princeton, Harvard, Yale, and Columbia—were named in honor of the Ivy League

Many walkers consider the San Juan Range of the Rocky Mountains to be the most beautiful section of the trail.

geologists who spent summers with their students studying the geology of the area. And the southern portion of the Sawatch Range where the names of the mountains honor another era of their history—Mounts Antero, Shavano, Ouray, and Chipeta—Ute Indian Nation chiefs and notables. The elk on Sargent's Mesa. Camping at Baldy Lake. Our layover day in Creede, a town directly off the pages of western history books, its "downtown" composed of several blocks of nineteenth-century buildings that sprang up overnight with the discovery of silver in the late 1800s. Celebrating that night with a pizza and bottle of wine on the balcony of our room at the Creede Hotel overlooking Main Street. Crossing the headwaters of the famous Rio Grande River. Walking through the high San Juan Range, what many people feel is the most striking part of the Rocky Mountains because the mountains are high and dramatic, their location on the western side of the Rockies bringing more rain and snow and supporting the greatest abundance of wildflowers. Fred and RJ, who gave us rides when we needed them.

The Colorado Trail represents the best of the natural history of the Rocky Mountains, but it's also a great cultural landscape. The towns adjacent to the trail are a reflection of the engaging history of the region, including its architecture, institutions, food, arts, and mythology. The people we met were as genuine and trustworthy as they were colorful. They and folks before them shaped the landscape over the years, and the reciprocal is just as true. This process continues today, and institutions like the Colorado Trail Foundation (which maintains the trail and produces its guidebook) and Gudy Gaskill (the trail's founder) are the latest and maybe greatest chapters.

Walking the full length of the trail normally requires five to six weeks (we walked 330 miles on our month-long trip). But it can be walked in sections that range from daytrips to weekends to longer vacations. We recommend several sections in particular.

The 12½ mile walk from Colorado Highway 9 to Copper Mountain is strenuous and well above tree line, but offers stunning views and lush

The Colorado Trail winds its way through large groves of aspen.

wildflowers. The free Summit Stage shuttle bus serves the local communities and offers convenient transportation back to your starting point, making it quite easy to hike without a car. Later the trail makes a sweeping turn around the town of Leadville that features access to several of the state's 14,000-foot mountains and a number of high mountain lakes. Nights can be spent in the funky Leadville Hostel, where proprietors "Wild Bill" and Cathy cook all-you-can-eat breakfasts in their pajamas and provide rides to trailheads for hikers. The day hike from San Luis Pass to Colorado Route 149 is the Rocky Mountains at their best. Much of the trail traverses the La Garita Wilderness, where the trail is faint in some areas and seems isolated everywhere; in fact, we saw no one along the trail that day. In places, the trail is marked with historic stone cairns that were built to guide a famous stock drive, and you feel like you're experiencing the true west. (We experienced some drama as well; thunderstorms built up early, menaced us with hail as we hurried across a broad saddle just under 13,000 feet, and then chased us

all the way across 3-mile Snow Mesa.) And, finally, we recommend any of the sections along the San Juan's for gorgeous mountain scenery.

Primary issues associated with walking all or part of the Colorado Trail concern its length and elevation. Of course, the trail can only be walked in summer, with some of the higher passes retaining snow well into June. It's common for thunderstorms to build on warm summer afternoons, so it's important to plan your hike to avoid high elevations above tree line after lunch. Take time to acclimate to the high elevations and lower levels of oxygen; arrive in the area a few days early and start your walk with short days, building distance as your body adjusts by producing more red blood cells. And be sure to drink plenty of water. Be prepared for warm, sunny days

"Perhaps the truth depends upon a walk around the lake."

—Wallace Stevens

The Durango and Silverton Railroad crosses the Colorado Trail in the Wemenuche Wilderness.

and use sun block liberally, and remember that temperatures drop rapidly at night due to high radiational cooling.

The Colorado Trail is long and full of potential adventures, but don't be intimidated. No one says you have to walk all 470 miles—pick an appealing section or two and start from there. The Colorado Trail is one of the finest long-distance walks in the U.S. and combines nature and culture in a harmonious whole. Whether you're looking for a backpacking trip or want to walk one day at a time—or perhaps you're thinking of combining the two into a slackpacking adventure—this trail's variety guarantees it'll have what you want. See for yourself.

Further Reading

www.coloradotrail.org

www.thecoloradotrail.com

The Colorado Trail Foundation. *The Colorado Trail.* Golden, CO: The Colorado Mountain Club Press, 2011.

The Colorado Trail Foundation. *The Colorado Trail Data Book.* Golden, CO: The Colorado Mountain Club Press, 2009.

Cotswold Way

Location England

Length 100 miles

Accommodations
Commercial: Yes
Huts/refuges: No
Camping: No

Baggage transfer Yes

Option to walk in sections All

Degree of challenge Low–Moderate

UNITED KINGDOM

Walkers along the Cotswold Way enjoy landscapes of prosperous farmland.

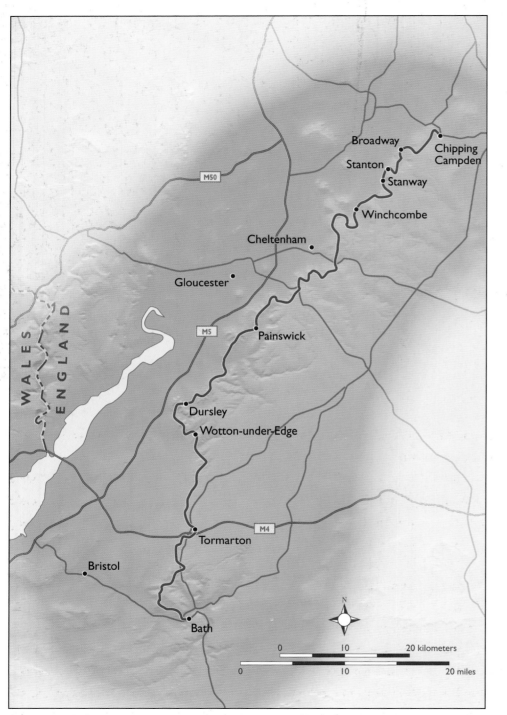

March was approaching and we had a window of opportunity—a little over a week available for an adventure. Of course, we wanted to do a walk, but where? The Cotswold Way had been on our "to do" list for several years, but early spring is hardly the traditional walking season in England. But the long-range weather forecast looked promising—cool, but little chance of rain (or snow!) so we decided to go for it. Soon we were delighted to be back on the trail, cold-weather gear at hand, and we were enjoying the benefits of off-season walking. Yes, it was brisk, but walking keeps you warm! Our nightly pub meals tasted better than ever and we always managed to find a table close to the fire. And, it seemed, we had the trail to ourselves. The trees had not yet leafed out so the views across the landscape were expansive and striking. March is lambing season in this country of sheep and we stopped time and again to watch the newborns running and jumping for the pure joy of it, playfully butting heads, and returning to nuzzle with their mothers when they were tired and hungry. Our recommendation? Consider walking in the off-season when the weather allows; it expands the walking year and offers a different kind of adventure.

The Cotswold Way is a national trail of England that runs just over 100 miles in the west-central region of the country, from Bath northeast to Chipping Campden. It wanders along the ridge of the Cotswold Hills, dropping down into the valleys to visit a series of historic towns and villages. Though the elevated features of this landscape are popularly called hills, the principal geologic feature of the region is more technically an escarpment, an elevated, tilted layer of rock. The Cotswold escarpment is nearly 100 miles long, rises gradually from the

Stately oaks are scattered along the Cotswold Way.

east to elevations around 900 feet, and drops off dramatically (the "scarp") to the west. The escarpment forms the eastern edge of the valley of the Severn River, the longest river in Britain, and the Cotswold Way offers outstanding views of this lovely valley from the raised land on which it is sited. The route deliberately meanders, visiting attractive towns and other cultural sites.

If there were an "England National Park" it would be in the Cotswolds—this area looks exactly as folks picture the country. History has flowed over Briton in successive waves since about 8000 BC, but time seems to have stopped in the Cotswold region around 1800 AD, when the area's wool industry began to collapse. The Industrial Revolution mostly bypassed the Cotswolds and left behind a living history of prosperous farms, thatched-roof cottages, well-to-do villages, and large market towns. And all of this is set against the Cotswold Hills, the Severn River, and the surrounding pastoral valleys. For many people, this is the idyllic, picture-postcard vision

of rural England, and this is validated by designation of the Cotswolds as the largest Area of Natural Beauty in England and Wales.

Most walkers start in Bath and walk north to keep the sun and wind at their backs. Stunning Bath is a UNESCO World Heritage Site. Celts worshipped there during the Iron Age, Romans built an elaborate bathing complex and enjoyed the natural hot springs for four hundred years, and later the Georgians erected magnificent buildings around and over the baths. It's easy to imagine you are in one of Jane Austen's novels because the center of town has changed so little since she wrote about it. Later still, fashionable Victorians travelled to Bath to "take the waters." It's fun to spend a couple of hours on one of the free, guided historical and architectural walks of the town. You'll undoubtedly find places that demand further exploration (the baths themselves or the Jane Austen Museum, for example), so it's best not to rush onto the trail itself. Stonehenge, one of the most famous

Walking the Cotswold Way in early spring offers lots of opportunities to see lambs.

archeological sites in the world, is a short drive from Bath, and it's easy to book a reasonably priced half-day tour if you wish to include this diversion.

The trail starts from the southern terminus of Bath Abbey and you walk through a parade of charming villages and towns. Painswick is known as "jewel of the Cotswolds" and its church boasts the area's largest collection of carved tombs. The hamlet of Stanway reveals a small cluster of historic buildings including a Jacobean manor and a twelfth-century church. Nearby Stanton has been restored and is considered "the perfect Cotswold village" with its thatched-roof cottages. Broadway boasts one of the most photographed main streets in England. Chipping Campden is an elegant old market town at the northern terminus of the trail and its High Street and "wool" church are showpieces. Most of the historic buildings along the walk are constructed from the native oolitic limestone (formed when dinosaurs roamed) that comprises the escarpment. This is a rich honey-colored stone that almost glows, and the buildings seem to be extensions of the very land on which they are built.

Just as geology has helped shape the Cotswolds, so have sheep. The Romans developed sheep farming on large estates in this region, and this farming expanded in Anglo Saxon times. The sheep were grazed in large "cots," meaning enclosures, on the "wolds" or hills. These weren't just any

The picture postcard–perfect village of Stanton features thatched roof homes.

There are several ancient burial mounds along the Cotswold Way.

sheep, they were Cotswold Lions—big, fast-growing, hornless animals with white faces and, most importantly, heavy, long fleece. These sheep were the foundation of the English wool trade with Europe and brought great prosperity to the Cotswold region. The Norman saying was, "In Europe the best wool is English; in England the best wool is Cotswold." In the thirteenth century there were half a million sheep in Britain, four times the human population. Most human landscapes along the route (towns, churches, manor houses, markets) can be traced to this wool trade and the money it generated. When the Industrial Revolution in the north of England offered more efficient means of production, the Cotswold wool economy declined precipitously. Fortunately, several flocks of Cotswold Lions still graze in the region's pastures and the breed is making a comeback.

You'll see evidence along the trail of habitation and prosperity that are much older than the sheep trade. Nearly one hundred Neolithic long barrows mark ancient burial sites; the most impressive of these is Belas Knap, started around 3000 BC. There are Iron Age hill forts that attest to the need for protection from warring tribes. There are ruins of Roman villas and fragments of Roman roads. There are medieval farming terraces and foundations of Norman buildings sometimes re-used by later Britons. The history rolls on and on, sometimes on top of itself as sites have layer upon layer of use. Various places along the trail are associated with some wonderful legends and myths, some Saxon, some Norman, some English. And the names of places leave no doubt you're in England—Birdlip, Crickley Hill, Old Sodbury, Wotton-under-Edge.

"Walking is a man's best medicine."
—Hippocrates

Allow a minimum of seven days to do this walk, and a few more would give time to explore the many highlights of this cultural landscape. Well served by delightful B&Bs and pubs along the route, the walk is not really appropriate for camping. The main gateway cities and towns are Bath, Gloucester, Cheltenham, Oxford, and Stratford-upon-Avon, with good train links and bus service and some local taxis. The Cotswold Way is one of the most effectively way-marked trails in England. The gentle route is sometimes on paths traveled by shepherds, priests, and tradesmen through the ages and sometimes on more modern country lanes and roads. The Cotswold Way is not for someone who seeks solitude and wants a sense of wilderness. It's a walk for someone who appreciates the human touch upon a welcoming land. This is a wonderful walk to sample and the many roads wandering through this area make it easy to arrange day walks. However, if you only hike for a day or two, you'll find yourself wishing you'd planned to walk the entire route. And remember to consider walking during the Cotswold Way's extended shoulder seasons.

Further Reading

www.nationaltrail.co.uk/cotswold

Burton, Anthony. *The Cotswold Way*. London: Aurum Press Ltd., 2010.

Cotswold Way. Doune, Perthshire, UK: Harvey Maps, 2005.

Hayne, Tricia, and Bob Hayne. *Cotswold Way: Chipping Campden to Bath*. Hindhead, Surrey, UK: Trailblazer Publications, 2009.

Rear, Mavis. *The Cotswold Way Handbook and Accommodation List*. Cheltenham, Gloucstershire, UK: Reardon Publishing, 2007.

Reynolds, Kev. *The Cotswold Way*. Milnthorpe, Cumbria, UK: Cicerone Press, 2011.

Ronald, J., and L. Cherry. *The Cotswold Way National Trail Companion*. Cotswold Way National Trail Office, 2007.

Sale, Richard. *A Guide to the Cotswold Way*. Ramsbury, Wiltshire, UK: The Crowood Press, 1999.

The Great Ocean Walk features the world famous Australian coastline.

Part 2: Extraordinary Hikes for Ordinary People

Great Ocean Walk

Location Australia

Length 60 miles

Accommodations
Commercial: Yes
Huts/refuges: Some
Camping: Yes

Baggage transfer Yes

Option to walk in sections All

Degree of challenge Low–Moderate

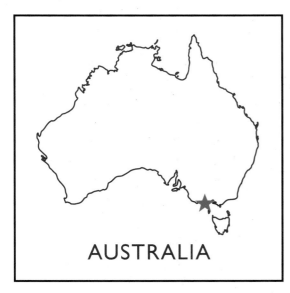

AUSTRALIA

The route of the Great Ocean Walk includes both beaches and headlands.

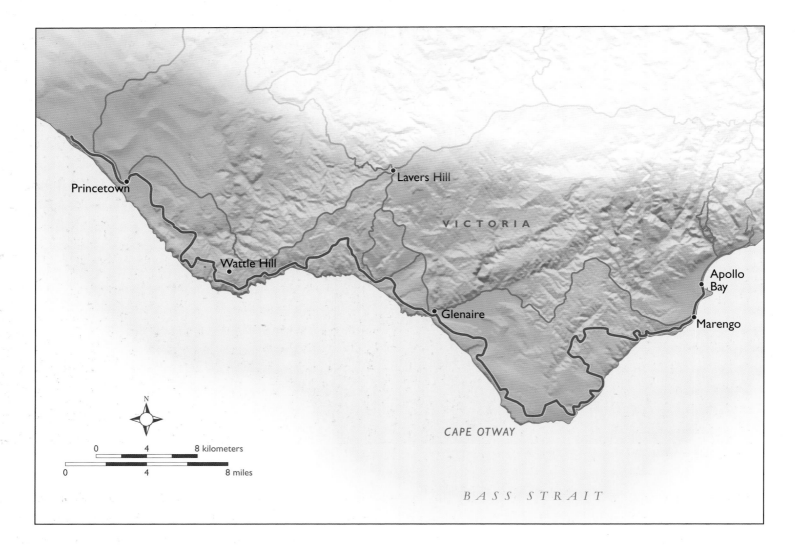

We've stayed in lots of mountain huts and hostels—you don't have to be a "youth" to do so. They were often rugged structures in remote places with, at best, a semi-private room, toilet and shower facilities, hearty dinners and breakfasts prepared by the hut master, and, of course, the company of fellow hikers. What hostels may lack in amenities they make up for in terms of location—and the food and company are always welcome no matter where you stay. But the Eco Beach Youth Hostel in Apollo Bay, Victoria, Australia, neatly situated at the edge of a lively fishing and tourist town that serves as the gateway to the Great Ocean Walk, breaks all the traditional rules. This is a relatively new structure that is leading hostels into the twenty-first century. It's an architecturally designed passive solar structure built to use 50 percent less water and energy than comparable accommodations, and it combines guest comfort with functionality and a big "wow" factor. There are two communal kitchens complete with everything a traveler could want and some things a traveler might not even think

The Twelve Apostles, giant sea stacks, mark the western end of the Great Ocean Walk.

of (bread-making machines, for example), comfortable lounges around a fireplace, Internet service, laundry facilities, a rooftop terrace, and patio space with grills. Oh, yes, there are also private rooms with balconies and spotless shared baths. We stayed at the Eco Beach Youth Hostel both before and after our Great Ocean Walk and found it to be (as one reviewer commented) "eco-tastic."

An encouraging trend in contemporary travel is the increasing interest in all things "eco," and the Great Ocean Walk, a 60-mile route along the beautiful coast of Victoria, Australia, is a good example. The walk itself was built to be "green." The trail is located to minimize degradation of the land and sometimes travels inland to avoid sensitive areas or to eliminate the need for elaborate engineering. Providing designated campsites reduces the overall impact of camping, and the Great Ocean Walk's campsites are tucked away to be visually unobtrusive.

Another good example of focus on the environment is the Great Ocean Ecolodge, where we stayed one night along the walk. It's an environmental research and education center as well as a refuge for injured wildlife, and includes several comfortable bed-and-breakfast-style rooms. Extensive grounds include both eucalyptus forests and open areas. The dusk wildlife walk was wonderful, but perhaps more impressive was the mob of kangaroos casually feeding outside the lodge. There was even a baby wallaby housed

Some of the Great Ocean Walk's beaches provide limitless beachcombing.

in an incubator in the living room! Income from the bed and breakfast helps fund the center, and, of course, staying there allows guests the time to appreciate the good work that's being done.

The Great Ocean Walk would be spectacular even without the ecological slant it showcases. Australia is known for its stunning coastline and wild beaches, and the Great Ocean Walk offers some of the country's finest. The route passes through two national parks—Great Otway and Port Campbell—and overlooks the Twelve Apostles Marine National Park and Marengo Reefs Marine Sanctuary. This relatively isolated geography on the southern coast of Victoria is tucked between the Otway mountain range to the north and the Bass Strait and Southern Ocean to the south. Some of the waves you'll see started in Antarctica—respect their power and temperature! The Great Ocean Walk follows some of the same coastline featured on the famous Great Ocean Drive, a 151-mile stretch of road in the southeast of the continent. The walk has been called the "back stage" of the road because it goes to the shore when the road heads inland, and the trail offers a much more intimate experience than driving. Or perhaps you'd like to combine driving and walking…

The Great Ocean Walk was designed so that one can easily "step on-step off" the trail. Many walking segments are less than three hours long, and it's easy to tailor the walk to your fitness level and interests. Because there are often low-tide and high-tide options (beach vs. headlands), "out and back" walks can easily become loop trails, an added bonus. Choose your type of overnight accommodation as well. Parks Victoria provides a system of walk-

"It takes days of practice to learn the art of sauntering. Commonly we stride through the out-of-doors too swiftly to see more than the most obvious and prominent things. For observing nature, the best pace is a snail's pace."

—Edwin Way Teale

Part 2: Extraordinary Hikes for Ordinary People

Many of the waves that wash up on the Great Ocean Walk had their origin in Antarctica.

in campgrounds with tent pads and tanks of rainwater, or you can stay in bed and breakfasts or hotels. Whether you prefer camp food with a view of the ocean or candlelit dining with just-caught seafood, this is your trail. Have the kind of experience you want!

Coastal beaches are isolated and deserted; be sure to build in plenty of time for lingering and beachcombing here. Our favorite beaches were Station Beach, with its magnificent waves and waterfall, and aptly named Wreck Beach with protruding anchors of two ships grounded there in the nineteenth century. Headlands offer open areas with wildflowers. There are wind-swept dunes and cliffs and patches of thick forests of eucalyptus, ancient myrtle, beeches, mountain ash, and blue gum trees. And in the rain forests there are tree ferns similar to those that were around when dinosaurs roamed this part of Australia. Inland portions of the route curve around rivers and bays, crossing biologically rich estuaries and occasionally

climbing to higher elevations that offer sweeping views of the seemingly endless coastline; our favorite was Gable Lookout, one of the highest sea cliffs on mainland Australia.

It's pretty exciting to see kangaroos and wallabies along the trail, and you've got a good chance of seeing both around the Aires River Escarpment and Hordenvale Wetlands. You also may be lucky enough to see koalas and echidnas. Sooty oystercatchers, king parrots, peregrine falcons, and cockatoos will delight even those folks not usually interested in birding. If the season is right (between June and October), look for migrating whales, and dolphins sometimes frolic in the waves.

The walk includes two especially iconic features. Cape Otway Lighthouse was the first lighthouse built in Victoria, and was designed to improve safety on what is locally called the "Shipwreck Coast." The lighthouse, scenic symbol of the state of Victoria, rises over 50 feet and is

Cape Otway Lighthouse was built to help guide ships in foggy conditions.

topped with a circular walkway that is open to the public. It offers striking views up and down the coast, though strong, gusty winds can make it difficult to hold the camera still. At the west end of the walk lie the Twelve Apostles in Port Campbell National Park; the Apostles are an exceptionally dramatic series of sea stacks just off the coast. These stacks (the largest of which is roughly 150 feet high) were originally part of the mainland cliffs, but the stormy ocean and blasting winds have gradually (over ten to twenty million years) eroded the soft limestone. This may be one of the most strikingly scenic views in all of Australia and is visited by over two million folks each year. The sea continues to erode these features (we counted only eight of the original Twelve Apostles), so you'd better do this walk soon!

The Great Ocean Walk is highly accessible, with several roads providing periodic access to the trail, making it easy to break the longer route into shorter walks. There are commercial shuttle services and lodgings will sometimes provide rides to walkers. Those wanting to experience the whole trail should allow five to seven days. If you are camping, a permit must be obtained from Parks Victoria, and campers must travel from east to west. As with all coastal trails, walkers must be mindful of tides and not find themselves stranded (or worse) by high tides—carry and use tide tables. Parks Victoria has thoughtfully provided signs noting "Decision Points" where the low-tide and high-tide trails diverge. Drinking water can be scarce so be sure to carry plenty of water, particularly in summer. Apollo Bay, a two and a half hour drive southwest of Melbourne, is the gateway town for the walk, and is a lively, friendly place. We used the good bus service between Melbourne and Apollo Bay, and the driver was kind enough to stop the bus to point out a family of wallabies in the trees beside the road.

We're partial to coastal walks (that's probably obvious from the walks included in this book). The Great Ocean Walk offers a sense of the best of Australian coastal life—its magnificent scenery, wild beaches, rich and exotic wildlife, and friendly, fun-loving people. It's a trail that offers lots of choices—we hope it's one you'll choose.

Further Reading

www.greatoceanwalk.com

Inca Trail

Location Peru

Length 30 miles

Accommodations
Commercial: No
Huts/refuges: No
Camping: Yes

Baggage transfer Porters

Option to walk in sections No

Degree of challenge Moderate–High

PERU

The Inca Trail includes many steps fashioned by the Incas.

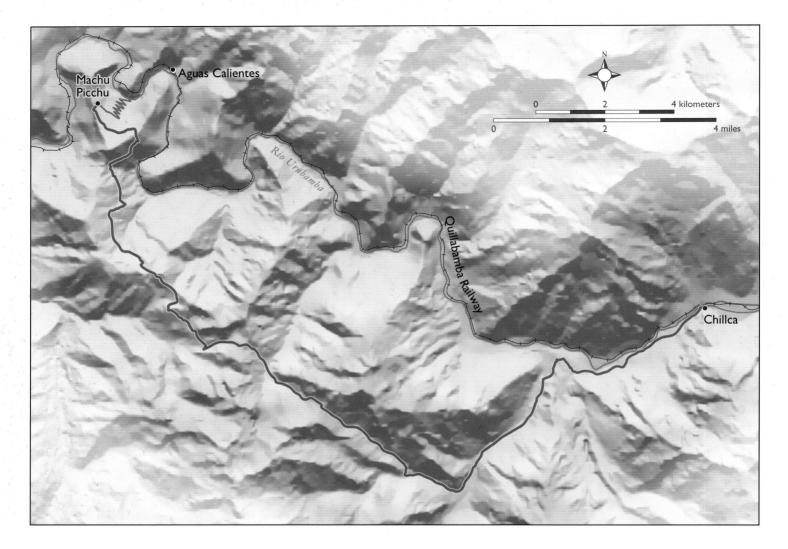

Like most people who walk the Inca Trail, we traveled to the small city of Cuzco, sometimes referred to as the "Katmandu of the Andes" and the jumping-off point for walking in this part of the world. Cuzco, translated as "navel of the world," was once the capital of the vast Inca Empire and home to an estimated fifteen thousand nobles, priests, and servants. Cuzco sits at 11,000 feet and it's highly recommended that walkers stay here a few days to acclimate to the thin air to be encountered along the Inca Trail. Cuzco has its own impressive attractions—the Inca ruins of Sacsayhuaman, Pukapukara, the Sun Temple, an historic Spanish cathedral, a thriving market, a large central square, and local people in colorful dress—so three days passed quickly. We had booked our walk of the Inca Trail with a local guiding service as is required by the Peruvian government. On our last night in Cuzco, we met with our guide and were surprised to find that we were the only two people to sign up for this trip. Thus, our "group" included our guide, a cook, a waiter, two

Machu Picchu includes a remarkable system of terracing on impossibly steep slopes.

porters, and us! A mini old-time African-style safari in the Andes! On the trail, our guide explained the natural and cultural history of what we saw, we ate all our excellent meals (prepared and served by our white-coated cook and waiter) in the "dining tent," we enjoyed hot water in the morning and evening for washing, and, of course, the porters carried nearly everything in enormous packs, leaving us with only day packs. On our last night in camp, our cook made us a cake to celebrate our successful walk of the Inca Trail and our impending arrival the next morning in much-anticipated Machu Picchu. What a luxurious alternative to conventional backpacking!

The Inca Trail and Machu Picchu are among the most iconic places in the world. The trail may be the world's most famous walking route and leads walkers to Machu Picchu, the mysterious "Lost City of the Incas," now a UNESCO World Heritage Site. The approximately 30-mile trail is actually just a fragment of the elaborate system of roads and trails that connected the

The Inca Trail climbs out of the Sacred Valley towards Warmiwanusca, Dead Woman's Pass, the highest point on the walk.

Inca Empire across much of what is now Ecuador, Peru, Argentina, and Chile. Though there are no written records, archeological evidence documents that the vast and powerful Inca civilization reached its zenith between 1100 AD and 1530 AD when it finally succumbed to the Spanish conquest. The trail is a marvelous example of the engineering prowess of the Incas, navigating the impossibly steep Andes, and the route reveals an astonishing civilization clinging to the sides of soaring mountains. It was an improbable, fascinating empire.

We were driven about three hours from Cuzco across the Sacred Valley to the trailhead at the tiny town of Chilca. Along the way we stopped at the authentic Inca town of Ollantaytambo to pick up our porters. The last twenty minutes were along a one-lane road with two-way traffic! At the trailhead the Peruvian government has established a checkpoint where all walkers must show their permit and passports are stamped. Porters pass through a separate checkpoint where their loads are weighed to ensure they are not so heavy as to be dangerous. After the checkpoint, we crossed a swinging bridge over the Urubamba River and were excited to start our trek to Machu Picchu. The first several miles were through lower-elevation, arid lands and the trail was busy with Inca Trail walkers and a variety of farm animals and occasional farmers from surrounding hamlets. But then the trail climbed toward the high mountain passes and the traffic (and the air!) thinned out. We camped the first night in a pasture that showed clear evidence of recent grazing animals. The stars of the Southern Hemisphere put on a great show, but we were asleep in our tent shortly after dinner.

We walked and camped for three more days. The trail quickly climbs out of the arid lands of the Urubamba Valley through high open grasslands, and ultimately into extensive and impressive rainforests with tree ferns, mosses, lichen, bromeliads (members of the pineapple family with short stems and rosettes of stiff leaves), and two hundred

Part 2: Extraordinary Hikes for Ordinary People

The Inca Trail passes many impressive archeological sites en route to Machu Picchu.

Machu Picchu is the dramatic finale to the Inca Trail.

and fifty species of orchids. Animals include nearly four hundred species of birds (we saw Andean condors and listened to screeching parakeets) and lots of butterflies. Views toward the tops of the surrounding mountains reveal glaciers and massive snowfields. Most of the trail is above 10,000 feet and there are three high passes to negotiate; the highest—colorfully named "Dead Woman's Pass"—is just under 14,000 feet. Guides often offer walkers coca tea as a mild stimulant to help with overcoming the elevation but we passed on this option. The trail isn't excessively steep or rough; in fact, it's "paved" in stone in some places. At one point, walkers descend 2,800 stone steps in a half-mile section of trail, all fashioned by the Incas.

But the stars of the show are the world-class archeological sites along the way—Llaqtapata, Runkurakay, Sayamarca, Winawayna, and more. Nearly all of the ruins are well preserved thanks to the remarkable engineering and construction by their builders. The stonework is impressive, especially when you realize no mortar was used and the rocks were cut with wooden wedges and stone knives and hammers. In some places these simple tools were used to cut steps and tunnels out of solid rock. Many of the ruins are sited on the flanks of seemingly unbuildable slopes and include extensive terracing for stability and to support agricultural production. Visitors are allowed to walk freely through these sites and our guide helped us understand their history and significance.

Our last night on the trail we camped at an overcrowded communal area with a beer hall—we thought it was an incongruous and unpleasant facility and hope the rumors of its impending replacement are true. Here walkers tingle with excitement about entering fabled Machu Picchu the next morning. Most groups wake well before dawn to get their first view of Machu Picchu at the Sun Gate as the sun is rising. This requires waiting in the dark in a long line to go through a final checkpoint where passports are stamped with the Machu Picchu insignia, but we decided to rise a little later and miss the crowds. From the Sun Gate it's about an hour's walk into Machu Picchu proper, a truly magical site. The extensive ruins are on a high saddle and seem even more impossibly located than the previous archeological sites. Llamas graze placidly among plazas, aqueducts, baths, and tiers. Archeologists still don't agree on the original use of Machu Picchu—was it an astronomical observatory, religious retreat, city, or palace? They do agree that it was abandoned and the memory of it lost before the Spaniards came to South America. Yale historian Hiram Bingham found the ruins of Machu Picchu in 1911 and spent several years supervising the clearing of the area; he's a local folk hero. Not surprisingly, Machu Picchu is usually crowded, averaging about two thousand visitors a day, most of whom arrive in nearby Aquas Calientes by train. Walkers arrive at Machu Picchu before most other visitors and this affords a more leisurely opportunity to stroll around the area.

From Machu Picchu, most visitors use a shuttle bus to travel to Aquas Calientes, a funky tourist town where we saw chickens casually scratching in front of luxury hotels. Visitors return to the Sacred Valley by train, an enjoyable and interesting three-hour ride along the Urubamba River that provides another perspective on the region—and views of even more ruins.

As noted earlier, walkers on the Inca Trail must use the services of a local guiding company and there is a great diversity to choose from. These companies help walkers appreciate the trail and make sure visitors don't disturb the ruins, and the policy also allows local people to enjoy more of the benefits of the tourist economy. Only five hundred people are allowed to start the walk daily, so it is advisable to make these arrangements well in advance. Our sense is that this number is too high, as camping areas were often crowded and toilet and other facilities over-taxed. Walking is allowed in one direction only to lessen perceived crowding. The trail is open all year,

"If I could not walk far and fast, I think I should just explode and perish."

—Charles Dickens

but the best weather is from May to October, with the peak season from June to August.

The classic walk of the trail is conducted in five days, including the return trip by train. This is a camping trip, but guides, cooks, and porters take much of the burden off walkers. The primary challenges are the elevation and the potential for bad weather in the form of rain. Recently, an alternative route called the Camino Salcantay has become popular. This is also part of the vast Inca Trail Network, but is served by a system of recently constructed upscale lodges.

Read all you can about the Incas and Machu Picchu before your trip—you will be more appreciative of the spectacular adventure that's the Inca Trail. Just realize that you still won't be fully prepared for the magic of this place.

Further Reading

www.incatrailperu.com

www.peru.info

www.perutravelguide.info

Danbury, Richard, and Alexander Stewart. *The Inca Trail, Cusco & Machu Picchu*. Hindhead, Surrey, UK: Trailblazer Publications, 2005

Megarry, Jacquetta, and Roy Davies. *Explore the Inca Trail*. Dunblane, UK: Rucksack Readers, 2011.

John Muir Trail

Location California, USA

Length 210 miles

Accommodations
Commercial: Few
Huts/refuges: No
Camping: Yes

Baggage transfer No

Option to walk in sections Some

Degree of challenge Moderate–High

UNITED STATES

The northern end of the John Muir Trail is iconic Yosemite Valley.

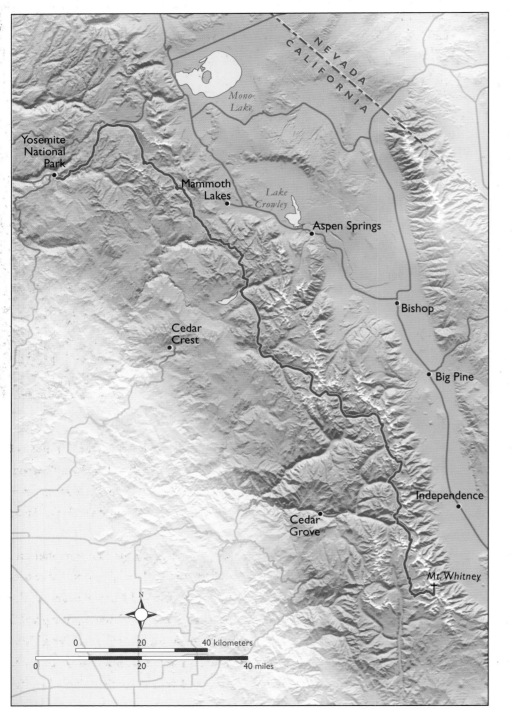

"I'll trade a mac and cheese dinner for a bag of Peanut M&M's." "Anyone want a package of beef jerky?" We were in the midst of a mini-marketplace at Muir Trail Ranch, the last resupply opportunity along the famous John Muir Trail. We'd backpacked just over 100 miles and we had another 120 to go—about nine more days at our current pace. Like all hikers, we'd mailed ourselves a resupply package to this remote outpost in the wilderness. Supplies had to be mailed in five-gallon buckets (with handles) because they were carried the last several miles to the ranch on the backs of pack animals. So here we sat, going through our new supply of food and a few other things—socks, soap, toothpaste, bandaids— thinking hard about what to take and what to leave behind. This is the eternal dilemma of backpackers: the luxury of food and other supplies versus the need to lighten the pack. There were two other groups sorting through their new supplies and we were all comparing notes, swapping things back and forth, and making painful decisions about what to leave behind. The most popular solution, of course, was to eat as much as possible now and we were doing a pretty good job of that. We calculated carefully what we thought we needed and added a little more for the sake of safety, repacked our gear, and walked south in the warm summer sun, the summit of Mt. Whitney still unseen, but beckoning.

Everyone knows about the beautiful, iconic sights of Yosemite National Park—towering granite cliffs and domes, some of the world's highest waterfalls, lush meadows, rivers rushing through virgin forests, high mountain lakes. Now imagine a trail that winds its way through more than 200 miles of this landscape, taking walkers on a spectacular, rollercoaster ride along the High Sierra. That's the John Muir Trail. John Muir

The Sierra Nevada Mountains have a rich stock of picture postcard lakes.

felt the Sierra Nevada's were the most beautiful mountains in the world, and we have no reason to disagree. "His" trail starts in Yosemite Valley and works its way over a series of high mountain passes to the summit of Mt. Whitney, the highest peak in the continental U.S., passing through Yosemite, Sequoia, and Kings Canyon national parks, and the Ansel Adams and John Muir wildernesses. This is one of the world's great walking adventures.

The trail starts at well-named Happy Isles along the Merced River in Yosemite Valley and immediately climbs toward the high country. The nearly 40 miles of the trail in Yosemite National Park are packed with scenery of the highest order, including Vernal and Nevada Falls, Half Dome, the Cathedral Peaks, Tuolumne Meadows, and Lyell Canyon. Take time for a day-long side trip to the top of Half Dome, but only if you are prepared to pull yourself up the cables that lead to the summit, a challenge for those of us who are even a little afraid of heights. Impossibly beautiful Lyell Canyon, its rich meadows fed by meandering Lyell Creek, leads walkers south, then it's up and over 11,000-foot Donahue Pass, out of Yosemite and into Ansel Adams Wilderness.

Ansel Adams is America's most famous landscape photographer and the High Sierra was his favorite subject. The trail passes along the shores of Thousand Island Lake with striking Ritter and Banner peaks in the background, the scene of some of Adams' most well-known photographs. Ruby, Emerald, and Garnet lakes are among the collection of "jewel"-like lakes in the 23-mile stretch of trail through this wilderness area. This area is also noted for its impressive evidence of volcanic activity including hot

A peaceful creek leads walkers through idyllic Lyle Canyon.

springs, cinder cones, and Devil's Postpile National Monument with its basilic columns formed by cooling magma.

The next 50 miles of the trail run through the massive John Muir Wilderness. Muir wandered extensively through the Sierras in the late nineteenth century, making many first ascents of the 13,000- and 14,000-foot peaks, successfully lobbying for creation of Yosemite National Park, and eloquently preaching the gospel of conservation. When many Americans seemed more concerned about material things, Muir wrote, "Everybody needs beauty as well as bread, places to play in and pray in." He called the Sierras the "Range of Light" not just because of the whitish color of the exposed granite peaks, but because they offered an opportunity to find higher, spiritual truths. Muir is the father of national parks in America and this trail and the wilderness it traverses are powerful monuments to all his good work. This portion of trail is classic High Sierra with towering snow-capped peaks, sparkling streams, patches of deep forest, and Virginia, Purple, and Marie lakes, some of the most beautiful in all the Sierras. Be sure to look back occasionally to see Ritter and Banner peaks fading 50

miles and more into the distance as evidence of your progress along the trail. And look off to the east and west into vast, seemingly untouched granite canyons. This extensive complex of national parks and forests offers many lifetimes of exploration.

Just past the 100-mile mark, the trail enters Kings Canyon National Park and then Sequoia National Park. Much of the trail through these parks is especially remote, and we were thrilled to camp on the shores of unnamed lakes, a marker of true wilderness. A highlight of this area is Evolution Basin, an especially dramatic 8-mile stretch well above timberline. The surrounding 13,000-foot peaks are named for famous scientists in the field of evolution—Mendel, Darwin, and Huxley. Nearly devoid of vegetation due to its elevation, this area looks much like it must have when the last glaciers retreated some ten thousand years ago. Just south are Rae Lakes, a chain of five lakes that offer plentiful campsites with five-star views. Speaking of stars, the night skies all along the trail are world class. And the meadows are the finest in the Sierras—every shade of green and sporting lush wildflowers, including lupines and Indian paintbrush. As walkers make their way south, the passes rise higher and higher: Muir Pass at 11,955 feet, Mather Pass at 12,100 feet, Pinchot Pass at 12,130 feet, and finally Forester Pass at 13,120 feet.

And then there's Mt. Whitney at 14,505 feet. As you approach the mountain look east and south for breathtaking views (if you have any breaths to spare) of the Great Western Divide. Most walkers make their last camp at Guitar Lake and wake early for the final push to the summit. About 2 miles from the top, the trail splits from the route that will be used to descend the mountain, so this is a good place to stash your pack and lighten your load for the final pitch. Short steps and frequent breaks are advised in this thin air. The summit is a sea of rocks with magnificent views in every direction. Be sure to sign the hikers' register in the small stone building housing meteorological equipment. We found ourselves with mixed emotions as we sat and luxuriously ate nearly all of our remaining stock of snacks, elated to have completed the trail, but sad to see our adventure come to an end. But there wasn't much time to romanticize because it's a 10-mile walk descending 6,000 feet from the summit to the nearest trailhead at Whitney Portal. And we wanted to get down in time for dinner and that cheeseburger we'd been dreaming about lately.

This trail offers an abundance of human and natural history. The place names celebrate the birth of America's Conservation Movement: Muir; Gifford Pinchot, first director of the U.S. Forest Service; Stephan Mather, first director of the National Park Service. Tectonic forces followed by centuries of glacial action and the eroding forces of water shaped the landscape. Forests of Jeffrey, white, lodgepole, and other pines and hemlock cloak the lower elevations. Animals include eagles, marmots, mule deer, and rarer mountain sheep and mountain lions. Walkers are almost guaranteed to see black bears.

The primary logistical concerns for walking the trail are its length and elevation. The trail is accessible only by backpacking and there are only a few reasonable options to get resupplied, so careful planning is required. It's wise to allow up to three weeks to walk the trail in its entirety. Elevations are high. With the exception of the trailhead in Yosemite (at

Cathedral Peak is a distinctive landmark along the John Muir Trail.

about 4,000 feet), the trail rarely drops below 8,000 feet and is usually substantially higher. The combined ascent over the length of the trail is nearly 50,000 feet. But the trail is well maintained and marked and the grades over the passes are generally moderate. A permit is required (make your reservation well in advance) and campers must use bear canisters, hard plastic containers that keep food and other aromatic items away from hungry or inquisitive bears; these canisters can be rented from the Wilderness Center in Yosemite Valley. Most walkers start at the northern end of the trail, acclimating gradually to the elevation as the passes increase in height. It's wise to camp within a few hours walking distance of the higher, exposed passes so you can get up and over them the next day before the chance of afternoon thunderstorms.

With a little creative map work, the trail lends itself to a number of section hikes of varying length. Examples include Tuolomne Meadows to Yosemite Valley (all down hill in this direction!), Tuolumne Meadows to Reds Meadow, and a loop hike that includes the Rae Lakes area. The hiking season is short—from July through most of September—due to heavy snows that start early and continue to clog the higher passes well into the summer. Summer days are usually sunny and warm, but nights cold. Walkers are blessed over most of the trail with plentiful supplies of water for drinking (which should be purified), swimming, and fishing. There are commercial shuttle services that will provide rides at the southern end of the trail, but they can be expensive.

The John Muir Trail makes nearly everyone's top ten list, including ours. In the words of the younger generation, it's "epic." *Backpacker Magazine* says, "Step for scenery-packed step, nothing else compares." We concur.

"In every walk with nature one receives far more than he seeks."

—John Muir

Further Reading

www.johnmuirtrail.org

Castle, Alan. *The John Muir Trail: Through the California Sierra Nevada.* Milnthorpe, Cumbria, UK: Cicerone Press, 2010.

Dodge, Kathleen. *Day and Section Hikes: The John Muir Trail.* Birmingham, AL: Menasha Ridge Press, 2007.

Harrison, Tom. *John Muir Trail Map Pack: Shaded Relief Topo Maps.* San Rafael, CA: Tom Harrison Maps, 2009.

Wenk, Elizabeth, and Kathy Morey. *John Muir Trail: The Essential Guide to Hiking America's Most Famous Trail.* Berkeley, CA: Wilderness Press, 2007.

Winnett, Thomas, and Kathy Morey. *Guide to the John Muir Trail.* Berkeley, CA: Wilderness Press, 1998.

Kaibab Trail

Location Arizona, USA

Length 21 miles

Accommodations
Commercial: Some
Huts/refuges: Some
Camping: Yes

Baggage transfer No

Option to walk in sections No

Degree of challenge Moderate–High

UNITED STATES

*Walkers on the Kaibab Trail enjoy dramatic
views of the Colorado River in the Inner Gorge of
the Grand Canyon.*

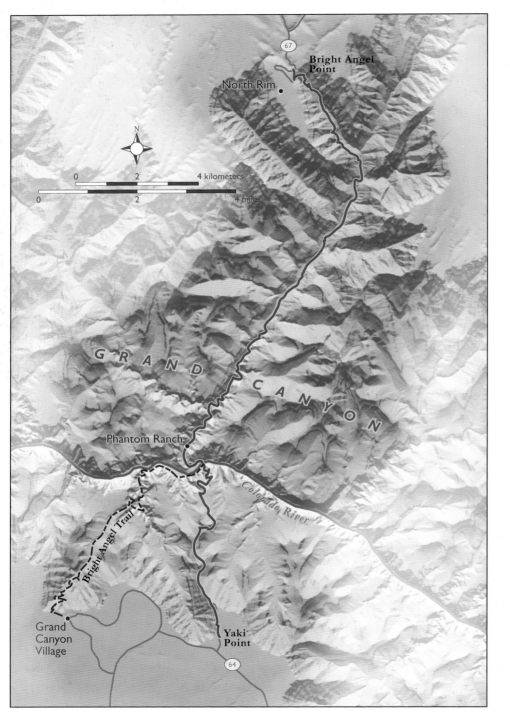

Grand Canyon National Park is one of our favorite national parks in the U.S. Like most of the park's nearly five million annual visitors, we were awestruck the first time we saw the canyon, its jaw-dropping scale and complexity seemingly beyond human imagination. The global importance of Grand Canyon is clearly manifested in its designation as a UNESCO World Heritage Site. But to more fully appreciate Grand Canyon, you must walk below the rim, ideally all the way to the Colorado River, the living heart of the park. This walk takes you roughly a mile beneath the surface of the earth, revealing nearly two billion years of geology in an orderly, step-by-step, layer-by-layer story more graphic than any written description. It's estimated that each step on the trail descending into the canyon represents one hundred thousand years of geologic history, and there are correspondingly dramatic changes in climate, plants, and animals. On our most recent walk of the Kaibab Trail, we met a young family on its first hike into the Canyon. They were so excited about what they were seeing and experiencing, that they could hardly find the words to express their feelings, and that's how we've felt sometimes, too. For many people, there's an emotional, even spiritual component of the Grand Canyon—an overwhelming sense of humility that only comes with walking through it. One writer calls walking the canyon the "physical price of admission," but it's well worth the cost.

Part 2: Extraordinary Hikes for Ordinary People

The Kaibab Trail is the only trail to traverse the Grand Canyon.

Grand Canyon National Park was established in 1919 and is one of the "crown jewels" of the U.S. National Park system. Of course, it's most famous for its massive gash in the earth—about 275 miles long, 5 to 15 miles wide, and about a mile deep—revealing much of the geologic history of the earth. The canyon was formed by a combination of uplift of the Colorado Plateau (an elevated area that comprises much of the southwestern U.S.) and the downward erosive force of the powerful Colorado River. The resulting exposed cross section reveals all three of the basic forms of rock that make up the earth: sedimentary (formed by deposition), igneous (formed through cooling and solidification of magma or lava), and metamorphic (changed molecularly by intense heat and pressure). The upper half of the canyon lays bare a succession of sedimentary rocks: deposits of marine organisms at the floor of deep seas (forming limestone) and windblown sand dunes (forming sandstone). The harder limestone erodes more slowly, forming steep cliffs, while the softer sandstone weathers more quickly, forming sloped layers. Over the eons the upper canyon has taken on a distinctive "stepped" appearance. Rocks at the bottom of the canyon, in what's called the Inner Gorge, are estimated to be as much as 1.7 billion years old and include volcanic intrusions (igneous rock) and schist (metamorphic rock). You'll want to spend some time at the National Park Service interpretive exhibits, particularly the Trail of Time Geology Exhibition on the south rim; learning about the geology certainly makes experiencing it more meaningful.

The word Kaibab is Paiute meaning "Mountain Lying Down," their term for the Grand Canyon. The South Kaibab Trail descends from the 7,000-foot South Rim of the canyon about 7 miles to the Colorado River. It leaves the rim at Yaki Point, just east of Grand Canyon Village. Much of the

Bright Angel Creek flows into the Colorado River near Phantom Ranch.

trail follows a natural ridgeline in the canyon and this results in spectacular panoramic views. However, the trail has been highly engineered (using dynamite and jackhammers where needed) and is steep in places. Notable points along the trail include aptly named Ooh Ahh Point, Cedar Ridge, Skeleton Point (named for the remains of a mule that fell to its death here), and the Tipoff (where the trail enters the canyon's inner gorge).

The North Kaibab Trail drops off the 8,000-foot North Rim of the canyon at Bright Angel Point and follows the natural fault line of Bright Angel Creek, an ancient Native American route through the canyon. It's considerably less steep, but consequently takes just over 14 miles to reach the Colorado River and join the South Kaibab Trail by means of a suspension bridge over the river. Notable points along the trail include Coconino Overview, Supai Tunnel (blasted out of the rock), Roaring Springs (a large natural spring that serves as the source of fresh water for most residents and visitors to Grand Canyon), Cottonwood Camp, and Phantom Ranch and Bright Angel Campground, both located on the substantial delta formed where Bright Angel Creek enters the Colorado River. This delta is a delightful oasis—a perennial source of water and shady cottonwood trees, willows, and tamarisk—for hikers who have just walked through miles of hot, desert conditions.

The only lodging in the canyon, Phantom Ranch is a rustic "resort" opened in 1922, designed by architect Mary Elizabeth Jane Colter at the behest of the Fred Harvey Company and the Santa Fe Railroad. The railroad helped open Grand Canyon to public use by building a spur line to the South Rim in the early 1900s, and this route has recently been restored (a ride that many visitors now enjoy). Phantom Ranch includes a series of cabins, a bunkhouse, and dining room, and it serves hikers and mule riders. The National Park Service manages nearby Bright Angel Campground.

The North and South Kaibab trails are among the most storied, historic and popular trails in the U.S. National Park system and have been designated as part of the National Trails System. The earliest trails in Grand Canyon were built by private entities primarily for mineral prospecting. Enterprising entrepreneurs charged a toll for use by the public. In response, the National Park Service constructed the Kaibab route in the 1920s. The Colorado River was a primary obstacle, and early crossings were made by ferry, and then a cable car. However, there are now two bridges that cross the river in the vicinity of Bright Angel Creek, the only crossings of the Colorado River within the nearly 300 miles of the river in the national park. The Kaibab Suspension Bridge (often called the "Black Bridge" because of its dark color) includes eight 550-foot braided steel cables that support the bridge, each weighing more than a ton; 42 men of the local Havasupai tribe carried each large strand down from the rim. Construction of this route was rarely easy!

Experiencing the Colorado River is one of the principal rewards for Kaibab Trail walkers. This mighty river drains much of the southwest quadrant of the U.S. and is a vital source of water in this arid land. It rises in the Rocky Mountains and flows 1,450 miles before emptying into the Gulf of California. The portion of the river that flows through Grand Canyon was first run in four wooden boats by one-armed Civil War veteran John Wesley Powell and his crew of ten men in 1869, one of the great American adventure stories. Powell was surveying the river and surrounding lands to help ensure wise use of the river's scarce water. Today, thousands of people raft the river each year for recreation, and Kaibab Trail walkers are likely to see one or more of these river trips.

Colorado is Spanish for "red river," and references the natural color of the water as a result of all of the sediment that is washed into the river from the surrounding arid lands. However, the section of the river that flows through Grand Canyon is now often clear as a result of the Glen Canyon Dam constructed just upstream of Grand Canyon in the 1960s. The dam slows the flow of the river, causing most of the sediment to be deposited at the bottom of the reservoir; when water is released through

Indian Paintbrush and agave are among the distinctive desert plants along the Kaibab Trail.

the dam it comes from near the bottom of the 600-foot deep Lake Powell and is clear and cold. Currently, the dam and lake are being managed in an experimental way to try to more closely mimic the natural flow of the river.

While geology and the Colorado River are the stars of the show for Kaibab Trail walkers, other elements of natural and human history add considerable interest. Walkers making the 5,000 to 6,000 feet of elevation change from the canyon's rims to the river (and back) pass through five of the seven North American life zones, representing highly unusual biological diversity in such close proximity. For every 1,000 feet of elevation loss from the canyon rims, air temperature rises 4 to 5 degrees. Snow is common on the canyon rims in winter, and temperatures at the bottom of the canyon can approach 120 degrees in summer. Because of this extreme temperature differential, plants and animals are highly varied. One can find mule deer, elk, and coyotes along with fir, spruce, and ponderosa pines on the canyon rims, and desert bighorn sheep and rattlesnakes, along with cacti and yucca deep within the canyon. California condors have recently been reintroduced into the Grand Canyon area and are frequently seen soaring. Utah agaves are also common, and they are a favorite of ours. This remarkable low-growing plant stores energy for about twenty-five years, then grows a stalk up to 12 feet high in a single season, flowers, and then dies, completing its life cycle.

Archeological evidence suggests that Native Americans settled in and around the canyon roughly eleven thousand years ago. These people, called Ancestral Pluebloans by contemporary archeologists, built small settlements and raised crops over a thousand years ago, but abandoned the area about 1140 AD. A nine-hundred-year old pueblo is located near the Kaibab Suspension Bridge. Spanish explorers looking for gold "discovered" Grand Canyon in 1540, but quickly moved on because the canyon presented such an impediment to travel. American prospectors combed the canyon in the

"If you pick 'em up, O Lord, I'll put 'em down."
—The Prayer of the Tired Walker

The Kaibab Trail uses a series of switchbacks to navigate the steeper sections of the Grand Canyon.

1800s, but found little of economic value. The canyon was first protected by Executive Order of President Teddy Roosevelt who, in a famous speech on the South Rim, admonished Americans to "Leave it as it is. You cannot improve on it. The ages have been at work on it, and man can only mar it."

The North and South Kaibab trails are well designed and maintained to a high level. While they are necessarily steep in a few places, the trail tread is wide and well groomed, making them a pleasure to walk. You're likely to see mule trains moving up and down the canyon carrying visitors and supplies in to Phantom Ranch. Walkers should stop and be still while the mules pass and follow directions given by the wranglers.

There are several options for walking the Kaibab Trail and Grand Canyon more broadly. The preferred option is to start on the north rim of the canyon and walk down the North Kaibab Trail to the Colorado River and then ascend the South Kaibab Trail to the south rim. Traversing the canyon from north to south saves walkers about a thousand feet of elevation gain (since the north rim is higher than the south rim). Most walkers leave their car at the south rim and take a commercial shuttle to the north rim to begin their hike. Be aware that this will take time: the north rim is only about 10 miles from the south rim as the crow flies, but the drive around the canyon is about 215 miles! Also note that car access to the north rim is usually only available from about mid-May to mid-September as snow closes the road the rest of the year. Plan on spending at least one night at either Phantom Ranch or Bright Angel Campground on this hike and preferably more; walking the North Kaibab Trail can be broken into two days by camping at Cottonwood Camp. If the north rim is not open, many walkers hike down the South Kaibab Trail and back up to the south rim via the Bright Angel Trail. Less steep than the South Kaibab Trail, the Bright Angel Trail is about 10 miles long. Again, at least one night should be spent at Phantom Ranch or Bright Angel Campground; there is also a campground at Indian Springs, about half way up the Bright Angel Trail. Some visitors do this walk (down

the South Kaibab Trail and up the Bright Angel Trail) in one day, but the National Park Service strongly discourages this. Walking in Grand Canyon is like mountain climbing in reverse; you walk downhill at first, but then have to climb up (way up!) out of the canyon.

You must always be prepared for hiking in desert conditions; don't be fooled if the air temperature is cool on the rim; it will get much warmer as you descend. Hikers are advised to drink a gallon of water per day on the trail. There is no water on the South Kaibab Trail, but water is available at several locations on the North Kaibab and Bright Angel trails. It's wise to hike early in the day, starting your hike out of the canyon at sunrise. Some walkers don't follow this advice and wind up needing assistance, and a few have even died in the canyon. No matter how tempting, don't swim in the Colorado River—its current is strong and dangerous and the water is cold. Reservations for accommodations at Phantom Ranch must be made well in advance, up to a year ahead to arrange a preferred date. Reservations for camping must also be made far ahead of time with the National Park Service.

A number of years ago, epic Grand Canyon walker Colin Fletcher wrote a book called *The Man Who Walked Through Time*. Walking the Grand Canyon and taking your own trip back in geologic time is one of the great walking experiences in the world. If walking all the way to the Colorado River is not advisable, then consider doing a day hike to any of the waypoints along the North or South Kaibab trails noted above; all these hikes will allow you to experience the magic of walking below the rim of Grand Canyon. We bet you'll be left speechless!

"People say that losing weight is no walk in the park. When I hear that I think, yeah, that's the problem."

—Chris Adams

Further Reading

www.nps.gov/grca

Adkison, Ron. *Hiking Grand Canyon National Park*. Nashville, TN: Falcon Press, 2006.

Roos, Constance. *The Grand Canyon: With Bryce and Zion Canyons in America's Southwest*. Milnthorpe, Cumbria, UK: Cicerone Press, 2010.

Thybony, Scott. *Grand Canyon North Kaibab Trail Guide*. Grand Canyon, AZ: Grand Canyon Association, 2005.

Thybony, Scott. *Grand Canyon South Kaibab Trail Guide*. Grand Canyon, AZ: Grand Canyon Association. 2005.

Thybony, Scott. *Phantom Ranch*. Grand Canyon, AZ: Grand Canyon Association. 2001.

Wenk, Elizabeth. *One Best Hike: Grand Canyon*. Berkeley, CA: Wilderness Press, 2010.

Kalalau Trail

Location Hawaii, USA

Length 22 miles (round trip)

Accommodations
Commercial: No
Huts/refuges: No
Camping: Yes

Baggage transfer No

Option to walk in sections No

Degree of challenge High

HAWAII, USA

The Kalalau Trail offers intimate views of Hawaii's famous Na Pali Coast.

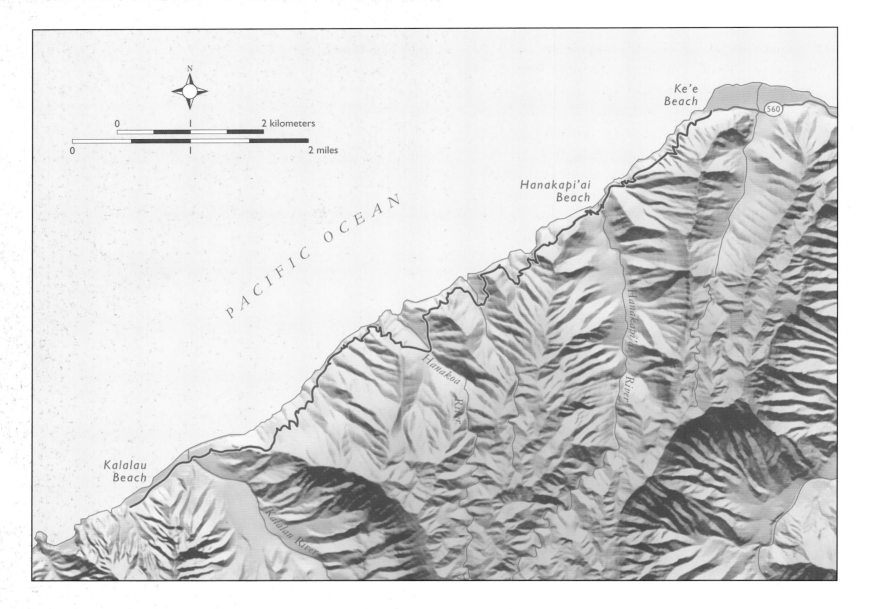

It was late afternoon by the time we reached the end of the trail and we were tired. The Kalalau Trail had been a harder hike than we were expecting, both physically and psychologically. But here we were at Kalalau Beach, a mile of golden sand and crashing surf at the mouth of a lush tropical valley. We pitched our tent in the shade of a cluster of trees and waded (carefully) into the surf. That evening, we walked to the far end of the beach and showered under a natural waterfall. At night we watched the stars in the clearest night sky we'd seen since we were kids and let the surf lull us to sleep (which didn't take long). You have to work some to experience this iconic bit of Hawaiian paradise, but we found it to be more than worth the effort.

Kauai is the "garden isle" of the Hawaiian Islands. Sounds like paradise, and in many ways it is. Lush rainforests and hanging valleys cling to steep 3,000-foot cliffs that rise out of the turquoise Pacific Ocean. The 11-mile (one way) Kalalau Trail is the only access to the famous Na Pali Coast, immortalized in dozens of Hollywood movies, including *Blue Hawaii* and *Jurassic Park*. But as usual, paradise comes at a cost. This can be an adventurous, hard, and even scary walk. The trail follows the folds in the cliffs, climbing in and out of deep, narrow valleys, rising and falling from beaches to more than a thousand exposed feet above the ocean, and seeming to periodically double back on itself. But the reward is some of the most beautiful scenery in the world, exotic vegetation, and camping at the end at a world-class beach with a waterfall as your personal shower.

Formed by lava from deep undersea volcanoes, Kauai was the first of the Hawaiian Islands to rise out of the Pacific Ocean. The island is estimated to be about five million years old—relatively young geologically—but this has allowed development of dense and rich vegetation that covers nearly every square inch of the island that will support it. The Kalalau Trail was originally built in the late 1800s and portions were rebuilt in the 1930s. The trail is easy to follow, but is not well maintained. In several places, the trail is very narrow with steep drop-offs to the ocean, and we found these places a little unnerving; we relied heavily on our hiking poles to get us through these sections.

Pali is Hawaiian for cliffs. The sheer cliffs of the Na Pali Coast are cut by waves from wind and water that collect over a vast expanse of Pacific Ocean, while its steep valleys are shaped by the many streams and waterfalls along its face. The rainforests that cover the cliffs are supported by prodigious precipitation; the summit of nearby Wai'ale'ale' Mountain holds the world record for rain at more than 600 inches in a year (it averages 420 inches). The trail starts at Ke'e Lagoon, often rated as the most beautiful beach on the planet, and traverses five valleys, ending at Kalalau Beach where further travel is blocked by a sheer, fluted pali that juts into the sea. Extensive stone-walled terraces

The Kalalau Trail follows the folds of the cliffs, climbing in and out of deep, narrow valleys.

The rocks and soil along the Kalalau Trail reveal the volcanic origin of the Hawaiian Islands.

can still be found in several of the valley bottoms where Hawaiians once lived and cultivated taro (an Asian starchy root vegetable) and coffee. Many rare plants grow on the trail's inaccessible cliffs, and wild goats are frequently seen. There are several campgrounds along the trail, including the one at the end of the trail, and camping is restricted to these areas. We strongly recommend spending at least two nights camping at Kalalau Beach to reward yourself and to fully appreciate "paradise."

"I have two doctors, my left leg and my right."
—G. M. Trevelyan

Even though this is a relatively short walk, it requires preparation, both physical and psychological. One might be tempted to try to walk out and back in one long day, but this would be a mistake. First, it would not allow for the time needed to fully appreciate this magical place. Second, it's a relatively demanding walk, requiring about 5,000 feet of accumulated elevation gain (one way) in a hot and humid environment, and on a trail tread that is sometimes narrow and rough, and that includes steep water courses and fording several (usually small) creeks. Rain can cause these streams to flood, and walkers should wait for the water to recede before attempting to cross (these small, steep streams tend to rise and fall quickly). Drinking water can be taken from streams, but must be treated. The bacterium leptospirosis exists in several creeks along the trail and can invade the body through small cuts and cause a sometimes fatal hepatitis-like sickness; be cautious about swimming in these waters. Caution is also needed in swimming at all ocean beaches because of unpredictable surf and dangerous currents and rip tides.

The trail begins in Ha'vena State Park about an hour and half drive from Lihu'e airport and ends at Kalalau Beach, though you

The Kalalau Trail clings to the steep slopes above the Pacific Ocean.

Kalalau Beach is the prize awaiting walkers at the end of the Kalalua Trail.

have to walk back to the start as this is an out-and-back trail. (It may be possible to arrange a boat ride to or from Kalalau Beach, thus shortening your walk by half. Check locally.) A permit (and nominal fee) are needed for the hike and the number of permits is limited. However, walking the first 2 miles of the trail (to Hanakapi'ai) does not require a permit and offers an appealing sample of the trail. The primary hiking season is May through September, when there is less rain, but it can be walked any time of the year as temperatures rarely drop below 60 degrees, even in winter. We walked in March.

Walking the Kalalau Trail has been described as having a strong spiritual component—*mana* in Hawaiian, meaning big medicine—representing the tension between the beauty of the area and the potential danger it represents. Consider walking the Kalalau Trail and getting a strong dose of this medicine. We feel we're better for it.

Further Reading

www.hawaiistateparks.org/hiking/kauai/kalalau.cfm

www.kalalautrail.com

Part 2: Extraordinary Hikes for Ordinary People

King Ludwig's Way

Location Germany

Length 80 miles

Accommodations
Commercial: Yes
Huts/refuges: No
Camping: Some

Baggage transfer Yes

Option to walk in sections All

Degree of challenge Low–Moderate

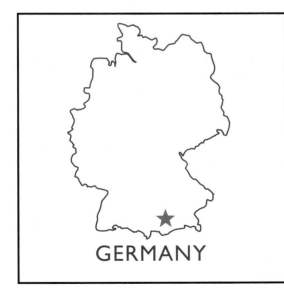

GERMANY

King Ludwig's Way often follows rural lanes through the Bavarian landscape.

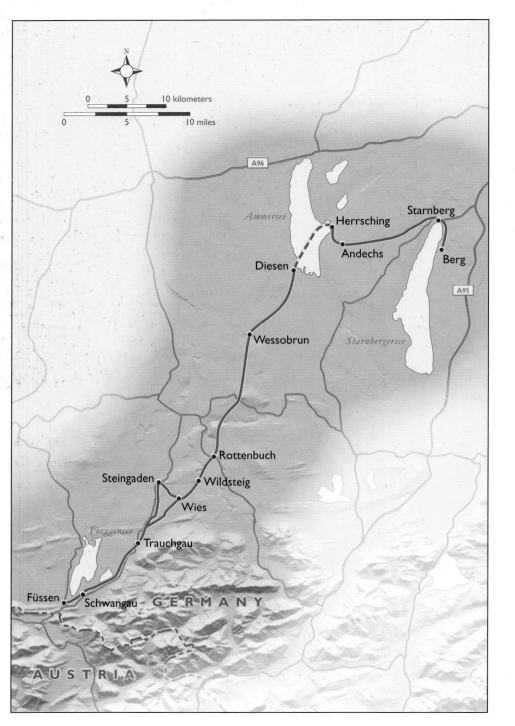

It was day five of our eight-day walk across Bavaria, following in the footsteps—literally and figuratively—of charismatic and eccentric King Ludwig, the nineteenth-century ruler of Bavaria when it was still an independent country. We were enjoying what we found to be the surprisingly rural character of the region: small-scale farms scattered across a rolling, pastoral landscape and dotted with a series of charming villages, each with a baroque church with an interior seemingly more ornate than the last. But on this August afternoon a thunderstorm was building and clearly heading our way. As the storm broke we were fortunate to find a small barn beside the country road we were walking, doors open and beckoning us to take shelter. Hay bales offered us comfortable seating and a good view of the lightning and accompanying sheets of rain. After an hour, the storm ended as quickly as it had begun and we continued on our way, the storm and our picturesque shelter another memorable and romantic moment of our delightful Bavarian adventure.

Popularly called the "Dream King," Ludwig ascended to the throne of Bavaria in 1864 at the vulnerable age of eighteen. He ruled erratically for twenty-two years until his mysterious death at age forty. While he was politically naive and spent beyond the country's means, he made lasting and increasingly valuable contributions in the areas of art and architecture. He was also an avid walker, and the trail that bears his name is an especially appropriate way to honor his legacy.

The ends of the trail mark the beginning and ending of Ludwig's reign, and the trail is usually walked in reverse chronological order, saving the best for last. It starts in the

A portion of King Ludwig's Way wanders through dramatic beech forests.

village of Berg on the shores of Lake Starnberg, where Ludwig drowned just a few days after he was removed from power for mental incompetence. Did he jump into the lake or was he pushed? This remains one of the great mysteries of European history. A simple cross in the lake and a small votive chapel on the shore mark the site of Ludwig's death. From the lake, the trail wanders south for 80 miles, stopping just short of the Austrian border. The end of the walk features the fairytale castles that are the most tangible manifestations of Ludwig and this period of Bavarian history.

The track wanders through the green countryside, passing among a dozen towns and villages that are attractive, offer numerous opportunities for accommodation or a hot lunch, and allow the trail to be walked in any number of days. Our favorites were Andechs, Diessen, Rottenbuch, Wildsteig, and Fussen. Andechs was founded in 1455 by Benedictine monks and sits on a hill, the "Holy Mount." The impressive abbey church is an historic pilgrimage site and is approached by a long lane featuring the Stations of the Cross. Today, most visitors drive to Andechs, attracted by the Andechs Abbey Brewery, including its restaurant and beer garden. Famous Andechs Bockbier, brewed by enterprising monks, is served by the traditional *maas*, a liter container shaped like a great vase, and, judging by the crowds the day we visited, the monks are good brewers. Diessen is an attractive lakeside town that is reached by ferry over Ammersee Lake, and features the Diessen Monastery Church, a striking example of Bavarian baroque architecture. Rottenbuch is a tiny but delightful monastery town, dominated by a grand church set on one side of a cobbled square and reached through a stone gateway. Wildsteig is an agricultural hamlet; the day we were there, the town was celebrating its

King Ludwig's Way passes a number of simple churches with dramatic baroque interiors.

nine hundredth anniversary, complete with antique tractors, residents in traditional costume, and an oompah band. Fussen is the largest town on the trail, a walled city located less than a mile from the Austrian border and featuring a castle, medieval streets, and a fine church. It's visitor-friendly, offering all services that walkers might need. All along the route nearly all houses (many of them traditional chalets) feature elaborate window boxes stuffed with geraniums.

The last day of walking presents the highlight of the trail, the two castles that mark the beginning and ending of Ludwig's reign. Hohenschwangau is the family castle where Ludwig was born. It's an impressive structure that features variations of the swan motif of the royal family on *everything*. But Ludwig yearned for something more than his birth home—a castle reflecting his fanciful interests in art and architecture—and he commissioned the building of Neuschwanstein, located in an improbable setting on the crest of a hill towering above the surrounding plains. It's a mix of architectural styles, including Romanesque, Byzantine, and many forms of Gothic, and Neuschwanstein is rumored to be the model for Cinderella's Castle at Disney World. To illustrate the lavish style in which the castle was created, fourteen wood carvers worked for four years on the bedroom furniture alone. More than two million visitors come to Neuschwanstein annually, so be prepared for long lines to purchase tickets. The trail approaches the castle through the steep Pollat Gorge at the base of the hill and leads to the Marie Bridge spanning the gorge and offering classic views of the castle. Tours of both castles are offered in several languages.

Other features of the trail include grand views of the surrounding Alps, two lakes (crossed by ferry), maypoles with the symbols of traditional occupations marking the entrance to all towns, Ammer Gorge (Bavaria's "Grand Canyon"), and the summit of Hofenpeissenberg Hill, which offers what many think is the finest view in Bavaria. We especially

Part 2: Extraordinary Hikes for Ordinary People

Neuschwanstein is the fairytale castle of King Ludwig.

liked the pilgrimage church at Wies, built in the eighteenth century and dramatically set in the midst of agricultural fields without any surrounding town; it's popularly called the "Meadow Church."

While most of the trail follows farm and rural roads, portions of the track cross patches of dense forest—beeches in the lower elevations and fir and pine at higher locations. Forests or *walds* are important in German folklore as places of wildness, beauty, and legend. Contemporary damage to these areas by air pollution and acid rain is taken very seriously by many Germans and is a contentious political issue.

King Ludwig's Way is a pleasant walk presenting only modest challenges. There are no long or steep climbs and daily walking distances average 8 to 12 miles, or even fewer if desired. This is a "lowland" walk, surrounded by the Alps, but through the valleys and forests at their base. All towns offer *gasthofs* (guesthouses) that are usually a combination of pub, hotel, and restaurant, and baggage transfers can easily be arranged. Part of the fun is eating traditional German food such as weiner schnitzel, sauerkraut, spatzel, apfelstrudel, and, of course, German beer. However, ordering can sometimes be an adventure as little English is spoken in some of the rural areas the trail traverses. Although our language skills were challenged, we always found the people we met to be friendly, helpful, and welcoming. The trail is well maintained and easy to follow—marked by a stylistic "K"—and access to the trail is easy by train from Munich and Fussen. The

The lively, historic town of Fussen marks the southern end of King Ludwig's Way.

peak walking season is June through August, but the shoulder months of May and September offer appealing options; October is also a possibility, though accommodations may be scarce during the Octoberfest, a tradition started by King Ludwig in celebration of his wedding.

Before this walk we didn't fully understand what an interesting figure King Ludwig was, nor did we appreciate his legacy for Germans in particular and Europeans more generally. King Ludwig's Way is an opportunity to experience the glorious Bavarian landscape and enjoy its modern rural character and people. Consider walking with King Ludwig across his native and beloved Bavaria.

····· Further Reading ······

Speakman, Fleur, and Collin Speakman, *King Ludwig Way*. Milnthorpe, Cumbria, UK: Cicerone, 1987.

Kungsleden

Location Sweden

Length 270 miles

Accommodations
Commercial: Some
Huts/refuges: Yes
Camping: Yes

Baggage transfer No

Option to walk in sections Some

Degree of challenge Moderate

SWEDEN

Long stretches of boardwalk keep walkers off the
wettest portions of the Kungsleden's tundra.

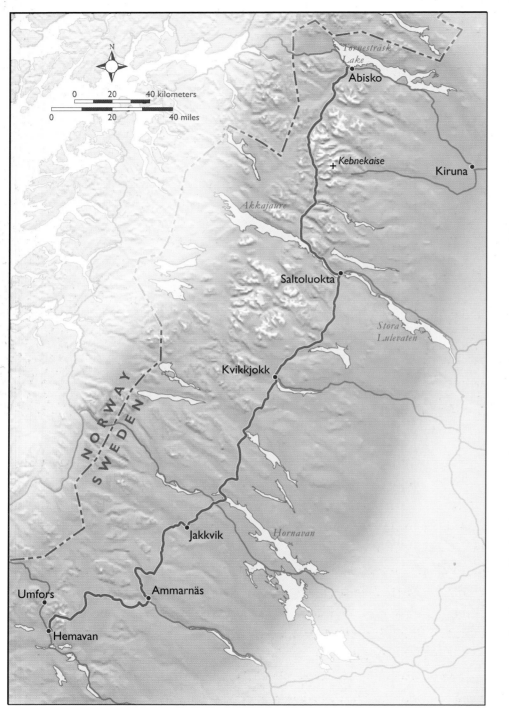

Our first day on the Kungsleden was just what we'd hoped—glorious scenery, beautiful weather, a good night's sleep in a warm, cozy hut shared with a friendly German couple about our age. Unfortunately, day two offered up an entirely different experience. We stepped out of our hut and back on the trail just as the rain started—and then came the wind. We walked (and occasionally slogged) all day across vast stretches of Arctic tundra, finally reaching our next hut about 4:00 that afternoon. We were cold and beat. But then came an unexpected reward. After the hut master checked us in, he casually asked if we would like to take a sauna before dinner. A sauna?! As it turns out, some of the more enterprising hut masters have built saunas for their guests, and this sounded like just what we needed. Of course, we didn't know exactly what a Swedish sauna was, but it sounded like a place to get clean and warm. And it was—for everyone at the hut, at the same time—co-ed, naked. A real cultural experience for two prudish Americans. We entered the sauna and washed with buckets of water heated on the woodstove and then sat on tiered benches soaking up the hot steam. When we were finally too hot, we dashed out of the building and plunged into the river, returning to the sauna to repeat the whole process. Our walk along the Kungsleden instilled in us a genuine appreciation for the tradition of the sauna—and the attractiveness of the Swedish people!

The Kungsleden's arctic tundra is biologically rich.

Kungsleden is translated as the "trail of kings" and sometimes the "king of trails." Both of these worked for us as the drama of the vast and stark landscape of Lapland is truly regal in scale and character. This 270-mile trail from Abisko south to Hemavan traverses the Lapponia UNESCO World Heritage Site, the largest area of wilderness left in Europe, and wanders through four national parks and a nature reserve, in all an area larger than some European countries. The Kungsleden is often referred to as the "national trail" of Sweden. The northern portion of the trail, about 120 miles—all north of the Arctic Circle—is acknowledged as the most scenic section, and that's what we walked, taking nine days.

This is a vast and dramatic landscape capped by an endless sky. Huge, shallow valleys lie at the foot of rolling, low-lying, snowcapped mountains with glaciers clinging to their sides. Big, fast-flowing rivers connect large, icy lakes. Deep forests of pine, spruce, and stunted birch cover much of the landscape the further south you go. The trail is well marked with stone cairns and red blazes and wayfinding is not difficult.

The trail tread is often wet, but miles of boardwalk have been constructed, and walking is easy in these places. However, other portions of the trail are rough with occasional steep, but short, climbs. All in all, this trail is of only moderate difficulty, though the weather and the trail's remoteness can add a substantial layer of challenge.

We enjoyed the wildlife: willow grouse, ptarmigan, golden eagles, and moose (what Swedes call elk). As we made our way along the edge of a small lake, an Arctic tern dove at us repeatedly, protecting its young in a nest near

A herd of reindeer flows across the Kungsleden.

the trail. And of course there are reindeer—herds of them flowing across the landscape. One afternoon we were taking a break, sitting on some rocks sunning ourselves, when a herd of reindeer walked slowly toward us, enveloping us, then moving on—a truly magical moment. We didn't see some of the more secretive wildlife: lynx, wolverines, wolves, and bears.

The Sami, northern Scandinavia's indigenous people who have lived in this area for ten thousand years, herd reindeer. Small clusters of Sami huts are seen periodically along the trail, and the Sami provide walkers with goods and services: local fish and other food, and ferries across lakes. Their knowledge of this land is so intimate that they divide the year into eight seasons.

Walking the trail offers adventures every day. Near the beginning, the trail takes walkers through the dramatic saddle known as Lapporten, the "Gates of Lapland." Four large lakes must be crossed along the trail, and this can be done in self-service rowboats. There are three rowboats at each lake. If there are two boats on your side, then you simply row one across, pulling your boat up on shore at the end. But if there is only one boat on your side, then you row to the other side, tow a boat back, and then row across again. This honor system ensures that there is always a boat for walkers approaching from either the north or the south. However, you must exercise caution in crossing these lakes—they are broad, deep, and icy. Local Sami guides will ferry walkers across the lakes in motorboats for a nominal fee, and this is a good idea if the water is rough or you are not experienced with boats.

Side trails lead into even more remote areas, and there are two especially attractive alternatives. At 6,932 feet, Kebnekaise is the highest mountain in Sweden (and all of Arctic Scandinavia), and it is accessible by a steep but not too difficult trail. Skierfe is not as high, but is especially dramatic and offers outstanding views into the heart of the wild and rugged mountains of Sarek National Park. Wild bilberries, cloudberries, and blueberries are more than plentiful (but can be sour!). The region is so pristine that water can be drunk directly

A series of tidy Swedish Tourist Federation huts are located an easy day's walk apart on the Kungsleden.

from rivers and lakes (one of the few places we've done this). Local smoked fish can sometimes be purchased for dinner. Take time to look closely—on hands and knees—at the tundra you're walking across and appreciate this biologically diverse, miniature "forest." Enjoy the midnight sun, meet walkers from around the world, and embrace the challenge of reading trail signs in seemingly unpronounceable Swedish.

An elaborate system of huts and lodges is scattered along the trail, an easy day's walk apart, and this means walkers do not have to carry tents, cooking equipment, and other camping gear. Huts are simple, but clean and efficient, providing duvets and pillows and communal kitchens stocked with gas stoves, pots and pans, and dishes. Some huts sell limited provisions. Hut etiquette demands that walkers take their boots off before entering, gather clean water for communal use, sweep floors, sort trash, shake and fold duvets, and store stools on tables before leaving. Walkers should also split wood when needed. Lodges (called *fjallstations*) are less common (there are three along the section of the trail we walked—Abisko, Saltoluokta, and Kivikkjokk) and are much more elaborate, offering hotel-like rooms, hot showers, and full-service restaurants. Lodges are the only places along the

"If you want to know if your brain is flabby, feel your legs."

—Bruce Barton

Walkers on the Kungsleden can use rowboats to cross the larger lakes.

trail that have road access. The Swedish Touring Federation operates all huts and lodges; because we had joined the organization prior to our trip, we received a substantial discount on fees.

As might be expected, the walking season is short on the Kungsleden: late June through some of September (depending on weather). (The trail also serves cross-country skiers in the winter.) Our walk was in the second half of August and temperatures dipped below freezing on a few nights. June and July can be wet, bringing out mosquitoes, but offer wildflowers in profusion. September offers fall colors. Huts and lodges take credit cards, but bring some cash for ferries and trade with the Sami. Camping is allowed along the trail with few restrictions, but nearly everyone uses the huts. Positioning for the Kungsleden takes a day or two on both ends of the walk. We took the eighteen-hour overnight train from Stockholm (an adventure in itself—our advice is to reserve a sleeping car, because the train was crowded). You can also fly to Kiruna and use buses to reach the beginning and ending points of the trail. Most people walk from north to south to keep the sun's warmth on their face. While in Stockholm, we mailed ourselves a resupply package that was delivered to one of the lodges. Unfortunately, there are no English guidebooks for the Kungsleden. Study maps carefully for both wayfinding (which was not difficult) and to find road access, if you wish a shorter or longer version of the trail than we walked.

Our walk on the Kungsleden was one of our favorites because the landscape and culture were so different and appealing. The trail is really a bit of a paradox as it tends to make lists of the world's best trails, but relatively few people actually walk it. On many days of our walk, we saw virtually no one on the trail and relatively few at the huts. In fact, most walkers haven't even heard of the Kungsleden. We suggest you walk this trail soon before the rest of the world discovers it.

Further Reading

www.svenskaturistforeningen.se/en

www.visitsweden.com/sweden/Attractions/Outdoor-activities/Hiking/Kings-trail

www.svenskaturistforeningen.se/en

www.svenskaturistforeningen.se/en

The Kungsleden features several large arctic lakes.

Fall foliage makes autumn an ideal time to walk the Long Trail.

Part Two: Extraordinary Hikes for Ordinary People

Long Trail

Location Vermont, USA

Length 273 miles

Accommodations
Commercial: Some
Huts/refuges: 3-sided shelters
Camping: Yes

Baggage transfer No

Option to walk in sections Most

Degree of challenge Moderate–High

UNITED STATES

The Long Trail crosses many streams flowing off the Green Mountains.

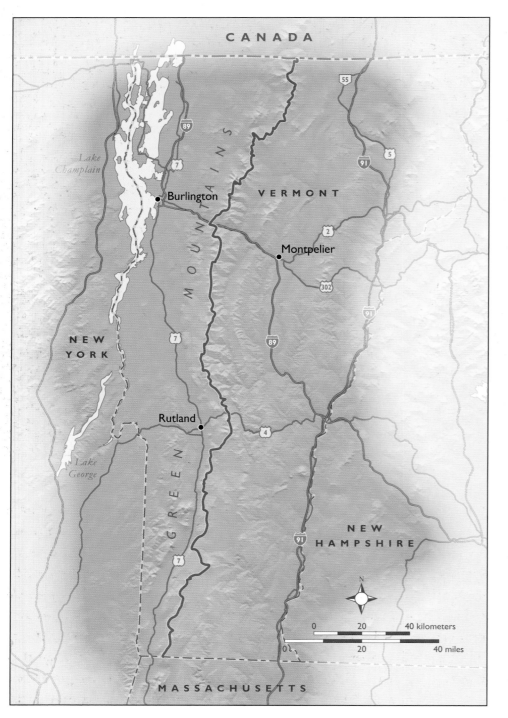

We love our Long Trail Guide. It's the compact source of all the information needed to walk this remarkable trail, the first long-distance trail in America. It provides detailed descriptions of the trail, including mileages, hiking times, difficulty ratings, locations of overnight shelters and campsites, water sources, and elevation profiles. It includes directions to trailheads and parking and even a small map. And it's designed to fit easily into the pack. There's only one problem with the guide—it's written in code. After a few days of walking we figured it out. For example, when the guide describes the terrain as "rolling," it means get ready for a series of significant ascents and descents. When the trail "drops steeply," hang on to exposed roots and whatever else is available. When it "climbs steeply," get ready for a half hour of anaerobic breathing. "Uneven" means extremely rough. "Rough going" means nearly impassable. "Wet area" means this bog will suck your boots off. Learning the understated language of Vermonters is just part of the fun of walking this trail. And the trail reflects its history. Developed prior to contemporary trail-building methods, the route tends to go from Point A (the trailhead) to Point B (a mountain summit) in the most direct line, without consideration of such niceties as switchbacks. But that's part of the adventure of the Long Trail—remember, the trail is "rolling."

The aptly named Long Trail is a 273-mile rollercoaster ride along the ridgeline of Vermont's Green Mountains, from Massachusetts to Canada, crossing the state's highest peaks and exposing much of its most beautiful scenery. It was conceived in 1909 by James P. Taylor, a teacher at Vermont

The Long Trail rises and falls along the ridge of the Green Mountains in Vermont.

Academy, who liked to take his pupils on hikes, but was frustrated that there weren't more trails connecting the major peaks of the Green Mountains. The Green Mountain Club ultimately achieved his vision of a "long trail" connecting all the major mountains in 1930. When the trail was officially opened that year, flares were lit from the tops of the mountain peaks along the route, a signal to all Vermonters. Today, the Long Trail, popularly called "A Footpath in the Wilderness," is one of the iconic features of Vermont and attracts thousands of hikers each year. The trail was the inspiration for the over 2,000-mile Appalachian Trail that runs from Georgia to Maine; in fact, a 100-mile section of the Long Trail is part of the "AT."

The Green Mountains are the geologic backbone of Vermont and give the Long Trail its distinctive "rolling" character. Part of the greater Appalachian Mountain system, the Greens run the length of the state, extending into Massachusetts and Canada, and ranging from 20 to 35 miles wide. The original mountains are thought to be over a billion years old and once rose to heights of 10,000 to 20,000 feet. But erosion, glaciation, and other geologic forces have reduced their heights to around 4,000 feet. The glaciers have given the mountains and surrounding landscape their distinctive form: mountains with relatively gentle north-facing slopes and steep south faces (rock "plucked" away by glaciers advancing to the south),

Occasional ladders help walkers up and down the steeper pitches of the Long Trail.

smoothed exposed peaks, broad U-shaped valleys, frequent ponds and bogs, and rocks everywhere. Two impressive rivers, the Winooski and Lamoille, bisect the range.

Long Trail walkers climb up and over all the major peaks—Glastonbury Mountain, Stratton Mountain, Killington Peak, Mount Abraham, Mount Ellen, Camel's Hump, Mount Mansfield, and Jay Peak. But of all the mountains in Vermont, Mansfield and Camel's Hump are the most iconic. Mansfield is the highest at 4,395 feet and looks like a person's profile (lying down) when viewed from the east. Distinctive knobs are known as "Forehead" (the highest point), "Nose," and "Chin." (Some close observers claim they can also distinguish upper and lower lips and an Adam's apple.) The view from the top is spectacular, and includes the White Mountains to the east, the Adirondack Mountains and Lake Champlain to the west, Montreal to the north, and a sea of peaks all around. Camel's Hump (a genteel version of the name "Camel's Rump" on a 1798 map prepared by Ira Allen, legendary Green Mountain Boy) is the only mountain in the state over 4,000 feet that has not been developed in some way. It, too, has a distinctive profile—a crouching lion. Both Mount Mansfield and Camel's Hump (as well as Mount Abraham) have substantive areas of arctic alpine tundra on their bald summits, remnants of the last glacial period some ten thousand years ago. The low-lying species of Bigelow's sedge, alpine bilberry, and mountain sandwort growing here are normally found only in areas a thousand or more miles to the north. These vegetative communities are highly fragile and walkers must be careful to stay on the trail in these areas and step only on bare rock surfaces. Green Mountain Club caretakers are posted on these summits to protect them and to help educate visitors.

Other prominent vegetation along the trail includes vast forests of northern hardwoods, including sugar maple (the state tree), red maple, beech, northern red oak, and yellow and white birch. Of course, this is the forest that provides the world-famous fall foliage of stunning reds, oranges, and yellows. Evergreen forests of spruce and fir grow at higher elevations and are responsible for the name "Green Mountains"; when first seen by explorer Samuel de Champlain from the lake that now bears his name, he exhorted "*Voila, les verds monts*" (Behold, the green mountains). As the forest approaches the highest elevations of 4,000 feet, trees become stunted by the short growing season and distorted by the wind and weather, forming the distinctive krummholz, meaning "crooked wood" in German. Spring wildflowers include trillium, violets, hepaticas, and spring beauties. Animals include plentiful white-tailed deer at lower elevations, beavers, bobcats, an increasing population of moose (we saw two on the trail), and black bears (we saw one). There is a great debate about whether there are still catamounts (Vermont's version of mountain lions) in the Green Mountains. There continue to be reported sightings, but scientists insist that they have been extirpated. Notable birds include partridge, wild turkeys, hawks, peregrine falcons, and bald eagles.

You'll encounter lots of interesting features along the trail. Several peaks, including Glastonbury, Stratton, and Belvidere, have fire towers that provide striking 360-degree views. Ski areas share several of the mountains, and a few offer chairlift rides to the top (or bottom) in summer and fall. Stratton Pond offers great swimming and is a favorite for many hikers. The trail passes through portions of six wilderness areas, all part of the Green Mountain National Forest. In these sections, the trail is more primitive and use levels tend to be low.

Vermont was home to Abenaki Indians long before it was colonized, and it's likely that portions of the Long Trail follow ancient aboriginal travel routes, but there is little physical evidence of the Native American presence. But you may be surprised to find evidence of historical occupation of this land as you walk the trail—occasional rock walls and cellar holes mark the locations of fruitless attempts to farm a land that was both steep and, because of the short growing season, unsuitable for growing crops. By 1850, 80 percent of Vermont had been cleared for timber, ships' masts, potash, and sheep farms. Now the state is 80 percent forested. The trail also includes a system of 173 miles of side

The Long Trail often offers great beauty underfoot.

trails that provide access up to the Long Trail and down to the many other delights of Vermont, including historic villages, bed and breakfasts, artisan cheeses and beer, breakfasts of pancakes and real maple syrup, and, of course, Ben and Jerry's ice cream.

The Long Trail is highly accessible with many road crossings and its extensive system of side trails, allowing for frequent resupply for through-hikers and easy access for day use. In fact, all of the trail can be walked in short sections of one to a few days. The trail is serviced with a system of three-sided shelters for overnight use and camping is allowed in most areas. A nominal fee may be required for some shelters and for the few primitive lodges. Many surrounding towns in Vermont have a range of bed and breakfast accommodations useful for hikers who don't want to camp. Wayfinding is generally easy as the trail is well marked by white blazes on trees and rocks; side trails are blazed in blue. Walkers are asked to refrain from using the trail until Memorial Day to give forest soils a chance to dry from the melting snow. Early summer offers impressive wildflowers, but mosquitoes and black flies as well—wear long pants and a long-sleeved shirt for protection. Fall is glorious with Vermont's renowned colors. The trail is not designed for winter use. Sturdy, waterproof boots are highly recommended in any season because the trail is often rough and wet. Vermont gets relatively few thunderstorms, but be wary when walking over the highest, exposed portions of the trail.

We advise you not to underestimate the Long Trail, neither the rewards it offers nor the challenges it presents. This is iconic Vermont. Though the Green Mountains aren't especially high, the trail climbs an accumulated 65,000 feet over the course of its length, and it is rough in places. (*Backpacker Magazine* deems it "curse-worthy.") We encourage you to walk the Long Trail, or sections of it; just dial down the normal daily mileage

expectations. We thank the Green Mountain Club for their heroic work in building and maintaining the Long Trail. The Club formed in 1910 with a mission to "make the mountains of Vermont play a larger part in the life of its people." Mission accomplished.

Further Reading

www.greenmountainclub.org

Long Trail Guide. Waterbury Center, VT: Green Mountain Club, 2007.

McCaw, Bob. *End to Enders Guide.* Waterbury Center, VT: Green Mountain Club, 2011.

"The longest journey begins with a single step."
—Lao Tsu

Lost Coast Trail

Location California, USA

Length 53 miles

Accommodations
Commercial: Some
Huts/refuges: No
Camping: Yes

Baggage transfer No

Option to walk in sections Some

Degree of challenge Moderate

UNITED STATES

Walkers enjoy views up and down the California coast in Sinkyone State Park.

Two hundred and thirty miles north of San Francisco lies the remote and solitary "Lost Coast" of California and what Backpacker Magazine calls "[o]ne of the premier ocean-hugging hikes in the world." In studying up for our hike we learned that Roosevelt Elk, one of the largest members of the deer family, had been reintroduced to this area several years ago and were thriving and reproducing. Male (bull) elk grow to be 1,000 pounds or more. We hoped we'd be able to get a glimpse of some of these magnificent animals, and on day four of our walk, we saw one of these bulls—up close and personal! That day found us high on the headlands and deep in thick rainforests watered by periodic storms blowing in off the Pacific Ocean. We were watching carefully where we placed our feet in this especially dense stretch of trail when we looked up to see a full-grown bull elk not more than 10 feet in front of us. It was grazing, had vines hanging off its substantial rack of antlers, and was almost perfectly camouflaged. Fortunately, it seemed totally unconcerned with us as we slowly backed away and waited for it to move on before we continued our walk south along the trail. Seeing wild animals on our walks is always a thrill, and the Roosevelt Elk we met on the Lost Coast Trail was one of the most thrilling ones indeed.

Decades ago when legendary U.S. Route 1 was being built along the coast of California, it was decided that it was not economically feasible to locate the road out and around the large area in the extreme northern part of the state that projects out into the ocean. Instead, the road "shortcuts" this area and goes inland, leaving what is now called the "Lost Coast," a region that remains generally inaccessible and lightly visited.

The Lost Coast Trail offers access to many pocket beaches that provide solitude for walkers.

For walkers, this has left a long stretch of beach and headlands in what is probably the longest length of wild coastline in the lower forty-eight states. Most of this land is managed by two public agencies, the federal Bureau of Land Management (King Range National Conservation Area) and the California State Parks Department (Sinkyone Wilderness State Park), and this provides ready public access.

The walk divides clearly into two distinct sections, separated by the community of Shelter Cove. The northern section begins at Mattole Beach at the mouth of the Mattole River; it's approximately 25 miles long and is nearly all directly on wild Pacific beaches strewn with massive piles of driftwood and other interesting flotsam. Dramatic sea stacks dot the ocean side of the walk while the inland side is composed of the steep slopes of the unusually high coastal mountains of the King's Range that culminate in 4,088-foot King's Peak. These coastal mountains are cut by several streams that spill their water out over the beach and into the Pacific Ocean, providing an important source of fresh water to walkers, interesting canyons to explore, and a series of natural benches that make good campsites. The walk offers close-up views of a wealth of marine life in the form of rich tide pools, pelicans, bald eagles, cormorants, playful sea otters, and barking groups of sea lions and harbor seals that frolic on the waves and form shoreline rookeries. Gray whales can be seen migrating in the winter and spring. Look closely for tracks of bears and mountain lions in the morning in the wet sand. Walkers have made elaborate driftwood structures that serve as good shelters and campsites. Fog is common and

Walkers can see impressive Roosevelt Elk on the high headlands of the Lost Coast of California.

adds to the wild character of the area. Each high tide wipes the beach clean of footprints and this—along with the general absence of other walkers—made us sometimes feel like we were the first people to ever walk these wild beaches.

"Walking is also an ambulation of mind."
—Gretel Ehrlich

The northern section of the hike comes to an abrupt end at a small promontory that juts still further into the ocean and has been developed into the remote community of Shelter Cove. Shelter Cove includes a number of small B&Bs that make a nice respite for walkers after a few nights of camping along the beach; our B&B owner even generously offered to do a load of wash for us. We enjoyed a simple meal and "people watched" the other visitors to this tiny community.

The southern half of the hike is a little longer—about 28 miles—and is distinctly different. Here, there are few beaches (the ocean meets a series of cliffs) and hiking is mostly along the striking high headlands that parallel the shoreline. These headlands are covered in a rich old-growth rainforest and offer panoramic views of the coastline. Significant forest trees include coast redwoods, Douglas fir with trunks up to six feet in diameter, and large tanoaks. The headlands are cut by occasional streams flowing into the Pacific Ocean and these sometimes offer access to beautiful pocket beaches, but also make for steep ascents and descents. The glamour wildlife species of these headlands is the Roosevelt Elk. This half of the walk ends unceremoniously at a parking lot at Sinkyone Wilderness State Park.

Of course, the Lost Coast has an important human history as well as natural history. Native Americans occupied this area as early as 6,000 BC and shell middens can still be seen on several beaches above the high tide line. Abandoned Punta Gorda Lighthouse ("massive point" in Spanish) was built in 1912 after the wreck of the *Columbia* killed eighty-seven people. Known as the "Alcatraz of lighthouses" because it was so isolated, it was decommissioned in 1950, and it must have been a lonely station indeed. Like many areas of California, the Lost Coast has supported farming, logging, and fishing and, if you look closely, you

The Lost Coast Trail of California is the longest stretch of coastal wilderness in the continental U.S.

can still see some evidence of these economic activities: some cattle and sheep ranching, abandoned logging roads, and the harbor at Shelter Cove. The area is also well known as a haven for the hippie generation and this adds interest; one foggy morning we were surprised to see a nude dancing group enjoying one of the more isolated driftwood structures.

There are several logistical concerns associated with walking the Lost Coast Trail. Though the area is accessible year round, the primary walking season is summer because there are Pacific storms in the winter and early spring, which bring more than 100 inches of rain annually. Even in summer, temperatures can be chilly as the area is cooled by the ocean and occasional fog. The primary concern is maintaining personal safety around the ocean. This area of the Pacific Ocean is cold and is subject to dangerous currents; we enjoyed wading in the water to refresh our feet, but wouldn't

risk swimming. Walkers must bring local tide tables with them and know how to use them (which is not difficult) because there are three stretches of beach in the northern half of the hike that can be walked when the tide is low, but that are inundated by high tide right up to the cliff faces. Be sure there is enough time to walk these stretches of beach before the tide comes in. An old saying among people who live along the coast is "never turn your back on the ocean"; occasional large or "rogue" waves can wash ashore and surprise walkers if they're not keeping an eye on the surf; we kept a wary eye just in case. Walking on the beach is a highlight of the northern part of the trail, but this makes for slow progress, especially with a backpack. Search out the harder sand, usually at the edge of the high tide line or the area of wet sand and this will make walking easier. We walked the trail from north to south to keep the prevailing wind at our backs. There is a commercial

Driftwood litters the beach along the Lost Coast Trail.

shuttle service that can be used to get you back to your car at the end of the walk; our driver even suggested a "dining spot," a converted gas station that served up one of the best burritos we've ever eaten.

We're partial to coastal walks; natural and human history seem to be so rich and dynamic where the ocean meets the land. The Lost Coast Trail offers what may be the best opportunity left in the lower forty-eight states for an extended walk along a wild section of a dramatic coastline. We highly recommend it.

Further Reading

www.blm.gov/ca/st/en/fo/arcata/kingrange/index.html

www.parks.ca.gov/?page_id=429

Brett, Daniel. *Hiking the Redwood Coast: Best Hikes along Northern and Central California's Coastline.* Nashville, TN: Falcon Press, 2004.

California's Lost Coast Recreation Map. Berkeley, CA: Wilderness Press, 2004.

Lorentzen, Bob, and Richard Nichols. *Hiking the California Coastal Trail.* Mendocino, CA: Bored Feet Press, 2002.

Trails of the Lost Coast. Berkeley, CA: Wilderness Press, 1999.

Lycian Way

Location Turkey

Length 330 miles

Accommodations
Commercial: Some
Huts/refuges: Some
Camping: Yes

Baggage transfer No

Option to walk in sections Some

Degree of challenge Moderate–High

TURKEY

Long portions of the Lycian Way follow the Turquoise Coast of Turkey.

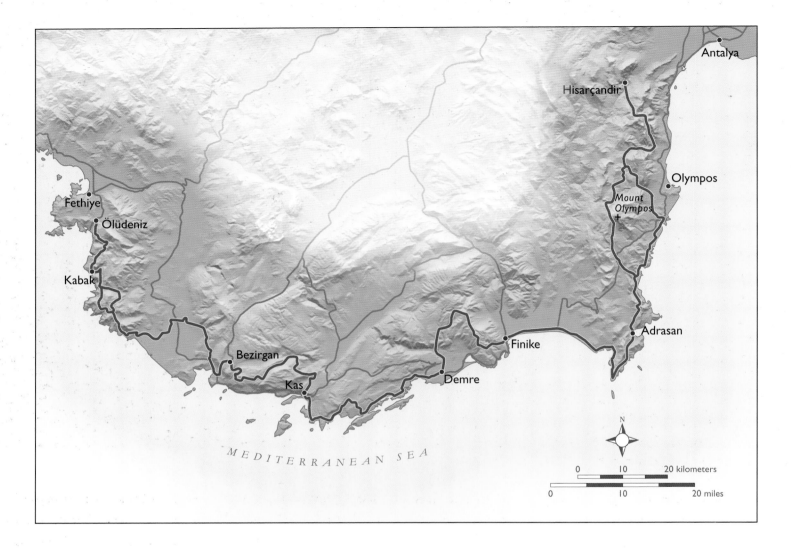

We'd finished our walk on the Lycian Way and were spending our last day in a small hotel in the rural fishing village of Adrasan before we traveled that evening to the city of Antalya to begin our journey home. Other guests who had walked several days with us encouraged us to celebrate our walk with a traditional Turkish bath, and that sounded like a good idea. Our two-hour "bath" began with a long session in the steam room where we sweated toxins. Then we were placed on large marble slabs where muscular Turkish

men first exfoliated us and then washed us—very thoroughly and at considerable length—with hot water and rich, soapy lather. This was followed by a facial in which local muds were painted on our faces and we were left with pots of tea, waiting for the mud to dry, after which the mud was washed from our faces, and the real action began. We were given massages that would best described as "vigorous." At the end of our massages, we were so relaxed that we each needed help getting up from the table. After heart-felt thanks

Graceful stone pines line portions of the Lycian Way.

to the towel-draped men (who spoke no English, but directed us by gestures), we showered to remove the massage oils. At the conclusion of our baths, we felt clean, refreshed, and invigorated—a perfect ending to our walk in Turkey.

Lycia is a large region on the southern coast of Turkey where the Taurus Mountains meet the Mediterranean Sea. The Lycian way, recently completed in 2000, offers a 330-mile walking route through the region, taking advantage of an assortment of Greek and Roman roads and aqueducts, mule paths, trading routes, backcountry roads, and forest trails. The western end of the trail is just south of the resort city of Fethiye, and the eastern end is southeast of the bustling port city Antalya. As you walk the Lycian Way, you follow in the footsteps of Alexander the Great and his army of ten thousand as they marched east through this area over twenty centuries ago. *The Sunday Times* of England recently called the trail one of the world's ten best walks.

Turkey is highly diverse in landscape and culture, and the Lycian Way is an accurate reflection of this. The trail leads walkers over high mountains, along deserted beaches, over coastal headlands, through forests of pine and cedars, and into rural villages where fishing and farming have been a way of life for thousands of years. This is a place where east meets west. Turkey is a Muslim country and every village has a mosque, but it is governed in a secular manner. Every village has a statue of Ataturk, who created the modern nation

Every town along the Lycian Way features at least one mosque.

of Turkey following World War I, and everywhere Turks proudly fly their distinctive red flag with a crescent moon and a single white star.

There were many highlights of our walk. We walked though the ancient and extensive ruins of the port city of Olympus with its temples, theater, and sarcophagi. The city was important to all the civilizations that occupied it, including Greeks, Romans, and Byzantines. An image of the city was struck on coins in 167-168 BC, and some of the buildings are thought to honor Roman Emperor Marcus Aurelius. We hiked over Mt. Olympus, at 7,763 feet the high point of the trail. We swam in the turquoise waters of the Mediterranean at deserted Pirates' Cove. We had lunch in an open-air restaurant where flatbread was being made and chickens occasionally strolled by the tables. We lingered at iconic Gelidonya Lighthouse, the symbol of the Lycian Way. We walked through the Chimera, the "eternal flames" that emanate from the earth. We know now that this phenomenon is related to natural gas deposits in the area, but legend has it that the flames are the breath of a mythical monster that is part lion, part goat, and part snake, and ancient mariners in this part of the Mediterranean used the flames for navigation. We walked through many coastal villages, most of which are located on river deltas and include extensive greenhouses and orchards where fresh vegetables and fruits—tomatoes, eggplants, oranges, and pomegranates—are grown for shipment to Istanbul and the north. We walked through a grove of cedars—remnants of the ancient "cedars of Lebanon"—where the Bible says, "The righteous shall flourish like the palm tree and grow like a cedar in Lebanon."

Flora and fauna are diverse. There are coastal forests of graceful stone (sometimes called Italian) pines, strawberry trees with their smooth red trunks, palms, carob trees, and higher-elevation groves of cedars as noted above. Cyclamen, an attractive houseplant in the western world, grows wild on the forest floor, carpeting it with flowers. Animals include deer, wild goats, badgers, porcupines, fox, and wild pigs or boars. The wild pigs use their long tusks to defend themselves and to dig for roots—we saw lots of evidence of their digging.

Part Two: Extraordinary Hikes for Ordinary People

This trail is long, remote, and rough in places; walking the length of the trail is a serious undertaking. A more feasible approach (which we recommend) is to walk selected sections that have support infrastructure. Good options include Ucagiz to Cape Gelidonia and Adrasan to Mt. Olympus, each representing about a week of walking. It's increasingly popular to find a small hotel in one or two of the villages in these areas to use as "home," and do a series of daily walks.

"When you have worn out your shoes, the strength of the shoe leather has passed into the fiber of your body. I measure your health by the number of shoes and hats and clothes you have worn out."

—Ralph Waldo Emerson

Best months to walk are April and May and September and October; it's too hot in the summer and too cold in the winter. We found the Turks we met to be friendly and helpful, but not much English is spoken. The sun is hot and stretches of the trail are dry, so be sure to carry water and use plenty of sunblock.

The Lycian Way leads walkers through a land that is diverse to the point of seeming paradoxical at times and places; it ranges from the mountains to the sea, it's old (the landscape and the culture) and new (the trail), its cities are modern and developed and its countryside rural and developing, its culture is borne out of both eastern and western traditions, its people are deeply religious but its civil affairs are conducted in a deliberately secular manner. We enjoyed this beautiful and seemingly exotic walk and hope you will too. And don't forget the Turkish bath at the end.

Walkers on the Lycian Way can see the eternal flames of the Chimera, once thought to be dragon's breath.

The Gelidonia Lighthouse is the scenic symbol of the Lycian Way.

Further Reading

www.lycianway.com

Clow, Kate. *The Lycian Way*. Hinckley, Leicestershire, UK: Cordee Publishing, 2009.

Milford Track

Location New Zealand

Length 33 miles

Accommodations
Commercial: Yes
Huts/refuges: Yes
Camping: No

Baggage transfer No

Option to walk in sections No

Degree of challenge Low–Moderate

NEW ZEALAND

The rainforests of the Milford Track give rise to many waterfalls and cascades.

We'd been warned about Kea birds, large parrots known for their intelligence and curiosity. If you leave your pack unattended, they'll find a way in, looking mostly for food, but known to carry away anything of interest, including small cameras and even one unfortunate walker's passport. But we weren't prepared when several birds kicked open the screen door of our cabin, one bird holding the door open while the others prepared to plunder our possessions. Regaining our composure and territorial instincts, we easily shooed them away. This organized raid was a clear demonstration of the social nature of these birds, often called "the clown of the mountains." New Zealanders simply call them "cheeky." Adult Kea are olive green and have a large, sharply curved beak, stand nearly 20 inches tall and weigh more than 2 pounds. They are one of only a few alpine parrots and are endemic to the South Island of New Zealand (found only there). Their name is derived from the language of the indigenous Maori people and probably refers to the sharp screech the birds utter. Kea were thought to attack sheep, and the population was sharply reduced by local ranchers, but the birds are now protected in parks and reserves.

The Milford Track has a long history and glowing reputation in the walking world. Developed in 1888, it was called by some "the eighth wonder of the world." A 1908 article in *The London Spectator* called the track "the finest walk in the world" and this moniker has stuck. More recently, *Outside Magazine* wrote that the trail includes a "syrup of superlatives."

The Milford Track is 33 miles long, traversing part of Fjordlands National Park, a major reserve in the southwest quadrant of the South Island of New Zealand. The park is part of the larger Te Wahipounamu UNESCO World Heritage Area.

Mitre Peak rises out of Milford Sound near the end of the Milford Track.

The track follows two glacially carved valleys that are connected by a gradual climb and descent of nearly 3,800-foot Mackinnon Pass. The Milford Track's most distinguishing feature is the biologically rich and strikingly beautiful rainforests. Of course, it takes rain to support them and the area is famous as one of the wettest places in the world, with an impressive average of 282 inches of precipitation annually. There are exotic (to us) plants, and the area's tree ferns were a highlight. They can grow to 60 feet high and have very large fronds; unlike conventional trees, their trunks are not woody, but are composed of a mass of fibrous roots. There are an estimated one thousand species of tree ferns in the world, many found only in New Zealand.

A variety of other features along the trail include rushing rivers, countless waterfalls and cascades, steep mountains topped with permanent snowfields, alpine wildflowers, small glacially formed mountain ponds called tarns, and, again thanks to the precipitation, thick coatings of moss on nearly everything. A highlight for most walkers is Sutherland Falls, a 1,900-foot cascade, fourth highest in the world, reached by a 45-minute side trail. Walkers emerge from the Milford Track at Sand Fly Point (more about the sand flies in a moment) near Milford Sound, a 12-mile-long fjord, and most stay overnight in the town of Milford for a boat trip the next day on the Sound, which we highly recommend. Distinctive Mitre Peak rises over a mile above the water and boaters are likely to see fur seals, dolphins, and possibly the rare Fjordland Crested Penguin.

"There is nothing like walking to get the feel of a country. A fine landscape is like a piece of music; it must be taken at the right tempo. Even a bicycle goes too fast."

—Paul Scott Mowrer

The Milford Track is not a demanding walk. The primary challenges are the climb over Mackinnon Pass, the rain, and sand flies (and, of course, defending yourself from Keas!). The climb over the pass is not steep and the trail is moderately graded and well maintained; it just requires resolve. Most of the rest of the walking is relatively flat, following the beautiful Clinton and Arthur rivers, and there are several swinging bridges over the rivers. The rain can be bothersome, but less so if you are prepared with good quality breathable rainwear. Encountering some rain can be advantageous as it produces dozens of ephemeral cascades and waterfalls. Some walkers encounter sand flies, a biting insect that can be pesky. Captain Cook visited Milford Sound in 1773 and described sand flies as "most mischievous animals that cause a swelling not possible to refrain from scratching." They didn't bother us.

The trail is very walker friendly with a series of well-developed huts (camping is not allowed). "Freedom walkers" (independent travelers also known as "trampers" in New Zealand) use the well-equipped public self-service huts. Huts sleep forty in large, bunkhouse-style rooms, and there are communal sitting areas and modern kitchen facilities. Organized groups ("pamper-trampers") use a series of private huts that are more like lodges or guesthouses, though most guest rooms are semi-private. These serve breakfast and dinner (complete with New Zealand wine) and provide supplies for packed lunches; they also offer hot showers and communal lounges. Companies that conduct

Much of the Milford Track winds through lush rainforests.

organized tours use local guides and rent equipment, a convenience for the walker who does not have the proper rain gear. Both types of huts have large heated drying rooms where wet clothes and packs can be dried overnight, but be careful drying wet leather boots in this manner as they may shrink substantially. And both types of huts offer good opportunities to meet other walkers from all over the world.

A permit is needed to walk the track and this must be secured well in advance, especially in the peak months of November to April, and the walk must be conducted from south to north (to minimize encounters among walking groups). Most walkers take five days to complete the trail, including a day to cruise on Milford Sound. Access to the Milford Track is generally through Queensland, which has developed a reputation as the adventure capital of New Zealand, offering bungee jumping, river rafting, sky diving, and parasailing. But walking the Milford Track may be the best adventure of all.

···· Further Reading ·····························

www.milfordtrack.net

DuFresne, Jim. *Tramping in New Zealand*. Melbourne,
   Australia: Lonely Planet, 2006.

Suspension bridges cross the major rivers along the Milford Track.

Sandhill cranes and other migratory birds are abundant along the Ocala Trail.

Part Two: Extraordinary Hikes for Ordinary People

Ocala Trail

Location Florida, USA

Length 71 miles

Accommodations
Commercial: Some
Huts/refuges: No
Camping: Yes

Baggage transfer No

Option to walk in sections All

Degree of challenge Low

UNITED STATES

Pine forests comprise the Ocala Trail's "Big Scrub."

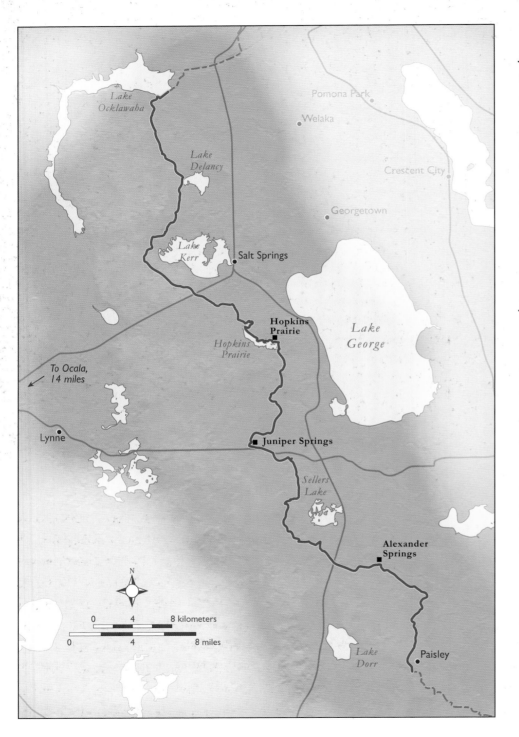

We meet the most interesting people on our walks. Take for instance Ken, a "trail angel." We had decided to walk the Ocala Trail in Florida in a series of day hikes and we needed some help with rides. Folks at the offices of the Florida Trail Association (the Ocala Trail is part of the much longer Florida Trail) suggested Ken as a volunteer who will help Ocala Trail walkers with logistics. So we contacted him, meeting for breakfast the first morning of our walk. Ken was well over eighty years old, but looked decades younger, and a few months earlier had led a two-week backpacking trip across Florida for other octogenarian walkers. Ken's worked on the Florida Trail for forty years and told us great stories about the area. One morning Ken couldn't help us with our daily shuttle because he had another engagement, so he recommended we ask Pat, owner of a hunting and fishing shop near the trail. Pat was retired from the Army where he had been an MP, and his size alone must have made him effective as a law-enforcement official! Born and raised in the Ocala area, Pat retired there to open his shop, and when he talked about the region, it was clear that he loved this place and wanted to share it with others. Pat was pleased to give us a ride one morning, and his courtly manners were a charming artifact of his southern roots. He cheerily told us lots of stories about fishing and "'gators," but when we asked him about snakes, his demeanor changed: "I'm a big ole boy myself, but I'm scared to death of snakes!" All trails have angels, and Ken and Pat are good examples on the beautiful Ocala Trail. We paid our new friends a nominal fee to cover their gas—that's all they would take—and left with an appreciation for

Part Two: Extraordinary Hikes for Ordinary People

The Ocala National Forest is dotted with shallow lakes that attract wildlife.

both the trail and the community of walkers who are pleased to help one another.

The Ocala Trail runs the length of the historic and ecologically important Ocala National Forest in north central Florida. This is the southern-most national forest in the continental U.S., covering nearly 400,000 acres. It was the first national forest in the eastern U.S., signed into law by conservation President Teddy Roosevelt in 1908. The Depression-era Civilian Conservation Corps developed many of the forest's recreation facilities in the 1930s, and they resonate with the CCC sensibility and aesthetic. Locally, the Ocala National Forest is simply known as "the forest." The Ocala Trail bisects this land on a north-south axis for 71 miles. It offers mostly dry, level walking through pine and hardwood forests, along the edges of ponds and prairies (large wet meadows), and across narrow sections of hardwood swamps. The trail is considered the "crown jewel" of the nearly 1,400-mile Florida Trail that goes from the Gulf Islands near Pensacola to just north of Everglades National Park.

This is an area that is rich in natural history. Much of Florida is only a few feet above sea level and the underlying bedrock is primarily limestone, a sedimentary rock composed mainly of the consolidated skeletal remains of marine organisms. Rainwater percolates quickly through this thick (up

Stately oaks covered in Spanish moss grace upland regions along the Ocala Trail.

to 2 miles) layer of limestone forming the Floridan Aquifer, a source of freshwater vital to both humans and wildlife. In places, water has dissolved the limestone and formed large basins, and springs discharge this fresh water to the surface. The Ocala Trail passes by or near several of these impressive water sources, including Alexander Springs, Juniper Springs, and Salt Springs, and these areas demand a visit.

Much of the trail passes through the largest forest of sand pines left in the world. These are short-lived trees (living about forty years) that grow to about 8 inches in diameter. They form a dense canopy with a shrubby understory, and this endangered ecosystem is commonly called the "Big Scrub." Other important ecosystems include slightly higher-elevation "islands" of longleaf pines (this ecosystem is also endangered), lower swamp forests of impressive bald cypress, with their buttresses and "knees," and stands of low-growing oaks with extensive and striking understories of saw palmettos.

There are many opportunities to watch interesting wildlife. You can count on seeing alligators in the area's ponds, rivers, and wetlands. There are many species of birds, including eagles and endangered Florida scrub-jays (found in family groupings), and red cockaded woodpeckers. These woodpeckers make their nests by boring out a cavity in pine trees, usually with a distinctive small round opening about 20 feet off the ground. To protect their eggs from snakes, they disturb the bark in a circle around the tree below the opening of the nest so sap runs down the tree, hardens, and makes a barrier too difficult for a snake to climb. One morning, we started our walk early at Rodman Reservoir at the northern end of the trail. In the mist and at close range, we saw three sandhill cranes that were "vacationing" in this area for the winter. They made their distinctive call and took to flight, displaying their impressive size and providing us with a magical moment. We also enjoyed watching several bald eagles rise and swoop at Hopkins Prairie.

One section of the trail crosses the Juniper Prairie Wilderness, portions of which had experienced a wildfire shortly before our visit. Since wilderness areas are supposed to be as natural as possible, the U.S. Forest

Sections of the Ocala Trail feature oaks with a dramatic understory of saw palmetto.

Service allows lightning-caused fires to burn, replicating nature in this fire-dependent ecosystem; on our first two days of walking, we saw smoke in the distance from wildfires in other parts of the forest. The Yearling Trail, a short side-trail in the Juniper Prairie Wilderness, leads to the area that was the inspiration for Marjorie Kinnan Rawlings's Pulitzer Prize-winning novel, *Cross Creek*, later made into the movie *The Yearling*.

We finished walking the Ocala Trail with an extra day to spare, and our trail angel friend Ken suggested we join an organized walk conducted by the Florida Trail Association on a portion of the nearby Cross Florida Greenway. This 110-mile corridor was originally intended to be the Cross Florida Barge Canal, a shipping route connecting the Gulf of Mexico with the Atlantic Ocean, a plan that was eventually stopped in the 1960s because of its massive environmental implications. Now the corridor is being developed into three trails serving walkers, bicyclists, and equestrians. We walked with a group of about eighty Florida Trail Association members; we were welcomed and enjoyed swapping trail stories, and we also enjoyed the organizational process necessary to manage such a large group! The highlight was walking over the "Land Bridge" that spans Interstate Highway 75. Here, an overpass has been constructed for walkers and equestrians only; it's covered in sandy soil and landscaped so well with local plants that you find it hard to believe that an interstate highway lies just below the vegetative barrier. It presents an odd appearance to the drivers below, too, as they see an overpass covered with trees and bushes.

The Ocala Trail requires no permits or reservations. It's well marked with orange blazes and the Florida Trail Association publishes a good guidebook that covers the entire Florida Trail. The U.S. Forest Service is also a good source of information and maintains a visitor center at Silver Springs. The nearby town of Ocala makes a good "base camp," and a number of road crossings allow the trail to be walked in a series of day hikes. The trail can be walked at any time of the year, though the best months are between October and April—it can get pretty hot and humid in the summer. We did our walk in January during an unusual cold snap. A few mornings, it was well below freezing, but bright sunshine warmed temperatures into the 50s each day, great conditions for walking. Walkers should be wary of deer hunters between November and January; these months are the only time primitive camping may be restricted.

The Ocala Trail offers walkers an up-close-and-personal view of some of the most exotic and endangered ecosystems in the southeastern U.S. It's a good option for a walk during the winter months when most other long-distance trails in the U.S. are snowed under. If you decide to walk it, we hope you meet interesting trail angels, too.

> *"I still find each day too short for all the thoughts I want to think, all the walks I want to take, all the books I want to read and all the friends I want to see."*
>
> **—John Burroughs**

······· **Further Reading** ························

www.floridatrail.org

www.fs.usda.gov/ocala

Friend, Sandra. *Florida Trail Companion Guide for Long Distance Hikers.* Gainesville, FL: Florida Trail Association, 2007.

Friend, Sandra. *The Florida Trail: The Official Hiking Guide.* Englewood, CO: Westcliffe Publishers, Inc., 2004.

Overland Track

Location Australia

Length 60 miles

Accommodations
Commercial: Yes
Huts/refuges: Yes
Camping: No

Baggage transfer No

Option to walk in sections No

Degree of challenge Moderate

AUSTRALIA

The Overland Track starts with a short climb above Dove Lake.

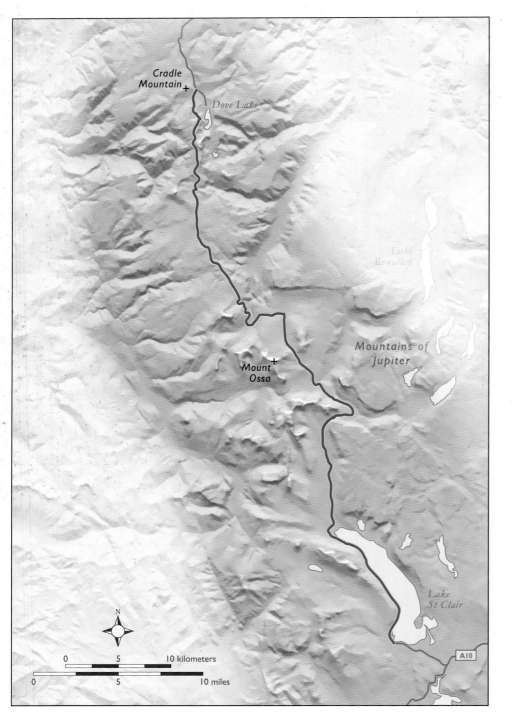

We usually do our walks as independent travelers because planning the trips can be both an educational and entertaining part of the walking experience. But we joined an organized group to walk the Overland Track, partly because it was too late to get the required permit (the company we booked with had reserved a block of permits) and partly to see first-hand the system of huts that had been built recently to accommodate organized groups. We were pleased to find a system of five simple, comfortable, "green" huts located a day's walk from one another and sited at inconspicuous locations, just off the main trail. These traditional "bush huts" were small and constructed largely of local materials. A wood stove provided heat and hot water, and the water supply was collected off the roof, stored in tanks, and pumped by walkers. Lights and cooking stoves were powered by propane. There were two Tasmanian guides for our fourteen-person group and they spent a good deal of time making sure we understood and appreciated the remarkable landscape through which we were walking. They also prepared our meals using local foods to the extent possible, including Tasmanian wines. Our group comprised eight Australians, four Brits, and two Americans, and we all seemed to enjoy each other's company. So what about our experiment with organized groups on the Overland Track? We enjoyed comfortable, environmentally sensitive huts, good company, informed guides, and distinctive local foods—what's not to like?

The Overland Track is a 60-mile route through Cradle Mountain-Lake St. Claire National Park in the heart of Tasmania (what the locals call "Tassie"), a large island off

An optional side trail of the Overland Track leads to the top of Mount Ossa, at 5,305-feet the highest mountain in Tasmania.

the southeast coast of Australia. It's widely regarded as the finest trek in Australia and is walked by some eight thousand people annually. (Aussies call this type of hiking "bushwalking," but that makes it sound harder than it really is because this is a well-groomed trail.) The route traverses the highest mountains in Tasmania and offers a stunning and diverse array of natural history that includes the mountains themselves, alpine lakes, rainforests, waterfalls, and some of the most distinctive plants and animals in the world. For these reasons, the trail and its surrounding lands are part of the UNESCO Tasmanian Wilderness World Heritage Area, a place of outstanding natural and cultural value to all people of the world.

"Not all who wander are lost."

—J. R. R. Tolkien

Cradle Mountain is the scenic symbol of the Overland Track.

Walkers must obtain a permit (of which there are a limited number) and pay a modest fee. In peak season walkers must travel from north to south as this reduces the number of encounters among groups along the trail and enhances the feeling of solitude. The walk begins by ascending distinctively shaped Cradle Mountain at 5,070 feet, though walkers don't climb all the way to the top. The geology of the Tasmanian mountains is revealed in the glacially carved Carter and Dove lakes at the foot of the peak. Other classic signs of glaciation include the generally U-shaped valleys (as opposed to V-shaped valleys, which were carved by rivers), cirques (roughly semi-circular basins on the side of mountains where rock has been eroded), moraines (mounds of sand and gravel deposited along the sides and feet of glaciers), and erratics (large rocks carried by glaciers and deposited elsewhere). The twin peaks of Cradle Mountain and many of the other high mountains are what geologists call "nunataks," peaks that rose above the glaciers and were largely unaffected by them. The tops of these mountains remain fluted and craggy, while the lower elevations have been smoothed by glacial action.

While the geology is interesting, it's the flora and fauna of Tasmania and the Overland Track that make it world famous, and justly so. Once part of the ancient supercontinent geologists call Gondwana, which included mainland Australia and parts of Africa and South America, Tasmania has been physically isolated for the last eighty million years, allowing for divergent forms of evolution. The island contains a remarkable thirty-one species of marsupials, a class of mammals in which newborns are carried by females in an exterior pouch (called the marsupium). Animals you are likely to encounter along the track include wombats (watch for their curious cube-shaped droppings), echidnas, wallabies, possums, and platypuses. Tasmanian devils, made famous in children's cartoons, are present, but they are declining due to a mysterious disease and are not often seen. There are also three species of poisonous snakes (whip snake, copperhead, and tiger snake), and some walkers prefer to wear gaiters because of this. Distinctive

Portions of the Overland Track pass through extensive meadows of distinctive button grass.

birds include the yellow-tailed black cockatoo (a large parrot), the yellow wattlebird (whose call sounds like someone having a good belch), the black currawong (a large black bird whose sharp metallic calls are synonymous with the Tasmanian wilderness), and several species of honeyeaters. Notable vegetation includes large moorlands of buttongrass, silver banksia, cushion plants, and forests of myrtle, eucalyptus, leatherwood, King Billy pines, and pencil pines.

The track has an interesting cultural history as well. Evidence—including quarries, stone artifacts, campsites, shelters, and fire sites—suggests that aboriginal people have lived in Tasmania for more than thirty thousand years. More recent history is focused on protection of the area and development of the Overland Track. Austrian immigrant Gustav Weindorfer built a chalet called Waldheim at the foot of Cradle Mountain in the early 1900s and encouraged Australians to visit the area; he worked hard to ensure the area was protected as a national park. The Overland Track officially begins at Waldheim, though the current structure is a reproduction.

"I can only meditate when I am walking. When I stop, I cease to think; my mind works only with my legs."
—Jean-Jacques Rousseau

Clear air and low humidity contribute to striking views along the Overland Track.

Trapper Bert Nicholls blazed the track in 1930 and the first through hike was completed the following year.

About halfway along the track, a side trail leads to the top of 5,305-foot Mt. Ossa, the highest peak in Tasmania. If the weather is good, we recommend this hike; from the top one can see nearly half of Tasmania. The walk ends at Lake St. Clair, the deepest lake in Australia, and the best place to see platypuses. The track runs along the lake shore, but most walkers complete the journey with a leisurely ferry ride across the lake.

The Overland Track is not a difficult hike if the weather cooperates and it certainly did for us. We experienced sunshine and some of the clearest air we've ever encountered—views were at times almost surreal because of their startling crispness. However, the rainforests along portions of the track suggest that stormy weather is not unusual and walkers should be prepared with waterproof outerwear and warm clothes. The track is well marked and includes a system of self-service huts (in addition to the private huts described above). The classic walk is six days. Portions of the track are boardwalked to facilitate walking in wet areas and to protect low-lying vegetation. The prime walking season is December through March when the track is usually at capacity. Access to Tasmania is by plane serving several small cities and by ferry from mainland Australia.

It was obvious that the Australians we walked the track with considered their trip a pilgrimage of sorts—a place every Australian should see and experience. Based on our hike, we'd extend that sentiment to the world more broadly. Walk this trail and you'll be glad you did.

Further Reading

www.parks.tas.gov.au/index.aspx?base=7771

The Overland Track: One Walk, Many Journeys. Hobart, Tasmania, Australia: Parks and Wildlife Service Tasmania, 2006.

Paria River Canyon

Location Utah and Arizona, USA

Length 38 miles

Accommodations
Commercial: No
Huts/refuges: No
Camping: Yes

Baggage transfer No

Option to walk in sections No

Degree of challenge Moderate

UNITED STATES

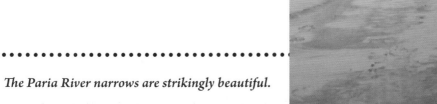

The Paria River narrows are strikingly beautiful.

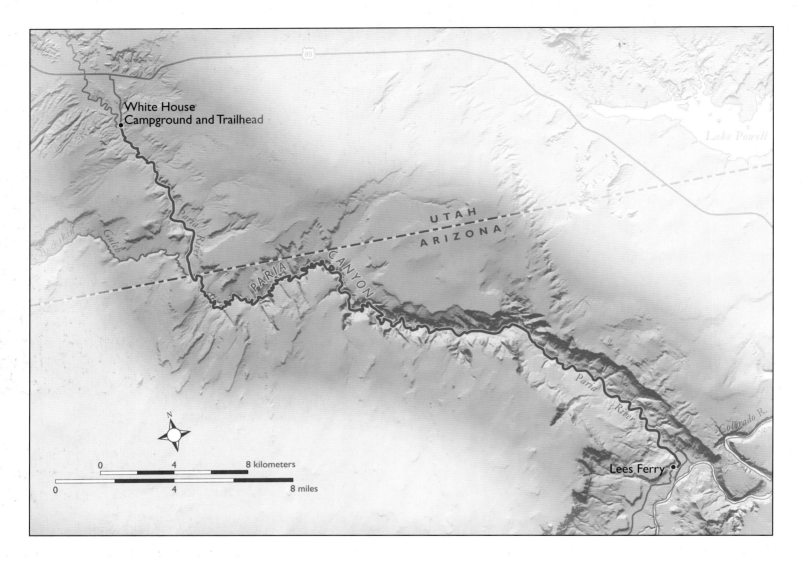

It was the middle of March, not the conventional time for visiting the dramatic Paria River Canyon in the glorious southwest of the United States. But travel had brought us to the region and this walk was too good to pass up. We watched the weather forecast closely and it was sure to be clear (no chance of rain—the most important consideration), but cold. Sure enough, there was a skim of ice on the river as we started the first day of our walk along the Paria River.

Soon the canyon walls narrowed and we reached a point where we had to cross the river. This was not a serious matter because the river was no more than knee deep and about 20 feet wide. But we were skittish about getting our feet wet, so we worked hard to find the shallowest crossing, strategically placing a few rocks and logs in the water, and made our move. Of course, our feet got wet anyway, and by the end of our four-day walk we laughed at our initial attempt to

Ancient rock art is evidence of the early presence of Native Americans.

keep dry. Over the course of the trek, we crossed the river a staggering 480 times, walking some of the narrowest stretches of the canyon right down the middle of the river! Fortunately, wet feet turned out not to be cold feet because our walking kept us warm.

"To walk in a sitting and riding society is always, at least potentially, the beginning of a Renaissance."
—Rebecca Solnit

The Paria River Canyon is a geologic marvel. It's one of the major "slot" canyons in the vast Colorado River Plateau in the southwest quadrant of the U.S. Slot canyons are formed by rivers that cut deeply into comparatively soft sandstone bedrock, forming narrow, sinuous, steep-walled canyons. The Paria River Canyon has been called "the premier narrows hike on the Colorado Plateau" and "one of world's best canyon walks." We're convinced. Long portions of the canyon are only a few yards wide, and sidewalls rise vertically for 1,000 feet or more. The river is a tributary of the legendary Colorado River (see the Kaibab Trail description for the classic Grand Canyon walk), starting in southern Utah and reaching the Colorado River at historic Lee's Ferry, Arizona, where all raft trips of the Colorado River through Grand Canyon begin. The walk through the "narrows" portion of the Paria River is 38 miles, most of this within the Paria Canyon-Vermillion Cliffs Wilderness Area.

The Paria River Canyon walk is more than geology, but that's where we have to begin. Paria means "muddy water" in the Paiute Indian language, and

Walking Paria Canyon requires many crossings of the shallow river.

this hints at the canyon's origin, including its geology and hydrology. The water is perpetually clouded with the tons of sediment it has eroded over the eons, and the granular character of the river water helps it cut into the sandstone bedrock. This erosive action is magnified by the simultaneous geologic uplift of the entire Colorado Plateau region. In this process, the Paria River has cut through and exposed seven major geologic formations (e.g., former sand dunes and sea bottoms) spanning eighty-five million years of geologic time, and all of this can be clearly read in the range of colors and form on the canyon walls. Water is vital to the arid southwest, and the Paria River is an integral component of the vast Colorado River drainage. The gauging station at the confluence of the Paria and Colorado rivers that measures water levels has been called one of the most important in the U.S. because it's the first on the Colorado River below Glen Canyon Dam.

The first few miles of the hike are relatively open and the surrounding landscape features a variety of "hoodoos"—domes, spires, and other formations carved out of the reddish sandstone. Then the walls close in sharply for the next 20 miles, with sun and shadow casting unusual plays of light and dark on the canyon's fluted, polished walls. In this deeply entrenched area, the sun reaches the riverbed for only a few hours a day. A number of side canyons flow into the Paria River, including dramatic Buckskin Gulch and Wrather Canyon. We recommend exploring both, the former an exceptionally narrow slot canyon featuring deep pools of cold water, and the latter offering a short hike to Wrather Arch, one of the largest natural stone arches in the world. Plan to linger a little at the confluence of the Paria and Buckskin Gulch, one of the most magical areas in the southwest, and be sure to notice the many hanging gardens of maidenhair fern and monkey flowers in the numerous seeps in the canyon walls. The last portion of the canyon—about 10 miles—widens substantially and the route climbs away from the river, crosses open desert, and requires some scrambling. Here you leave the wilderness portion of the hike and find several abandoned ranches and mines. This area also has petrified wood and dinosaur bones and tracks.

When you reach Lonely Dell Ranch, turn around and look back to see all of the canyon's geologic formations rising 2,800 feet above the river.

Paria Canyon harbors many interesting plants and animals. Large cottonwood trees offer shade and often mark good campsites. A number of animals make their home in Paria Canyon, or at least pass through looking for food and shelter. These include pronghorn antelope, coyotes, bobcats, mountain lions, desert bighorn sheep, mule deer, foxes, porcupines, beavers, cottontails, and ground squirrels, though walkers rarely see many of these animals. Birds include California condors (reintroduced to this area in 1996), bald and golden eagles, peregrine falcons, red-tailed and Coopers hawks, great blue herons, great horned owls, and hummingbirds. Listen for the call of canyon wrens, a melodious series of descending notes characteristic of all of the canyon country of the southwest. There are also rattlesnakes, black widow spiders, and scorpions—be sure to shake out your boots in the morning.

Of course, the Paria River Canyon has an interesting historical and cultural component as well. It's thought that Native Americans used the area for at least ten thousand years, but that it was primarily a travel route. Walkers can find a number of ancient rock art panels, groups of images and symbols carved into (petroglyphs) and painted onto (pictographs) flat rock surfaces. And Lee's Ferry was an important Colorado River crossing for early settlers who tried (in vain) to develop ranching and mining in this arid land.

This is a world-class walk. From a purely physical standpoint, it's not overly difficult in that there is very little elevation change. But it's not without some important safety considerations. This is a wilderness backpacking trip; once you enter the canyon, there is no way out except returning to the start or continuing to the end. You will be walking a route, not a maintained trail. For the most part, it will not be difficult to find your way (just follow the river downstream), but you will have to pick the places you want to cross the river. By far the most important consideration is avoiding periodic flash floods that can occur, primarily in July, August, and early September. We noticed flood debris—logs, brush,

Hiking the lower end of the Paria River Canyon involves some scrambling and wayfinding.

etc.—lodged between the canyon walls at heights of 50 feet or more above the riverbed. Avoid this walk (and other slot canyons) if there is the threat of thunderstorms anywhere in the vicinity; flash floods can be caused by heavy rain anywhere in the extended watershed, not just in the Paria River Canyon narrows. Other potential hazards are deep mud and even occasional pockets of quicksand. Finally, there is no water available the last 10 miles of the hike; be sure to stock up on water before you reach this point. Earlier in the hike, water is available from several natural springs that are marked on hiking maps. This water must be treated for drinking; it's not feasible to purify river water for drinking because it's too full of silt. When it's hot, the general rule for hiking in arid lands is to drink a gallon of water per day.

Three trailheads serve the hike—Buckskin Gulch, Wire Pass, and White House. The first two require hiking all or most of challenging Buckskin Gulch to reach the river, so we recommend White House, which is located directly adjacent to the Paria River. A permit and nominal fee are required (available from the U.S. Bureau of Land Management, which administers most of the canyon) and only twenty people are allowed to start the hike each day. The prime months to walk are April and May when days are long, wildflowers (including flowering cacti) are at their peak, cottonwoods and other trees have leafed out providing shade, freshwater springs are running, it's not too hot, and flash flood danger is relatively low. A convenient commercial shuttle services this hike; park your car at Lee's Ferry and the shuttle takes you upstream to the White House trailhead.

The Paria River Canyon is unlike any other walk described in this book; in fact, it's almost like being on another planet. Consider walking the Paria River Canyon—it's worth getting your feet wet!

Further Reading

www.americansouthwest.net/slot_canyons/paria-river/canyon.html

Kelsey, Michael. *Hiking and Exploring the Paria River.* Brigham City, UT: Brigham Distributing, 2010.

"It is good to have an end to journey towards; but it is the journey that matters in the end."
—**Ursula K. LeGuin**

South Downs Way

Location England

Length 100 miles

Accommodations
Commercial: Yes
Huts/refuges: No
Camping: No

Baggage transfer Yes

Option to walk in sections All

Degree of challenge Low–Moderate

UNITED KINGDOM

The "Cathedral of the Downs" is made of native flint, as are most buildings along the South Downs Way.

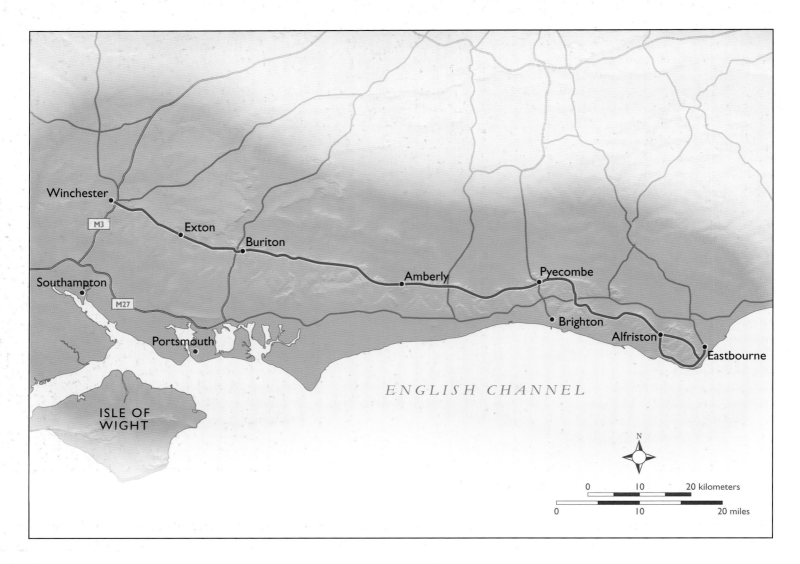

The English tradition of afternoon tea is lovely; teatime combined with walking is divine! Nothing compares to strolling into yet another quaint English village, pleasantly fatigued and always hungry, and finding a beckoning tearoom. Here we enjoyed the refreshing and revitalizing nourishment of homemade scones, cakes, or even sandwiches (with their crusts properly removed, of course) and an invigorating pot of freshly brewed tea. The English have perfected this mini-meal to an art form, and we thoroughly appreciated the times we could share in this ritual while walking the South Downs Way. Because the route runs from town to town, we timed our daily walks with our afternoon break in mind. When a convenient tearoom wasn't available, we made do with store-bought treats carried in the pack (we recommend the coconut macaroons); the elevated route along the trail always provided us with inviting vistas out over the beautiful English countryside for these self-service teas.

Walkers on the South Downs Way must come off the Downs to get to town.

When is "down" really up? When walking the South Downs Way, of course! The word "down" has its origin in the Old English "dun" meaning "hill." The South Downs Way is a trail perched on the gentle ridgeline that winds its way across much of southern England. People seem to be drawn to the high places in a landscape; perhaps this preference has its origins in the life of early humans when being uphill had strategic advantages. Whatever the motivation, we all like viewpoints that allow us to see and understand the landscape in ways that are just not possible where the earth is flat. The South Downs Way offers a nearly continuous succession of viewpoints that meander across this beautiful section of southern England. The tops of the downs have been used throughout history and before for burial sites, fortifications, homes, signaling beacons, and farming. In the most recent iteration, paragliders and hang gliders (even whole schools of eager pupils!) delight in the updrafts associated with this elevated landscape. In a sometimes uneasy combination of old and new uses, one of our guidebooks suggested that standing on tumuli (ancient burial sites) affords the best

"After dinner sit awhile, after supper walk a mile."
—English proverb

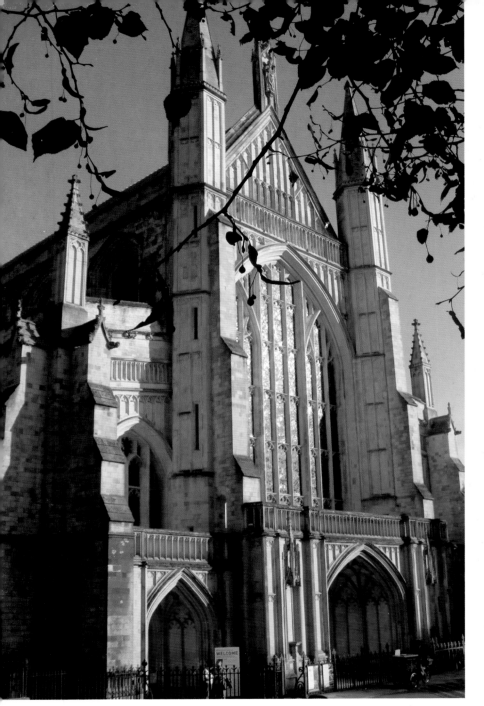

Historic Winchester Cathedral marks the western end of the South Downs Way.

views, and we saw folks happily picnicking on a large tumulus. The South Downs Way is a beautiful and gentle landscape that can be easily walked and appreciated for its many natural, historical, and recreational features.

Located roughly an hour south of London, the South Downs Way is a 100-mile walk in one of the newest national parks in England. South Downs National Park, established in 2011, celebrates the downs, gentle hills of chalk that meet the sea in spectacular white cliffs. Originally the bottom of a shallow sea, the land was formed seventy to one hundred million years ago (during the Cretaceous Period) from the tiny shells of marine organisms. These shells fell to the sea floor and slo-o-o-w-ly accumulated and consolidated at a rate of one foot every thirty thousand years. Then, approximately twenty million years ago (during the Tertiary Period), tectonic plates collided and the land was raised into a huge dome. Erosion has worked on the downs since this time, and transformed this dome into gentle rolling hills and valleys. Originally 1,000 feet high, this chalk layer is still impressive, with some of the cliff faces measuring over 500 feet.

Deep chalk is underfoot at all times, and you'll see bands of flint as well; these are fossilized sea sponge skeletons. These fist-sized nodules of stone are one of the primary building materials in this region, and many buildings and fences are constructed of these fossils cemented together. There are trees in some of the gentle valleys, but most of the downs are now open, having been denuded of trees in Neolithic times (roughly five thousand years ago). Erosion has worked aggressively on this deforested land and now the topsoil is too thin in many places to support trees. However, the topsoil does support a wonderful green turf that makes walking on much of the downs as smooth as walking on a golf course.

We chose to walk the South Downs Way from east to west (from Eastbourne to Winchester), from the more open and exposed sections to the more wooded, because we thought Winchester made a fitting finale—it's a lively market town full of interesting history and it's very tourist friendly. But the walk can easily be done in either direction, or you might choose to do a segment or two anywhere along the trail. Eastbourne is

Part Two: Extraordinary Hikes for Ordinary People

Walkers often must share the trail with farm animals along the South Downs Way.

only 75 minutes from London by train and the trip from Winchester back to London is just over an hour. Trains run several times per hour, so it's easy to position yourself. There is even train service from one end to the other. Eastbourne is a Georgian/Victorian seaside resort town and there are signs directing you to the South Downs Way right outside the train station.

We started the walk with a modest ascent of the downs to Beachy Head, where we could see the first of the Seven Sisters (we counted eight), a series of gentle rises with impressive white cliff faces meeting the sea. These cliffs continue to erode and slump into the English Channel, evidence of geology in action—it's best to stay back from the edge! Mostly you follow the rim of the South Downs escarpment, gaining surprisingly panoramic

views from roughly 650 feet above sea level. The trail stays on top of the downs, dropping only to cross river valleys called "wind gaps." Rivers include the Cuckmere, Ourse, Arun, Ardur, and Meon. (There's a saying that after the River Ardur, "the way gets 'arder and 'arder," but we didn't notice much difference.) You also occasionally cross or travel parallel to beautiful chalk streams.

One of the driest and warmest parts of England, the South Downs are home to many wildflowers. Cowslips are the symbol of the downs and grow on southern slopes. There is surprisingly diverse plant life in the "grass deserts" of the downs, with up to fifty species per square yard. There are lots of butterflies in summer; you have the chance to see over twenty species. Crossing the rivers and their estuaries (on bridges) offers the best opportunity to see lots of bird life. Our first wide water was Cuckmere Haven and we saw tufted ducks, swans, dabchicks, cormorants, and herons. Other days we watched larks, and saw many gray pheasants and partridges. We weren't fortunate enough to see hares, but there certainly are lots of their holes along the Seven Sisters. We want to believe that the cows we saw (mostly black and white ones like those of our native Vermont) mooed with a British accent, but we just couldn't hear it. At any rate they provided a picturesque punctuation for the pastoral vistas.

The trail opened in 1972 (in places following trails worn by nomadic tribes) and is well maintained and well marked with the white acorn symbol on posts. The landscape is wonderfully British, a mixture of pasture, arable fields, and woodlands, and the landscape is bigger and more open than in other parts of the country. We think of it as Britain's "Big Sky Country." Towns are in the lowlands and are conveniently located about a day's walk apart.

Gently up and down you go, passing rich remnants of early human history along the way. Of course there are impressive and historic buildings in the towns, notably Saxon and Norman churches. Alfriston has a large flint church called "The Cathedral of the Downs" and this town is home of the first property—the Clergy House—adopted by the National Trust (a now powerful conservation organization).

But it is up on the high land that we found the most interesting history. No matter what your favorite period of history, the South Downs Way can accommodate you. Neolithic man farmed the downs and mined them for flint to use for tools. The Bronze Age saw primitive farm sites, burial barrows (places where a internment was followed by the building of a mound of soil) and hill forts (areas of earthwork-enclosed high ground used for defense).

"Civilized man has built a coach, but has lost the use of his feet."

—Ralph Waldo Emerson

There are four hundred burial barrows (sometimes called long barrows) and many tumuli (individual burial mounds) along the path's route. There are Iron Age lynchets (ancient field systems), defensive dykes, and ancient tracks. Later, Romans built trade and communication routes, now used as rights of way. Near Bignor Hill there's a sign at the remains of a Roman road pointing the way to Londinium (Latin for London) to remind walkers of the Roman period of history. This road dates from about 70 AD and there are villa remains nearby.

Many of the summits along the downs have been used for coastal defense and communication. Ditchling Beacon (now part of a nature reserve) was one of a chain of bonfire sites used for centuries to send signals along the coast. Bonfires here and further along the coast were used to warn Queen Elizabeth I of the approach of the Spanish Armada and are still used for celebrations such as the Diamond Jubilee of Queen Elizabeth II.

History is represented in other ways as well. Chanctonbury Ring, a circle of beech trees planted in 1780, marks one especially beautiful hilltop. (Iron Age people also used this site, and there are remains of a Roman temple.) One of the many legends associated with this site has it that if you run around the ring of trees seven times the devil will come—but we decided it was best not to test this. On several hilltops dew ponds were built about two hundred years ago; these large, shallow depressions collected rainwater for sheep rearing; once there were over two hundred thousand ewes and lambs in the region, and the dew ponds were necessary because there's virtually no surface water on the downs. The two Clayton windmills (local landmarks known as Jack and Jill) date from 1866 and 1821, respectively. You walk right past a large white chalk horse (the figure of a horse outlined in chalk on the side of a hill) from the 1920s, but have to detour if you want to see the Long Man, which is England's largest chalk figure and the largest representation of a human in Western Europe. General Eisenhower addressed the Allied troops prior to D-Day from Cheesefoot Hill, where the landscape forms a natural amphitheater. After the war the downs were used for growing grain. A huge telecommunications tower is on Butser Hill, highest point of the walk at 889 feet.

Amberley was our favorite village, an especially picturesque town with thatched roofs and the ruins of a fourteenth-century castle (now an upscale hotel where a guest had parked his private helicopter on the lawn). At the end of each day, you come off the downs and spend the night in one of the communities dotted along the way; there you'll find B&Bs, pubs, and youth hostels. There aren't as many towns as in some parts of England, so you may have to walk an extra mile or two. If the distance between lodgings is greater than you want to walk, it's possible to arrange rides; baggage service is doable, too. There are only a few designated campsites, and you must ask the landowner for permission before camping elsewhere. It's important that you close all gates you pass through—and the ingenuity of some of the closures themselves is entertaining.

Of course, everyone enjoys Winchester, our end to the walk. It was a clear day and we could see the steeple of Winchester Cathedral several miles before we reached town. Once the Saxon capital of England, Winchester is now a small city with a college founded in 1382, and it has a ramparted town wall. Its impressive cathedral was started in 1079 and finished in 1404 and incorporates many different building styles. It's one of the longest cathedrals in Europe at 556 feet, but has a short tower. We finished our walk on a Saturday and this allowed us to attend the Sunday service the next morning; we found it to be an interesting cultural experience and especially enjoyed the boys' choir.

When the weather is dry it's possible to walk the South Downs Way in trail-running shoes; the path is sometimes on a bridleway, sometimes a footpath, sometimes a country lane. Be aware that you'll want some cushioning because the chalk and flint are right under the vegetation, and, if it's wet, the chalk can be a little slippery. On weekends we saw some equestrians and bikers, but there are also horse and bike variants to the trail in places. Lots of folks enjoy the South Downs Way—in ways

The eastern section of the South Downs Way parallels the white chalk cliffs of the English Channel.

as varied as training dogs to mountain biking—so this is not the trail for someone seeking solitude.

There is little opportunity to get fresh water on the trail, so you will have to carry some. Many of the sections are fully exposed, so this trail is more safely enjoyed when the weather is cooperative.

Perhaps you'll enjoy standing on the high ground to savor the views of the sea or the attractive inland towns. Or maybe you'll like imagining folks from an earlier period of history living their lives in this gentle landscape. Maybe you'll prefer studying the area's plants, or perhaps it's the animals that are of greatest interest. It doesn't matter—the South Downs Way can accommodate all these interests and more. And be sure to take time for afternoon tea!

"With a rotating periscope head, strong legs, and unbounded dreams, the walking species became the ruler of the earth."

—Joseph Amato

Further Reading

www.nationaltrail.co.uk/southdowns

Barltrop, Fiona. *South Downs Way*. Dunblane, UK: Rucksack Readers, 2011.

Manthorp, Jim. *South Downs Way: Winchester to Eastbourne*. Hindhead, Surrey, UK: Trailblazer Publications, 2009.

Millmore, Paul. *South Downs Way*. London: Aurem Press, 2010.

Reynolds, Kev. *The South Downs Way*. Milnthrpe, Cumbria, UK: Cicerone Press, 2004.

South Downs Way. Doune, Perthshire, UK: Harvey Maps.

Superior Hiking Trail

Location Minnesota, USA

Length 300 miles

Accommodations
Commercial: Some
Huts/refuges: No
Camping: Yes

Baggage transfer Some

Option to walk in sections All

Degree of challenge Moderate

UNITED STATES

*Split Rock Lighthouse is the symbol of the
Superior Hiking Trail.*

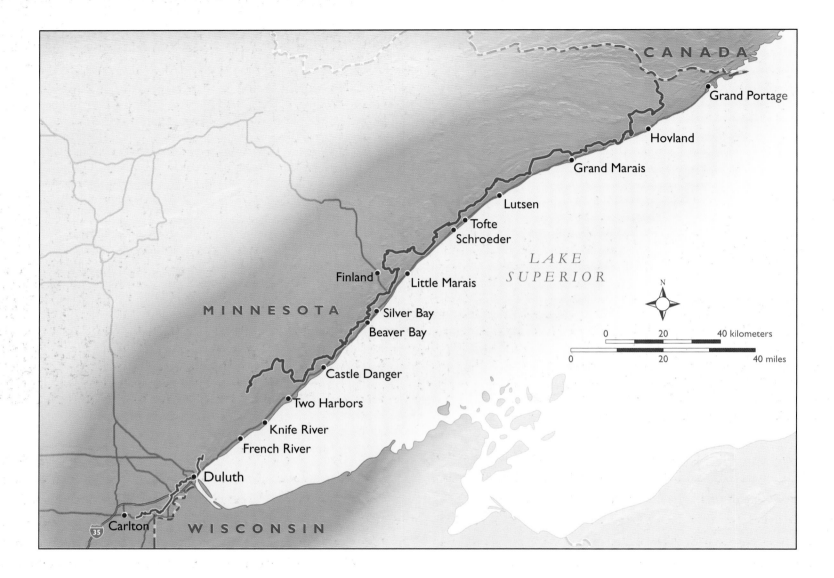

The bull moose lifted its head from the pond where it had been grazing, vines draped across its impressive rack of antlers. The beaver stopped its work on the dam that formed the pond and followed the glide of the bald eagle overhead. Sunlight illuminated the red maple leaves and the bright yellow leaves of the birch trees fluttered in the light breeze. That night the wolves and coyotes serenaded the shimmering northern lights. Okay, so we didn't really experience all these things on our walk of the Superior Hiking Trail. But the point is that we could have. The Superior Hiking Trail offers a glimpse into the vast north woods, an important component of America's natural and human history. The trail remains relatively unvisited despite its accessibility and growing reputation.

The Superior Hiking Trail passes many ponds with beaver lodges.

With a name like "Superior," it's got to be great. And it is! The nearly 300-mile Superior Hiking Trail follows the North Shore of legendary Lake Superior, the largest freshwater lake in the world (as measured by surface area). Excavated by glacial action some ten thousand years ago, Lake Superior is the greatest of the Great Lakes, comprising 32,000 square miles (about the size of the state of Maine). Moreover, much of the trail is carved out of the historic three-million-acre Superior National Forest, by far the largest national forest in the eastern U.S. No wonder *Backpacker Magazine* named this one of the top ten long-distance trails in America, "leaving all others in the dust."

The trail is in far northern Minnesota (what the tourism marketers have dubbed the "North Coast of America"), bounded by the Duluth area to the south and the Canadian border to the north (with a gap just north of Duluth). It's exceptionally diverse in both natural and cultural history.

Most of the trail winds through the Sawtooth Mountain range overlooking the lake, with occasional forays and side-trails to the lake's shore. Landscape features include mountain summits, deep gorges, waterfalls carved by mighty and historic rivers such as the Cascade, Temperance, and Devil Track, extensive inland lakes, ponds and bogs, and the rocky shores of Lake Superior. Most of the land is heavily forested—classic northern hardwoods

"People usually consider walking on water or in thin air a miracle. But I think the real miracle is not to walk either on water or in thin air, but to walk on earth."

—Thich Nhat Hanh

Numerous steep mountain streams cut the Sawtooth Mountains along the Superior Hiking Trail.

(maple, oak, basswood) in the lower elevations and boreal forest (balsam, pine, spruce, cedar, and tamarack) cloaking the higher areas.

This diverse, protected landscape supports a great variety of animal life, including black bears, moose, deer, coyotes, bobcats, mountain lions, eagles and other raptors, snowshoe hares, and marten. The area is the last stronghold of the gray wolf in the lower 48 states. While most hikers won't be fortunate enough to see many of these animals, it's exciting to know that you're walking through a vast wilderness that still provides home to many of America's most iconic wildlife species.

The human history of this area is equally impressive. Native Americans first settled in the North Shore region in 8,000 BC after the glaciers retreated. Frenchmen were the first Europeans to explore the area in the early 1700s searching for a northwest passage and later, in spite of conflicts between the native tribes, began the fur trade. They were supplanted by the British, who continued the trade, establishing a series of trading forts, including Grand Portage. Grand Portage National Monument, a part of the U.S. National Park system, commemorates this colorful history near the northern terminus of the Superior Hiking Trail. Henry Wadsworth Longfellow's epic poem *The Song of Hiawatha* is set here on the shores of what he called "Gitchee Gummee" and tells of the love of Hiawatha and Minnehaha. Longfellow exercised substantial editorial license in this poem, but his lines conjure up the romantic north woods mystique.

When Americans started moving west, surveys showed rich mineral resources in this area. In 1854 all Native American lands were ceded by treaty to the U.S. and, after some boom and bust stages, growth began in earnest in the region in the 1880s. Fishing became a major industry. Iron mining was followed by taconite (an iron-bearing rock) mining, and the railroad built during the mining boom allowed the lumber industry to flourish after 1890. In the early twentieth century tourism began to grow as extractive industries declined. Large and exclusive resorts were built along the shore of the lake, and some (Lutsen Resort and Cascade Lodge, for example) are still in operation, offering meals and accommodations for those not rich and famous, including walkers on the Superior Hiking Trail.

The Superior Hiking Trail occasionally descends to the shores of Lake Superior.

The Superior Hiking Trail is a relatively new addition to the stock of long-distance trails in the U.S. It was officially opened at a ceremonial "log-cutting" in 1987, and was built and is maintained by the Superior Hiking Trail Association, a group that now numbers over three thousand members. The trail connects seven state parks, two state forests, the Superior National Forest, and several stretches of private lands (where walkers must remain on the trail). The trail is highly accessible, crossed by mostly small country roads every 5 to 10 miles, allowing for relatively easy day walks. Eighty-six backcountry campsites are scattered along the trail at relatively regular intervals, though there are none in the Duluth area. A number of small towns and resorts are adjacent to the trail, providing a ready supply of motels, bed

and breakfasts, and historic inns for those who choose not to camp. Duluth and the larger towns of Two Harbors and Grand Marais offer walkers a full range of supplies and services. Two Harbors houses the Superior Hiking Trail Association offices and store, and tourist-friendly Grand Marais includes a concentration of art galleries, shops, and restaurants. The Superior Shuttle bus runs regular routes along the trail's numerous parking areas and this is a much appreciated service. A commercial lodge-to-lodge service will arrange treks of any length along part of the trail; the service includes maps, shuttles, lodging, breakfasts, and packed lunches. The trail is slated to ultimately become a part of the 4,500-mile North Country Scenic Trail from New York to North Dakota, but it will retain its identity as the

Superior Hiking Trail. The Superior Hiking Trail Association's *Guide to the Superior Hiking Trail* is a must for walkers.

We enjoyed our walk on the Superior Hiking Trail—the rich history and culture of the North Shore and the beauty and naturalness of this off-the-beaten-track geography. Highlights were seemingly unending views over Lake Superior, including the distant outlines of Apostle Island National Lakeshore and Isle Royale National Park; visiting the habitats of so many animals that now live only in the remote corners of the U.S. such as northern Minnesota; the solitude we experienced along the northern sections of trail (some days we saw no one else); and the accessibility of colorful towns and hospitable people when wanted. We found the trail to be well marked (with blue rectangular blazes) and maintained, but the natural topography can make walking long distances challenging; hikes of more than 8 to 10 miles often seemed hard. Even though the highest point on the trail is only about 1,800 feet in elevation, most days on the trail require several steep (but short) climbs and descents.

The trail is accessible from May through October. Spring offers abundant wildflowers, summer warm days and unending shades of green (but biting insects can be a nuisance—or worse), fall colorful foliage, and late fall extended views otherwise hidden by billions of leaves. Our best advice: walk when you can and as much as you can—and you'll be glad you did.

Further Reading

www.shta.org

Guide to the Superior Hiking Trail. Two Harbors, MN: Superior Hiking Trail Association, 2010.

"Walks. The body advances, while the mind flutters around it like a bird."

—Jules Renard

Tahoe Rim Trail

Location California and Nevada, USA

Length 165 miles

Accommodations
Commercial: Most
Huts/refuges: No
Camping: Yes

Baggage transfer No

Option to walk in sections All

Degree of challenge Moderate–High

UNITED STATES

High mountain lakes along the Tahoe Rim Trail offer opportunities for mid-day swims.

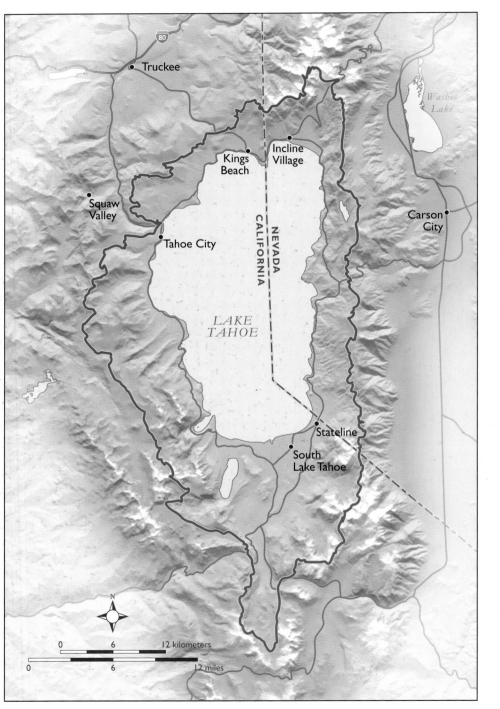

We made a lot of new friends on the Tahoe Rim Trail—well, sort of. John Muir, the preeminent walker of these Sierra Nevada Mountains, wrote that recognizing the plants and animals he encountered on his walks was like greeting old friends. So we decided to take his advice and introduce ourselves to the impressive trees along the Tahoe Rim Trail. The Tahoe Basin's range of elevations, aspects, geology, and climate offer a special richness of trees that vary widely and impressively in form and function. Learning about these trees—telling one species from another, how they've adapted to their environment, what they tell us about the places they live—can deepen our appreciation of the natural world, and add to our enjoyment of walking among them. Take, for example, ponderosa pines, stately trees that grow in open groves at lower elevations and derive their name from their "ponderous bulk." They can grow to nearly 250 feet high and 8 feet in diameter, living up to five hunded years. The bark on their massive trunks is a distinctive cinnamon-brown to orange-yellow, but their most distinguishing (and pleasing) characteristic is that they smell like vanilla when warmed by the sun. Walking through a ponderosa pine forest on a sunny day can delight many of the senses. Trees can be interesting friends indeed. They're beautiful, of course, but they also help us by controlling soil erosion, providing wildlife habitat, moderating the weather, improving air quality, conserving water, providing building materials, and helping to neutralize excessive emissions of carbon dioxide that contribute to the threat of global climate change. Trees do a lot for

Part Two: Extraordinary Hikes for Ordinary People

us, but are we responding in kind? Joyce Kilmer wrote in his most famous poem:

> I think that I shall never see
> A poem lovely as a tree.

More recently, humorist Ogden Nash replied in parody:

> I think that I shall never see
> A billboard lovely as a tree.
> Perhaps, unless the billboards fall,
> I'll never see a tree at all.

The Tahoe Rim Trail (most walkers call it the TRT) makes a 165-mile loop around gorgeous Lake Tahoe, the third largest lake in the U.S. (eighth largest in the world) at roughly 12 by 22 miles, covering over 500 square miles. It sits on the California/Nevada state line with extensive shoreline in both states. But Lake Tahoe is more than big—it's strikingly beautiful. Its depth (more than 1,600 feet) and purity (you can see objects more than 100 feet below the surface) manifest themselves in the rich, deep blue color on the open lake and sparkling turquoises along its beaches, coves, and bays.

Most of the TRT is set back off the shore along the ridges and slopes of the surrounding Sierra Nevada Mountains in California and Carson Range in Nevada, offering sweeping views of the lake as well as stately forests, mountain wildflowers, and peaks of more than 10,000 feet. If you choose to do the entire trail, you have the option of backpacking or doing a series of day hikes, as roads (mostly paved) break this loop into eight neat sections ranging from 13 to nearly 20 miles. By utilizing side trails and some more minor Forest Service roads (as we did) you can shorten some of these sections even further. Loop trails are fun because you can see where you're going as well as where you've been. We hiked by day and rested in comfort by night in nearby towns, but be forewarned that some of the pockets of strip development on Tahoe's shore can shock the senses after a blissful day on the trail.

Emerald Bay is one of the most popular destinations on Lake Tahoe.

The Tahoe Rim Trail runs through the granite peaks and high mountain lakes of the Desolation Wilderness, thought by many to be the most beautiful section of the trail.

It took a lot of geologic history to make the lake and the surrounding lands, including faults, volcanoes, and glaciers. Initially, the Tahoe Basin sank along two fault lines, making a deep depression. About two million years ago, lava created a dam where the Truckee River now flows and the lake reached a height of 600 feet higher than its current surface elevation of 6,200 feet. Subsequent glacial action reduced the height of the dam and shaped the surrounding landscape by scouring out the Tahoe Basin and polishing the surrounding granite.

The TRT also reflects the human history of this area, following travel routes of Native Americans (the Washoe tribe) and pioneers. Historical artifacts along the trail include remnants from the silver mines that started with discovery of the famous Comstock Lode in nearby Virginia City in 1859 as well as enormous stumps of trees cut to fuel those mines and support their underground labyrinths. Lake Tahoe became a retreat for the rich families of San Francisco, Sacramento, and Virginia City around the turn of the twentieth century and was opened to the masses when improved roads and the prevalence of cars made travel easier after World War II. The 1960 Winter Olympics were held in Squaw Valley and that brought the Lake Tahoe Basin into the international spotlight.

"An early-morning walk is a blessing for the whole day."
—Henry David Thoreau

Interesting plants and animals are found in abundance and variety in this area as the elevations along the trail range from 6,200 feet at the surface of the lake to over 10,000 feet at the summit of Relay Peak. Bald eagles and red-tailed hawks soar, but black bear, mountain lion, bobcat, mule deer, and coyote sightings are less common. Wildflowers are abundant in the open slopes and meadows—our favorite was the distinctive yellow mule's ears.

But it's the trees that stole the show for us. In addition to the ponderosa pines noted earlier, the sugar pine was a favorite. This is

Part Two: Extraordinary Hikes for Ordinary People

The turquoise waters of Lake Tahoe tempt walkers to stop long enough for a refreshing swim.

a tree of superlatives, the tallest of all the pines and growing the longest cones, which sometimes reach over 20 inches. When you see a sugar pine cone, you'll know it! In keeping with their name, sugar pines produce a sweet resin that John Muir liked better than maple syrup. White fir is probably the most common tree in the Tahoe Basin. These are large trees that favor moist soils; look for them near the lake. Red firs also form extensive forests in the area; they are larger than white firs and present a classic, narrow, conical, symmetrical crown, and this "magnificent" character is reflected in their scientific name, *Abies magnifica*. The name lodgepole pine also suggests something about its character. These trees grow especially straight in their conventional dense groves and the resulting poles were used by Native Americans to support their lodges.

Western white pine, whitebark pine, and western juniper are all higher-elevation trees, growing between 10,000 and 12,000 feet. Western white pine is a large tree—sometimes massive—and we measured one by the side of the trail with a circumference of 24 feet! Whitebark pine tends to grow in exposed locations and its crown is often distorted by the wind with most of its substantive branches clinging to the leeward side of the trunk. Western juniper can live as long as a thousand years. It grows in dry, rocky areas that are often exposed and it can take on a twisted, gnarly appearance. The principal deciduous tree in the Tahoe Basin is quaking aspen. It is readily recognized by its white (sometimes pale yellow-green) bark, its toothed, egg-shaped leaves with flat stems that "quake" in the breeze, and its yellow, gold, and occasionally orange fall colors. It prefers

"You need special shoes for hiking—and a bit of a special soul as well."

—Terri Guillemets

wet areas and its presence suggests that surface or ground water is nearby. The seeds of aspen are so small (it takes two million to make a pound!) they are easily and widely distributed by the wind.

The TRT is located primarily on national forest lands and passes through three wilderness areas—Mt. Rose, Granite Chief, and Desolation. The 35-mile stretch through the Desolation Wilderness may be the most dramatic: a quintessential Sierra Nevada landscape, with exposed granite peaks, high mountain passes, and more than a hundred lakes to swim in or just admire. Look closely at the granite outcrops and see the glacial polish and the grooves and chatter marks where the glaciers advanced and retreated. A side trail leads to world-class views of Emerald Bay, the most photographed spot in the Tahoe Basin. From Meiss Meadows to Twin Peaks (on the western shore) the trail coincides with about 50 miles of the Pacific Crest Trail, which runs from Mexico to Canada—we enjoyed talking with the extraordinary PCT hikers we encountered.

The Tahoe Rim Trail is a fairly new addition to the world of long-distance walking, officially opened in 2001. Over ten thousand volunteers toiled to make this trail happen, and now they are working on a trail to connect to Reno, Nevada. The TRT is a multi-use trail with just over half the trail open to mountain bikers and all of it open to equestrians. The rules state that hikers yield to horses, and bikers yield to hikers and horses, and, for the most part, it works pretty well.

Lake Tahoe is roughly 200 miles north of San Francisco, 100 miles east of Sacramento and 60 miles west of Reno, so access to the area is fairly easy; you'll want to spend a little time in the basin to acclimate to the elevation. The trail is open year-round to allow for cross-country skiing and snowshoeing, but the hiking season is July through September. Water is an issue. Although many streams drain into Lake Tahoe, most of these are seasonal, so it's important to check locally about both drinking water and any remaining snowfields; you want to avoid walking through challenging wet spring snowfields, locally called "Sierra cement." Camping is allowed just about everywhere, although you need a permit for the Desolation Wilderness (you need a permit to hike there, too) and you are restricted to two primitive campgrounds while walking through Lake Tahoe Nevada State Park. There are no fees.

If you want to experience the most sensational portion of a truly sensational trail and are willing to backpack, most folks recommend the three days from Echo Lake to Barker Pass in the Desolation Wilderness. If you're into long-distance views, the best is from the top of Mt. Rose, where you can look into the Sierra Nevadas, the Carson Range, out over the lake, and north to Mounts Lassen and Shasta—a 360-degree view that's worth the uphill pull. The TRT is well maintained and wayfinding is easy. There is substantial elevation change over most sections, but the trail was designed to maintain a modest grade. Neither a front country trail nor a true wilderness experience, the Tahoe Rim Trail is challenging in places, but the rewards are great.

You'll see lots of our tree friends along the trail, living together in some of the most impressive forests in North America. Take time to meet them and say thanks for all they do for us. And tell them we sent you.

Further Reading

www.tahoerimtrail.org

Hauserman, Tim. *The Tahoe Rim Trail: The Official Guide for Hikers, Mountain Bikers and Equestrians.* Berkeley, CA: Wilderness Press, 2012.

Tour du Mont Blanc

Location France, Italy, Switzerland

Length 100+ miles

Accommodations
Commercial: Most
Huts/refuges: Yes
Camping: Some

Baggage transfer Most
(except refuges)

Option to walk in sections Most

Degree of challenge Moderate

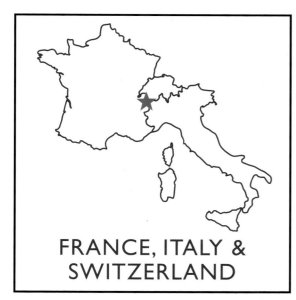

FRANCE, ITALY &
SWITZERLAND

The Tour du Mont Blanc winds through many
valleys of the Mont Blanc region of France,
Italy, and Switzerland.

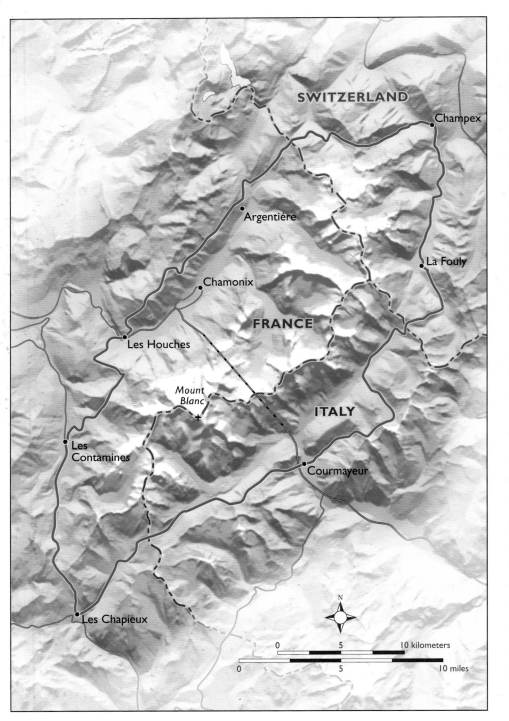

We were walking the three-day Swiss section of the Tour du Mont Blanc through the farming region appropriately named Bovine. It was mid-afternoon, and we'd been serenaded on and off all day by the bells of the local cows grazing in the high pastures. Now, the sounds were growing louder. As we rounded the next bend in the trail, we understood why—one of the local farmers had converted part of his barn into a small outdoor restaurant for walkers, and his herd of milk cows was there to greet us. In fact, the large cows had congregated on the trail and were a little intimidating; fortunately they were used to walkers and it was easy to sweet-talk enough of them off the trail so we could reach the barn, where we enjoyed our afternoon snack of fresh-baked bread and local creamy cheese. Other walkers were enjoying a late lunch of soup, sandwiches, and wine, and we were all admiring the lovely views of the valley below and preparing ourselves for the last leg of the day's climb.

The Tour du Mont Blanc (TMB) is one of the most historic and popular walks in all of Europe. This is a circular journey around Mont Blanc, affectionately known as the "Monarch of the Alps," the highest mountain in western Europe. More properly, the trail encircles the Mont Blanc massif, a complex of some four hundred summits and the forty glaciers that flow off these mountains in all directions. The trail wanders a little more than 100 miles (depending upon a range of alternative routes) through three countries (France, Italy, and Switzerland). Most walking days start in one of the major valleys that radiate from the mountain. The trail then climbs a high pass and descends into the next valley, each with its own character and each seeming more dramatic and beautiful than the last.

Walkers above Chamonix enjoy striking views of the Mont Blanc massif.

Walkers have been trekking around Mont Blanc since the late eighteenth century, though its popularity began in earnest during the Victorian Age, when the area began attracting the English gentry. Now an estimated ten thousand walkers take to the trail each year, and for good reason, as this is a walk worthy of its reputation. The classic TMB walk is conducted in eleven days, but this leaves no time for rest days, or more importantly, exploring the famous mountaineering centers of Chamonix, France, and Cormayeur, Italy, along the way. We highly recommend two weeks for this walk.

The classic walk is conducted in an "anticlockwise" direction (as the British guidebooks say), and starts in the village of Les Houches, just a few miles from Chamonix (though, of course, the hike can be done in either direction and can be started at any of the many accessible towns and villages along the route). We suggest a day in Chamonix at the beginning or end of the hike (or both!) to soak up the mountaineering history of this area and to generally enjoy this tourist-friendly town.

After a few days in France, walkers enter the historic Italian village of Dolonne and cross the glacier-fed river to Cormayeur. Sometimes called the "Italian Chamonix" (which Italians probably don't appreciate), Cormayeur is a relatively large town with its own history of mountain culture and a thriving tourism infrastructure. A layover day here is a good idea, not just to rest the legs, but to have an adventure on Mont Blanc itself. A short ride from Cormayeur on the public bus takes you to Palud, the base of a network of

The Tour du Mont Blanc offers close inspection of the south flank of Mont Blanc.

cable cars that traverse Mont Blanc and ultimately descend (dramatically!) into Chamonix. The engineering of these cable cars is a marvel, and views are truly stunning, including the surrounding Alps in all directions, glacial crevasses, and groups of climbers roped together as they move to and from the summit. A return trip to Cormayeur at the end of the day is easy by local bus through the 16-mile Mont Blanc Tunnel.

The next day of walking climbs steeply to gain the long, open ridge line of Mont de la Saxe, and, if the weather is fine, this day is stunning. The whole eastern profile of the Mont Blanc massif is presented for close inspection, and the grassy meadows along the ridge offer suitable viewing platforms and lunch spots. Listen carefully for distant avalanches and rock falls if you need any convincing that this is a dynamic landscape, a masterpiece of nature still in the making.

When you reach the cultural landscape that is Switzerland, you know it. The following few days are distinctly Swiss, with traditional wooden chalets, flower-filled window boxes, meadows filled with cows, and the melodies of cow bells that seem to "yodel" through the hills. Views of Mont Blanc have receded as the trail is now a considerable distance north of the massif. However, there are fine views of the impressive Grand Combin mountain complex (which can be inspected more closely on the Walker's Haute Route, the next walk that we describe).

Upon re-entering France, the trail ascends a series of ladders and handrails to the Grand Balcon Sud, where it traverses the slopes and ridges on the Aigulles Rouges and looks across Chamonix to the impressive western face of the Mont Blanc massif. Be sure to look for chamois and ibex (wild goats) through this section of the trail; and you'll undoubtedly be impressed by the avalanche barriers, wooden structures erected at right angles to the steep slopes to minimize avalanche danger. Mountain refuges offer simple accommodations with five-star views, or you can descend by numerous cable cars to the creature comforts of Chamonix, returning to the trail the next morning. The last stage of the hike is a gentle descent back to the village of Les Houches where you began your journey some two weeks ago.

A complete list of highlights for this walk would be unwieldy. We particularly enjoyed the views of Mont Blanc and its glaciers, and it was very satisfying to know we had walked all the way around "The Monarch." We also delighted in being outdoors in areas of great beauty by day and indoors in great comfort by night. This trail is one that energizes its walkers—remember the uphills are always followed by complementing downhills!

The TMB is generally rated as moderate, although there are several long, but gradual ascents. Though Mont Blanc is an impressive 15,770 feet, the trail does not go *over* the mountain, as that would require technical climbing. Elevations along the trail generally range from about 4,000 feet to just over 8,000 feet. Most sections are well graded and maintained, and the trail is clearly marked, though the markings vary by country. There is some exposure to steep dropoffs in a few isolated spots, but there are fixed chains, ladders, and metal handrails to compensate where needed, and there are a number of alternative routes that can be taken to avoid steep climbs and bad weather. Occasional ski lifts and good local bus and train service offer convenient options to shorten the hike or walk the trail in sections. Luggage transfer service is generally available, but not at refuges. Just be warned that, if you do only a few sections or a "best of" hike, you'll want to come back for more.

Because of its elevation, the walking season for the TMB is short—July through the middle of September. Depending on snowfall, several of the higher passes may be snow covered in June, requiring gaiters and even an ice axe. Mountain refuges begin closing as fall snowstorms approach in the latter half of September. August is the traditional French holiday period and reservations are necessary for accommodations during this time. The trail is well served by an especially diverse range of accommodations, including refuges in the higher elevations, small hotels and B&Bs in valley villages, and even (if you wish) five-star hotels in Chamonix and Cormayeur. Walkers should take maximum advantage of the fine quality local foods of the region, with special emphasis on cheese, bread, and (possibly) wine carried in the pack for lunch. For example, we particularly enjoyed the Beaufort d'Alpage, a cow's milk cheese from the tiny village

Refugio Elizabetta sits at the foot of one of Mont Blanc's many glaciers.

of Les Chapieux, which has been made in the region since Roman times. These foods complement the scenery by offering other sensory perceptions of the region's distinctive landscape.

Despite the multinational nature of this walk, French is the unofficial language of the TMB. English can be spotty, so brush up on your French or carry a simple phrase book. Though the Swiss are not part of the EU, the euro is generally accepted. Most refuges do not accept credit cards, so carry some cash; there are cash machines in several of the largest towns along the trail.

This is more than a fine walk—the TMB is a unanimous choice among lists of "the world's greatest hikes." The landscape is overwhelming with its soaring height, its massive scale, its active and powerful glaciers, its flower-filled meadows, and its gentle, sculpted valleys. The cultural overlay complements the landscape with its French, Italian, and Swiss adaptations of lifestyle, language, architecture, food, and mythology. Be sure to put a checkmark on your life list next to the TMB.

"Walking: the most ancient exercise and still the best modern exercise."

—Carrie Latet

Further Reading

www.walkingthetmb.com

Manthorpe, Jim. *Tour du Mont Blanc*. Hindhead, Surrey, UK: Trailblazer Press, 2008.

McCormack, Gareth. *Explore the Tour of Mont Blanc*. Dunbane, UK: Rucksack Readers, 2005

Reynolds, Kev. *Tour of Mont Blanc*. Milnthorpe, Cumbria, UK: Cicerone Press, 2010.

Walker's Haute Route

Location France and Switzerland

Length 114 miles

Accommodations
Commercial: Most
Huts/refuges: Yes
Camping: Some

Baggage transfer No

Option to walk in sections Most

Degree of challenge Moderate–High

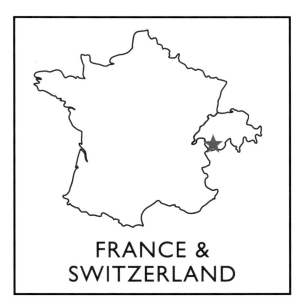

FRANCE &
SWITZERLAND

*Active glaciers still shape the landscape
along the Walker's Haute Route.*

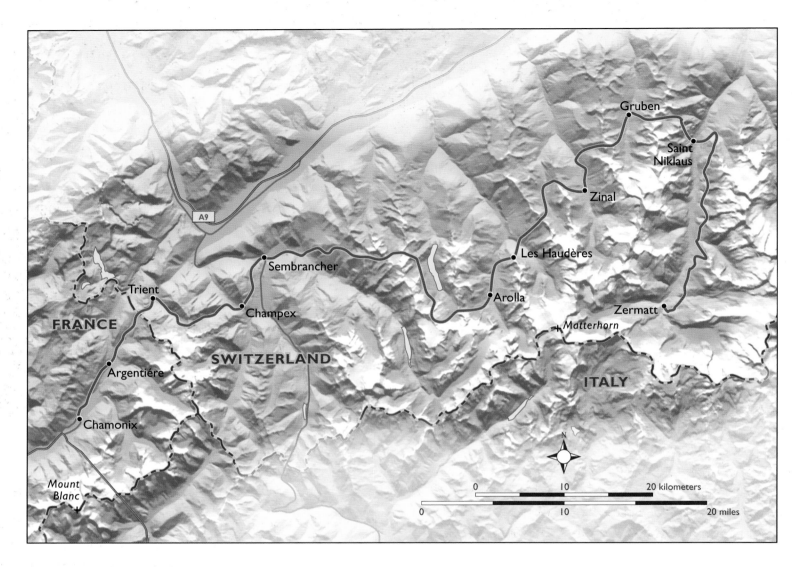

Everyone knows about glaciers—rivers of ice that "flow" downhill, advancing and retreating, sculpting the landscape. But for most people, all this is learned in textbooks and can sound very abstract. The Walker's Haute Route brought it all to life for us in one special day. There, right before us, was a river of ice flowing off the mountain we were traversing. Our route led us directly across the surface of the glacier where we saw the fissures (crevaces) in the ice as it turned downhill more sharply, and we walked carefully among the rocks and other debris the glacier had excavated from the mountain. We climbed and walked atop long, linear deposits of rock and gravel—lateral glacial moraines, just like the textbooks describe. We climbed a large (and rough) terminal moraine and skirted some glacial erratics (large rocks carried and eventually dropped by the flowing ice far from their origin). And we walked around a series

A traditional hamlet with buildings of native larch clings to the mountainside alongside the Walker's Haute Route.

of tarns, small ponds formed from glacial meltwater. Never again will we be confused about glaciers and their impact on the land. The Walker's Haute Route should be a required field trip for all students of geology and glacial action—and it's a delightful walk as well!

Mont Blanc and the Matterhorn are arguably the two most famous Alps, and Chamonix, France, and Zermatt, Switzerland, two of the greatest mountaineering centers in the world, sit at their respective bases. The Walker's Haute Route is a glorious 114-mile hike that connects these two centers of outdoor activity. Winding through the largest collection of high peaks in Western Europe, the route crosses eleven passes of almost 10,000 feet. Although occasionally challenging in difficulty, the Walker's Haute

"Thoughts come clearly while one walks."
—Thomas Mann

Route's combination of scenery, cultural experience, and availability of creature comforts make it well worth the effort, and, in fact, it is such a wonderful walk that the effort required is often completely overshadowed by the rewards of the experience.

In the 1860s a route was developed between Chamonix and Zermatt, but this could only be done as a mountaineering expedition. In the early twentieth century, the towns were linked by a ski touring route popular in the spring, and this route forms the basis for what is now the Walker's Haute Route. Climbing an accumulated 39,000 feet, the trail crosses the grain of the landscape. Typically, each day involves climbing over a mountain pass

The Matterhorn rises above Zermatt, the eastern end of the Walker's Haute Route.

and dropping through forests and high pastures to the next valley town to refresh for the following day's walk. The towns offer varying (sometimes quite luxurious, if you're interested) types of accommodation as well as places to eat and (usually) to resupply. On the few occasions where staying overnight at the higher elevations is best, there are mountain refuges offering a bed, shower, dinner with local wine or beer, breakfast, and the company of other like-minded walkers from all over the world.

It's best to allow two weeks if walking the entire route as progress can be slow over some stretches and you want to allow adequate time to appreciate the landscape and the towns of Chamonix and Zermatt. One appealing aspect of the Walker's Haute Route is that there are variations available if the weather deteriorates or the legs need a break. We suggest a variant from Cabane de Prafleuri to Arolla, the alternate route via Cabane des Dix. Cabane des Dix has an especially dramatic setting, and offers lunch on the deck (we had delicious homemade soup which was served in a warmed bowl by a smiling server who looked like an adult cherub). If you choose to spend the night at Cabane des Dix, be forewarned that the water (from the glacier just up the hill) for the outdoor shower is solar heated and has a long recovery time. Be early in line! All the villages along the trail are accessible by local buses or train so walking the trail in sections (or skipping some sections if needed) is easily done. Access is complemented by the occasional chairlift as well, making this an easy trail to "sample."

Expect some of the best weather in all of Switzerland with warm days, sunshine, and relatively little precipitation. Nights are cold—good for sleeping. June is the earliest the trail is open and September is best with clear bright days. Marmots, chamois, and ibex may be seen—in this order of likelihood. You definitely will see the wonderful Herens cows with their melodious bells. Descended from the almost extinct European aurochs and raised to fight each other in the ring, these placid-seeming giants and the milk cows of Switzerland add a "Heidi-like" quality to an already achingly beautiful walk. If that weren't enough, the route passes

The Walker's Haute Route passes through a series of attractive French and Swiss villages.

through the richest flora in all of Switzerland. There are meadows filled with wildflowers and lots of edelweiss, the unofficial national flower.

The latter stages of the Walker's Haute Route pass from French-speaking to German-speaking Switzerland, and there are some subtle changes in building forms. For the most part, though, you're looking at chalets, more chalets, and even more chalets, each seemingly competing with its neighbors in floral display. Of particular interest are the Valasian buildings. Built of local larch trees (which blacken after centuries) and roofed with heavy stone slabs up to several inches thick, these buildings are further distinguished by rounded stone plates (like large thick pizzas) which rest between the wooden pillars that lift the structure off the ground and the upper building itself. These stones protect the building's contents from rodents, although the technique means that nothing is binding a

Valasian building to the ground—each structure represents a strong faith in the forces of gravity!

Other highlights of the walk were dining on the terrace of Cabane du Mont Fort (one of the mountain refuges) and watching the sunset, the Grand Hotel La Sage with its conservatory (complete with pool table) and gourmet meals, and tourist-friendly Zermatt, where automobiles are not allowed. And, of course, let's not forget the Alps themselves with their massive (though retreating) glaciers.

No special equipment is needed for the Walker's Haute Route, although trekking poles are helpful with the descents and for a little extra security at the few exposed areas. (There are fixed chains in a couple of spots.) Of course, you should be prepared for rain and/or snow whenever you hike at altitude.

Refuges along the Walker's Haute Route offer spectacular settings.

The Walker's Haute Route is not the easiest hike in the Alps (the Tour du Mont Blanc—previously described—is similar, but less demanding), but it richly rewards the walker in terms of truly awe-inspiring scenery, rich cultural experience, and the ease with which "civilization" can be incorporated with the natural. And don't forget—this is an ideal hike to treat with a "cherry picker's" approach!

It's easiest to fly to Geneva and use public transport to get to Chamonix. Don't overlook the possibility of taking the Mont Blanc Express train partway as it is an engineering marvel and a good introduction to the Alps. Zermatt is served by the Glacier Express, proud of its reputation as "the world's slowest express train" and a good first step to returning to Geneva and home. Remember, this is Switzerland and public transportation is clean, efficient, and on time—to the minute! The contrast between the wild beauty of the Alps and the civilized lifestyle makes this an unforgettable experience—and in the future you'll truly understand glaciers.

Further Reading

Reynolds, Kev. *Chamonix—Zermatt: The Walker's Haute Route.* Milnthorpe, Cumbria, UK: Cicerone Press, 2010.

Stewart, Alexander. *The Walker's Haute Route: Mont Blanc to the Materhorn.* Surrey, UK: Trailblazer Publications, 2008.

West Coast Trail

Location British Columbia, Canada

Length 50 miles

Accommodations
Commercial: No
Huts/refuges: No
Camping: Yes

Baggage transfer No

Option to walk in sections No

Degree of challenge High

CANADA

The 50-mile West Coast Trail follows the rugged coastline of British Columbia, Canada.

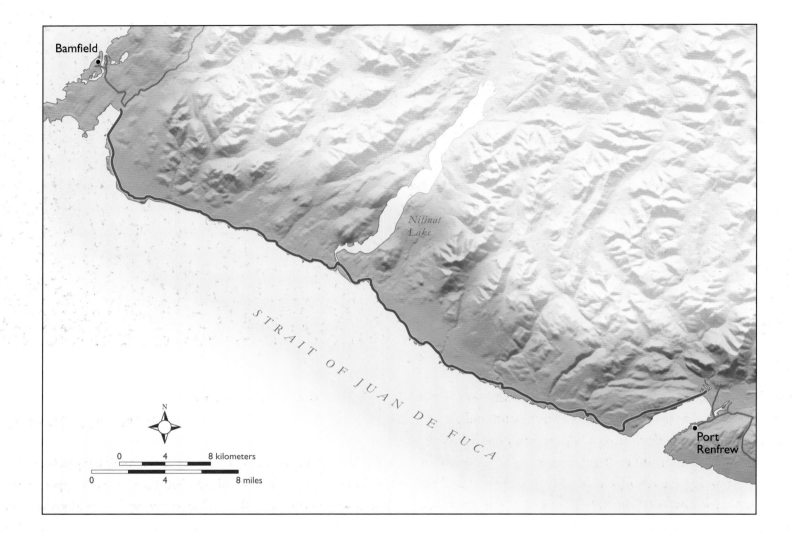

It was the first day of our backpacking trip along the West Coast Trail and the weather was good. More importantly, the weather forecast was good—little or no chance of Pacific storms—and that meant we were in an equally good mood (more about the weather later). It was late in the day when we approached Camper Creek, the first of five rivers along the trail that the guidebook said must be crossed by cable car. We were intrigued, but a little anxious as well; how does one go about using a personal cable car? We smiled as we reached the river to find a shiny, two-person cable car strung across the river on steel cables and pulleys—sort of like a carnival ride in the middle of the wilderness. But the car was resting above the midpoint of the creek, hanging in the slack of the cables. We mounted the wooden platform at the side of the creek and read the directions. Accordingly, we both pulled on one of the cables and moved the car slowly toward us. When it reached the platform, one of us hopped in and stored both our packs. Then the other got in and we let go of the

The West Coast Trail offers miles of wild beaches in Pacific Rim National Park.

platform. Wheee! Using gravity, we were racing (it seemed) across the river—until we were just beyond the halfway point and gravity began to work against us. From this point, we pulled on one of the cables, hauling ourselves toward the platform on the other side of the river, all this becoming increasingly difficult as we approached the platform. It was with great satisfaction that we successfully completed our journey across the river, unloaded our packs and ourselves, and continued along the trail, looking forward to our next cable car ride.

Pacific Rim National Park is a gem in the outstanding system of parks managed by Parks Canada. As the name suggests, this park hugs the Pacific coast and is located in the southwest part of Vancouver Island, British Columbia. Following the Pacific Coast for some 50 miles, the West Coast Trail has been described as "the best the west coast has to offer" and "the definitive hike of the temperate rainforests on the west coast of North

"It is a great art to saunter."
—Henry David Thoreau

America." And it delivers. The trail is cut from the lush temperate rainforests that cover the park's steep headlands, but there are many opportunities to drop down and walk along the area's expansive and pristine beaches, and we recommend taking advantage of these opportunities when possible. When walking the beaches, search out the more firmly packed sand at the edge of the high water mark where walking is easier, and look for old fishing buoys that are tied to trees marking the points where walkers should return to higher ground.

The contemporary version of the trail was opened in 1980, but it has a much longer history. In fact, it has many histories, beginning as a gathering and trading route for people of the First Nations. In the latter half of the nineteenth century it provided a route for a telegraph system connecting

Walkers find massive piles of driftwood along the beaches of the West Coast Trail.

the city of Victoria in the south to the frontier town of Bamfield in the north. Walkers will see occasional poles and wires along the trail from this era. Later, the trail was used primarily as a life-saving route in response to the more than sixty shipwrecks along this section of the coast (known as "The Graveyard of the Pacific"). The sinking of the *Valencia* in 1906 was especially tragic, as many survivors were able to swim ashore, but ultimately perished due to the difficulty of reaching civilization. Today, the trail has been upgraded and serves as one of the world's great coastal walks.

It's hard to decide which of the trail's environments is the more compelling—the beaches or the headlands. The beaches are frequent and expansive, and with tides and waves constantly washing the slate clean, each walker gets the sense that he or she is the first to traverse this area. Waves crash, broad tidal shelves extend into the sea, sea stacks and caves add drama, tidal pools teem with sea life, beds of kelp and rock outcrops demand closer inspection, and marine mammals—gray whales and orcas, harbor seals, dolphins, and porpoises—swim just off shore. Beaches are littered with massive piles of driftwood and offer many lifetimes of beachcombing.

The headlands offer a rare and intimate experience with the continent's majestic and cathedral-like old-growth rainforests of Douglas fir, western hemlock, western red cedar, and Sitka spruce, some of the tallest trees in the world, with a rich understory of ferns, trillium, and bunchberries. Animals of this forest include black bears, mountain lions, and wolves, clear manifestations of the remote and wild character of this area. The forests and sea together support diverse birdlife, including eagles, herring gulls, Steller's jays, cormorants, and red-beaked oyster catchers.

Every mile of this trail is an adventure. Walkers often have their choice of beach or headland trail, but this decision has to be made wisely. Some portions of beach are flooded at high tide right up to the steep cliffs they adjoin, and walkers must carry a tide chart (and be able to read it) to avoid the danger of entrapment and exposure to the sea. Headland soils are wet and boggy (after all, these are *rain*forests) and can make for slow going. Miles of boardwalk have been constructed to keep walkers up and off these fragile environments, and they are a convenience to walkers as well. While there is only moderate

Part Two: Extraordinary Hikes for Ordinary People

elevation to be gained along the trail (the highpoint is only 600 feet above sea level), the land is steeply cut by many rivers emptying into the sea. Many ravines are so steep that they're impassible without the extensive system of dozens of ladders that lead walkers up and down. The longest ladder is 70 feet, but there are often many ladders joined together. Five of the rivers are too wide to bridge, and these are serviced by cable cars. Two of the rivers are broader still and must be crossed by ferry.

Other distinctive features of the trail are more cultural and include reserves for three tribes of First Nations people: Pacheedaht, Didadaht, and Huu-Ay-Aht. These groups have inhabited this area for over four thousand years, and the First Nation village of Clo-oose is thought to be one of the oldest on the west coast of all of North America. "Guardians" from these tribes help maintain the trail and provide ferry service across the two largest rivers. Walkers must stay on the trail when passing through these reserves (clearly marked on trail maps) and no camping is allowed in these areas. The trail also includes two historic lighthouses: Carmanah Point Lighthouse constructed in 1891 and Pachena Point Lighthouse, the last original wooden light tower on the west coast of Canada. And when you're walking on the beach, watch for remains of the many shipwrecks that are periodically exposed by tides and storms.

The striking beauty of the West Coast Trail must be weighed against the challenges it presents. Parks Canada calls it "one of the most grueling hikes in North America." The most common danger is the weather that can sometimes legitimately be called horrendous. Periodic storms blow in from the Pacific Ocean with high winds and days of rain. The trail should not be attempted when the weather report is bad. Even when the forecast is good, be prepared for the unexpected and take warm clothes, serious rain gear, a good tent, and extra food. The extensive boardwalks and system of ladders make walking easier, but they are often coated with slippery moss and are sometimes in disrepair. Muddy bogs can suck your boots off. Gaiters are highly recommended for the upland portions of the trail. Rock shelves sometimes extend into the sea and can be walked in low tide, but be careful of "surge channels," where water flows quickly out to the sea and can be very dangerous. Use the cable cars and

Two-person, self-service cable cars help walkers across several of the larger rivers that flow into the Pacific Ocean.

Portions of the West Coast Trail traverse dense rainforests.

ferries when crossing the larger rivers and don't be tempted to try to wade or swim across these cold and dangerous waters. This is a remote area that must be backpacked, where there are no resupply points, and where rescue is difficult and time consuming. Be prepared and enjoy it on its own terms.

The primary walking season is May through September. During the "high season" (June 15 to September 15), a permit and fee are required and permits are limited to approximately fifty each day. A Parks Canada information station is located at each end of the trail and walkers must watch an information and safety video prior to being issued a permit. Most walkers complete the trail in five to seven days. Camping is allowed in most locations (except the First Nations reserves noted above) and we recommend planning your trip to camp at least one night on the beach at Tsusiat Falls, where the river drops directly onto the beach, providing a convenient (but cold!) shower. The villages of Port Renfrew in the south and Bamfield in the north reflect their timber and fishing heritage and offer limited services to walkers. Commercial shuttle bus service from both ends of the trail is provided from the beautiful and tourist-friendly city of Victoria.

The West Coast Trail asks a lot of walkers, but it gives back even more. Carefully prepare yourself for this walk and you will be richly rewarded. We were.

Further Reading

www.parkscanada.gc.ca/pacificrim

Gill, Ian. *Hiking on the Edge.* Vancouver, British Columbia: Raincoast Books, 2002.

Leadem, Tim. *Hiking the West Coast of Vancouver Island.* Toronto, Ontario: Greystone Books, 2005.

Leadem, Tim. *Hiking the West Coast Trail: A Pocket Guide.* Toronto, Ontario: Greystone Books, 2006.

West Highland Way

Location Scotland

Length 96 miles

Accommodations
Commercial: Yes
Huts/refuges: Some
Camping: Some

Baggage transfer Yes

Option to walk in sections All

Degree of challenge Moderate

UNITED KINGDOM

The West Highland Way crosses numerous streams that flow into Loch Lomond and other lakes.

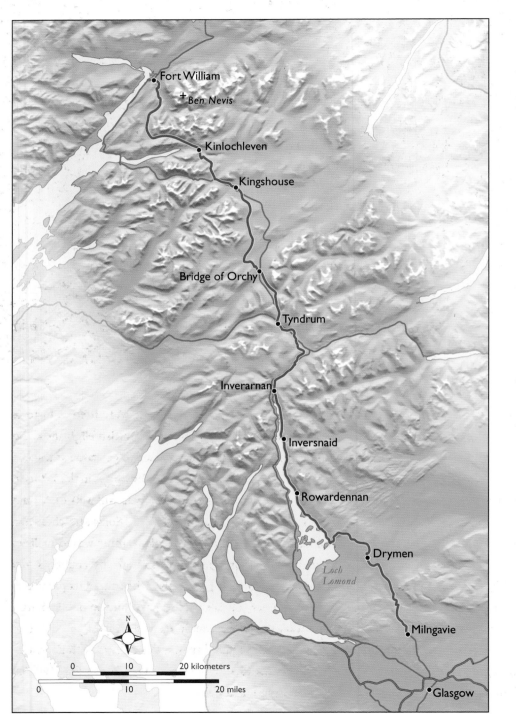

The West Highland Way had been on our list for a number of years, a classic trail that all reasonably serious walkers should consider. Once we'd selected our dates, we studied our guidebook, planning the details of our walk. Because English is the native tongue in Scotland, we thought it would be easy to arrange reservations at the accommodations—mostly bed and breakfasts—we'd selected. But we weren't expecting the Scottish version of English that we encountered on the phone—thickly accented and loaded with colorful idioms, most of which we didn't understand. We also wondered just how comprehensible we were as well, speaking "American." In each case, we'd stated the date of our arrival as clearly as possible and thought we'd heard a confirmation (or maybe it was just wishful thinking). But no money had changed hands and no confirmation numbers were given, just a friendly, seemingly casual agreement over the phone. However, as it turned out, in every case, our proprietors were expecting us and we were warmly welcomed. Apparently we were all speaking English after all!

The West Highland Way is officially the most popular long-distance trail in Scotland (and all of Britain as well). Over fifty thousand trekkers per year make the 96-mile journey from near Glasgow to Fort William, leaving the romantic and picturesque lowland village of Milngavie (pronounced "mull-guy"), passing by the wild shores of "bonnie" Loch Lomond and over the desolate wilds of Rannock Moor to the very foot of Ben Nevis, at 4,077 feet the highest mountain in the United Kingdom.

Conic Hill, one of the highest points of the West Highland Way, offers sweeping views of traditional Scottish countryside.

Yes, Loch Lomond is the largest freshwater lake in Britain (with a surface area of 27 square miles). Yes, Rannock Moor is the largest moor in Britain and stretches for roughly 50 square miles. And, yes, Ben Nevis is surrounded by the untamed wildness and grandeur of the Scottish Highlands. But this hike is definitely more than a collection of outstanding topography, although those features alone make the walk well worth doing (to say nothing of the dramatic waterfalls, peaty pools, mysterious woods, and other romantic landforms). Don't overlook the appeal of humanity's mark on the land. Whether this human history is represented by Bronze Age stones at Dumgoyach Hill, early Christian sites on wooded islands on Loch Lomond, a cave and prison used by Rob Roy (Scotland's version of Robin Hood), or more modern day farms and forests, the cultural record of tensions, conflict, trade, and traffic greatly enrich the walking experience, and this trek is a wonderful combination of the "civilized" with the "wild."

Offering surprising variety, the West Highland Way follows historic routes from the lowlands around Glasgow into the Scottish Highlands. You will walk on ancient footpaths and drove roads used to get cattle and sheep to market, you will walk on old military roads built by troops in the 1700s to help control the uprising of Jacobite clansmen, and you will walk on former coach roads and even abandoned railway rights of way. Some stretches were always open to walkers, but designation of the official route was formalized into a coherent entity in 1980, and part runs through the country's first national park. This route is definitely greater than the sum of its parts and, while day hiking sections is easy because of the availability of public transit, we recommend you walk the entire trail. In fact, we suggest you consider adding on the Great Glen Way, Scotland's newest long-distance trail (created in 2002) to make a total walk of 170 miles from Glasgow to Fort William and then across the country to Inverness.

Country paths make for delightful walking along the West Highland Way.

Although hardy souls walk the West Highland Way in every season, our advice is to skip the unpredictable winter weather (and the risks associated with potential hypothermia in a desolate spot) and enjoy this walk from April through August and, our favorite time to walk in Britain, September to early October. The West Highland Way has a reputation for rain and there's just no reasonable hope of walking in dry weather the whole way. Waterproof boots, jacket, pants, gloves, and hat, as well as a plastic bag lining your pack will prove invaluable. This is Scotland—it's supposed to be wet! And the rains do encourage the lush vegetation. The eastern shore of Loch Lomond supports one quarter of all known British flowering plants and ferns, and the forests are spectacular. The heathers and heaths on the moor are particularly lovely, and you'll enjoy them more if you've tucked some extra cold-weather clothing in your pack. Remember, if you engage one of the local luggage-carrying services, you are guaranteed a complete change into dry clothes for the evening's pub meal.

Milngavie, the trail's southern terminus, is a 7-mile train ride from Glasgow, the best staging point. The hike can be divided into seven or eight moderate stages and each night offers a bed and breakfast or hotel. Pubs (including the Clachan in Drymen, the oldest pub in the country), cafes, and hotels are available for most lunches. In most cases you'll be spending the night in a quintessential Scottish village, with the exception of an overnight in the Kingshouse (sometimes "Kings House") Hotel a couple of days from the end. This lodging dates from the seventeenth century and the building was used as a barracks for George III's soldiers. While it was somewhat funky, we appreciated the enormous bathtub attached to our room—and the King's House is the only place to stay unless you leave the trail for a town 11 miles away. Kinlochleven, the next stop, has an old electrical-generating plant that has been turned into a climbing center complete with an indoor ice-climbing room, a fun and unexpected diversion. Should you choose to break your journey at atypical junctions, area B&Bs often will provide rides. We highly recommend making reservations, as this route is very popular.

"Bonnie" Loch Lomond is the largest lake in Scotland.

Most folks walk south to north, working their way from the more pastoral to the "savage" (by U.K. standards). The West Highland Way is well signed with the thistle and hexagon motif and can be supplemented (if one is a "peak bagger") by climbing some of the nearby mountains. We were quite happy without those additions though it's important to respect the munro-collecting tradition. (A munro is a mountain over 3,000 feet, named after the man who catalogued all 284 of them in Scotland.) It is also helpful to recognize some of the other local idioms: "glen" = valley, "loch" = lake, "moor" = heather slope, "burn" = creek, "fell" = hill, for example. It's best to learn the correct pronunciation of names locally as they are often, shall we say, surprising.

In terms of fauna, you'll mostly see domestic animals (particularly sheep) at the beginning of the walk. Later you'll encounter some Highland cattle; they are large-horned, furry beasts. On the moors you might see red deer and, if you're lucky, wild goats. Golden eagles may soar overhead. But the fauna you're most likely to encounter and remember are the midges, wee mosquito-like insects that can be most irritating. Bring insect repellent and a headnet. Hiking either early or late in the season greatly diminishes the likelihood of these critters and we only had a few brief encounters, none deemed worthy of net or repellent.

Geologically speaking, the West Highland Way is rich. Glacial action scoured the valley and there are obvious fault lines as well. For example, as you view Loch Lomond's 22-mile length from the top of Conic Hill, a highlight of the second day, you note the islands that mark the Highland Boundary Fault, which divides the two distinct environments of Scotland's lowlands and highlands.

Heather covers most of the moorlands of the West Highland Way.

Scottish folks are warm and welcoming. They are not known for their culinary efforts, but we found the hearty pub meals to be tasty and regenerative. We fondly remember the piping hot French fries ("chips") served with everything, though they are perhaps best when accompanied by fish and mushy peas (a specialty of the north of Britain). Of course there is lots of beer for the thirsty walker, and single malt liquor is a specialty in Fort William, where a toast to completing the West Highland Way is a rich tradition.

Further Reading

www.west-highland-way.co.uk

Loram, Charlie. *West Highland Way: Glasgow to Fort William.* Hindhead, Surrey, UK: Tailblazer, 2010.

Megarry, Jacquetta. *The West Highland Way.* Dunblane, UK: Rucksack Readers, 2011.

Smith, Roger. *The West Highland Way: Official Guide.* Edinburgh, Scotland: Mercat Press, 2010.

West Highland Way. Dunblane, Perthshire, UK: Harvey Maps, 2008.

West Highland Way: Map/Guide. Stirling, Scotland: Footprint, 1999.

"We live in a fast-paced society. Walking slows us down."

—Robert Sweetgall

References

Amato, Joseph A. *On Foot: A History of Walking*. New York: New York University Press, 2004.

Auerbach, Paul. *Wilderness Medicine (5th Edition)*. New York: Mosby, 2007.

Auerbach, Paul, Howard Donner, and Eric Weiss. *Field Guide to Wilderness Medicine*. New York: Mosby, 2008.

Axcell, Claudia, Vikki Kinmont Kath, Diana Cooke, and Bob Kenmont. *Simple Foods for the Pack: More Than 200 All-Natural, Trail-Tested Recipes*. San Francisco: Sierra Club, 2004.

Baudrillard, Jean. *America*. Translated by Chris Turner. London: Verso, 2010.

Beffort, Brian. *Joy of Backpacking: Your Complete Guide to Attaining Pure Happiness in the Outdoors*. Birmingham, Alabama: Wilderness Press, 2007.

Benjamin, Walter. *Charles Baudelaire: A Lyric Poet in the Era of High Capitalism*. Translated by Harry Zohn. London: Verso, 1997.

Bradbury, Ray. "The Pedestrian." (1951). In *S is for Space*. Hornsea, England: PS Publishing, 2008.

Brame, Rich, and David Cole. *Soft Paths: Enjoying the Wilderness Without Harming It*. Mechanicsburg, Pennsylvania: Stackpole Books, 2011.

Burns, Bob, and Mike Burns. *Wilderness Navigation: Finding Your Way Using Map, Compass, Altimeter, and GPS*. Seattle, Washington: Mountaineers Books, 2004.

Connors, Christine, and Tim Connors. *Lightweight Trail-tested Recipes for Backcountry Trips*. Guilford, Connecticut: Three Forks Publishing, 2000.

Fletcher, Colin, and Chip Rawlins. *The Complete Walker IV*. New York: Alfred Knopf, 2010.

Harmon, Will. *Leave No Trace: Minimum Impact Outdoor Recreation*. Nashville, Tennessee: Falcon, 1997.

Harvey, Mark. *The National Outdoor Leadership School's Wilderness Guide*. Beaverton, Oregon: Touchstone, 1999.

Ikonian, Therese. *Fitness Walking (2nd Edition)*. Champaign, Illinois: Human Kinetics, 2005.

Jordan, Ryan. *Lightweight Backpacking and Camping: A Field Guide to Wilderness Equipment, Technique, and Style*. Bozeman, Montana: Beartooth Mountain Press, 2005.

Leakey, Mary. Footprints in the Ashes of Time. *National Geographic*. April 1979.

Louv, Richard. *Last Child in the Woods: Saving Our Children from Nature-Deficit Disorder*. Chapel Hill, North Carolina: Algonquin Books, 2008.

McGurney, Annette. *Leave No Trace: A Guide to the New Wilderness Etiquette*. Seattle, Washington: Mountaineers Books, 2003.

McKinney, John. *The Joy of Hiking: Hiking the Trailmaster Way*. Birmingham, Alabama: Wilderness Press, 2005.

Morley, Christopher. "The Art of Walking." In *The Magic of Walking*. New York: Simon and Schuster, 1969.

Mumford, Lewis. *The Highway and the City*. Westport, Connecticut: Greenwood Press, 1981.

Muybridge, Eadweard. *The Human Figure in Motion* (1901). New York: Dover, 1955.

Some long-distance trails can be walked in the off-season. (Long Trail)

Nicholson, Geoff. *The Lost Art of Walking*. New York: Riverhead Books, 2009.

Rousseau, Jean-Jacques. *The Reveries of a Solitary Walker* (1782). Translated by Charles E. Butterworth. Sudbury, Massachusetts: Dartmouth Publishing, 2000.

Rousseau, Jean-Jaques. *The Confessions*. Translated by J. M. Cohen. Harmondsworth, England: Penguin Books, 1953.

Schimelpfenig, Tod. *NOLS Wilderness Medicine (4th Edition)*. Mechanicsburg, Pennsylvania: Stackpole Books, 2006.

Seidman, David. *The Essential Wilderness Navigator: How to Find Your Way in the Great Outdoors (2nd Edition)*. Camden, Maine: Ragged Mountain Press, 2000.

Solnit, Rebecca. *Wanderlust: A History of Walking*. New York: Penguin Books, 2001.

Spilner, Maggie. *Prevention's Complete Book of Walking*. Emmaus, Pennsylvania: Rodale Books, 2000.

Thoreau, Henry David. "Walking." *Atlantic Monthly*. June 1862.

Waterman, Laura, and Guy Waterman. *Backwoods Ethics: A Guide to Low Impact Camping and Hiking*. Woodstock, Vermont: Countryman Press, 2003.

Wilford, John Noble. "The Transforming Leap, from Four Legs to Two." *New York Times*, September 5, 1995, B5.

Wolfe, Linnie Marsh (Editor). *John of the Mountains: The Unpublished Journals of John Muir*. Madison, Wisconsin: University of Wisconsin Press, 1979.

Books and Essays on Walking/Hiking

The Complete Walker IV (Colin Fletcher and Chip Rawlins, 2010). The latest edition of the "how to" book that *Field & Stream Magazine* called "the Hiker's Bible."

Feet of Clay: Her Epic Walk Across Australia (Ffyona Campbell, 1991). The story of the young author's remarkable 2,500-mile walk in 1988 from Sydney to Perth, Australia.

In Praise of Walking (Leslie Stephen, 1902). An essay about the importance of walking to the development of English literature.

Labyrinths: Ancient Paths of Wisdom and Peace (Virginia Westbury, 2001). A study of the history, location, and meaning of the "paths of peace."

The Lost Art of Walking (Geoff Nicholson, 2008). A quirky, entertaining history of walking.

The Man Who Walked Through Time (Colin Fletcher, 1988). The author's story of his epic walk in 1963 through the Grand Canyon.

The Mindful Hiker: On the Trail to Find the Path (Stephen Altschuler, 2004). A self-help book on "seeing" more clearly through hiking.

On Foot: A History of Walking (Joseph Amato, 2004). An academic but readable treatment of the history of walking.

On Foot through Africa (Ffyona Campbell, 1994). A follow-up to her book *Feet of Clay*.

"The Pedestrian" (Ray Bradbury, 1951). A short story about the disappearance of walking in the future.

Planetwalker: How to Change Your World One Step at a Time (John Francis, 2005). Inspirational story of the author's silent walk

Some long-distance trails require walkers to backpack. (West Coast Trail)

across America in the 1970s and '80s to promote environmental consciousness.

The Reveries of the Solitary Walker (Jean-Jacques Rousseau, 1782). An autobiographical description of ten walks and associated philosophical insights.

The Roads to Sata: A Two-Thousand Mile Walk Through Japan (Alan Booth, 1997). The author's account of his 128-day walk in Japan in 1977.

Romantic Writing and Pedestrian Travel (Robin Jarvis, 1997). A study of how walking influenced Romantic poetry.

Sauntering (Christopher Morley, 1920). An essay about walking in the city.

The Thousand-Mile Summer (Colin Fletcher, 1964). The author's story of his walk from one end of California to the other in 1958.

Thousand Mile Walk to the Gulf (John Muir, 1916). The author's description of his 1867 walk from Indiana to the Gulf of Mexico.

Tracks (Robyn Davidson, 1995). The author's thoughtful and sometimes funny account of her 1,700-mile walk across the Australian desert in 1977.

The Vintage Book of Walking (Duncan Minshull, 2000). A literary anthology of walking.

A Walk Across America (Peter Jenkins, 1973). The author's description of his 1970's walk across America in search of himself.

A Walk Across America 2 (Peter Jenkins, 1981). A sequel to his best-selling book, *A Walk Across America*.

A Walk in the Woods: Rediscovering America on the Appalachian Trail (Bill Bryson, 2006). The author's humorous account of his misadventures during his 1990s walk along the Appalachian Trail.

"Walking" (Henry David Thoreau, 1862). Thoreau's famous lecture and essay about "sauntering."

Walking in America (Donald Zochert, 1974). An edited collection of essays on walking.

Walking the World: Memories and Adventures (Alan Cook, 2003). A book about walking by a confirmed long-distance walker.

Walking to Vermont (Christopher Wren, 2004). The author's insightful account of his walk from New York City to Vermont upon retirement.

Wandering Home (Bill McKibben, 2005). A hopeful story of the author's three-week walk in Vermont and the Adirondacks of New York.

Wanderlust: A History of Walking (Rebecca Solnit, 2000). A smart, original book about the history of walking.

The Whole Story: A Walk Around the World (Ffyona Campbell, 1996). A follow-up to her earlier books, *Feet of Clay* and *On Foot through Africa*.

Worldwalk (Steven Newman, 1989). The author's story of his four-year, 15,000-mile walk around the world in the 1980s.

Index